One in Christ™

Student Book

Grade 3

CONCORDIA PUBLISHING HOUSE • SAINT LOUIS

Writers: Angela Achong, Clarence Berndt, Heather Burhop, Tanya Calendo, Victoria Cordt, Christine Dehnke, Nicole Dreyer, Carol Geisler, Abigail Genig, Kriss Glaeser, Lyla Glaskey, Betsy Graham, Diane Grebing, Stephenie Hovland, Salina Huebner, Julaine Kammrath, Sharon Kembel, Sara Knea, Sarah Koehneke, Juanita Krueger, Judy Lilliquist, Mark Lucas, Anna Maschke, Remkea Ockander, Christina Oka, Jane Ellen Pase, Michele Pickel, Pamela Rellstab, Al Renard, Christine Ries, Eileen Ritter, Mary Rowell, Elaine Rubel, John Rubel, Kathleen Schelp, Naomi Schimm, Annette Skibbe, Amanda Szymanski, Gayle Timken, Kendra Trosper

Edited by Lorraine Groth, Cynthia Wheeler, Jane Fryar, Arnold Schmidt

Series editors: Rodney L. Rathmann, Carolyn Bergt, Brenda Trunkhill

Editorial assistant: Amanda G. Lansche

Manufactured in Shenzhen, China/055760/414108

9 10 11 12 13 14 15 16 17 18   28 27 26 25 24 23 22 21 20 19

Table of Contents

Unit 1—God and His Word

Unit 2—The Holy Spirit Blesses the Church

Unit 3—God the Father's Gracious Gifts

Unit 4—Jesus Brings Salvation

Unit 5—God Hears and Answers His People

Unit 6—God's Love Leads Us to Respond with Love

Unit 7—God Comes to Us through the Means of Grace

Unit 8—God Works in Me to Follow His Ways

Unit 9—God Makes Us His Witnesses

Appendix   224

How We Learn about God

We see the true God's work in **Natroe**.

The **Bible** shows us the true God.

The Bible Tells Us about God

Find the green words in the Bible verses and highlight them.

1. God is spirit.

God is spirit, and those who worship Him must worship in spirit and truth. John 4:24

2. God is the Creator.

The LORD is the everlasting God, the Creator of the ends of the earth. Isaiah 40:28

3. God is eternal and does not change.

Now to the King eternal, immortal, invisible, the only God, be honor and glory for ever and ever. 1 Timothy 1:17 (NIV)

I the LORD do not change. Malachi 3:6

4. God is love.

God is love. This is how God showed His love. . . . He loved us and sent His Son as an atoning sacrifice for our sins. 1 John 4:8–10 (NIV)

Word Study

Match the words with the correct definition.

____**B**____ spirit   A. Maker of the universe

____**A**____ Creator   B. A personal being without a body

Why I Want to Know God

God made me. God loves me and cares for me!

God is always with me and knows everything about me. He knows my thoughts and how many hairs are on my head (Luke 12:7).

God knows that I was born in sin and that I sin every day. He knows I need help and cannot save myself.

Because God loves me, He sent His only Son, Jesus, to pay for my sin. Jesus lived without sin and then died on the cross to pay for my sin and the sins of all the world. He rose from the dead to give me and all who believe in Him new life, now and forever.

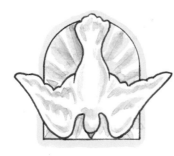

Through the Bible, the Holy Spirit calls me to faith, keeps me in true faith, and helps me learn about Jesus and live as His follower.

Bible Words to Remember

God is spirit, and those who worship Him must worship in spirit and truth. John 4:24

2

Who Is God?

These words describe God. Find and circle the words in the Bible verses.

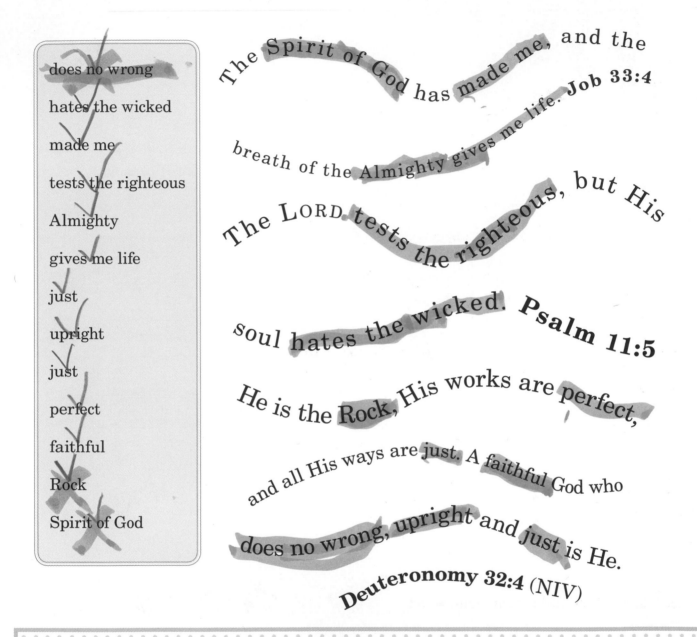

does no wrong

hates the wicked

made me

tests the righteous

Almighty

gives me life

just

upright

just

perfect

faithful

Rock

Spirit of God

The Spirit of God has made me, and the breath of the Almighty gives me life. **Job 33:4**

The LORD tests the righteous, but His soul hates the wicked. **Psalm 11:5**

He is the Rock, His works are perfect, and all His ways are just. A faithful God who does no wrong, upright and just is He.

Deuteronomy 32:4 (NIV)

Word Study

Use these words to fill in the blanks below: Savior, perfect, sin.

1. Jesus is _perfect_, because He never sinned.

2. God does not like _sin_, bad things we do because of our sinful nature.

3. Jesus is our _Savior_ and forgives our sins when we do wrong.

Who Is Jesus?

Let's sum things up.

God is faithful, perfect, and just. People are unfaithful, sinful, and unfair. God hates sin because it separates us from Him.

God hated sin so much that He sent His own Son, Jesus, to earth to become our Savior.

Jesus sacrificed Himself on the cross to pay for all the sin in the world and make us right with God.

What Does This Mean for Us?

Those who believe in Jesus receive forgiveness of sin, His righteousness, and perfection. We know God through His Son, Jesus Christ.

My Advocate

Jesus became my advocate when . . . he died for my sin

Because Jesus is my advocate . . . we will aways pray

I can be an advocate for someone when . . . falls down and hurt them self

Bible Words to Remember

If anyone does sin, we have an advocate with the Father, Jesus Christ the righteous. 1 John 2:1

3

The Bible Is . . .

The Word of God → inspired by the Holy Spirit → written down by God's people → for God's people.

To know God, know the **Bible**.

God is perfect. The Bible is **true**.

God is holy. The Bible tells us **law**, commands from God to obey.

God is love. The Bible tells us **gospel**, the Good News that Jesus saves us from sin.

Josiah Treasured God's Word

READER 1: The Bible tells about Josiah, who became king when he was eight years old.

JOSIAH: I wanted to do what was right. I wanted to serve the true God, like my ancestor King David did.

READER 2: King David wasn't perfect, but he loved and served God. He listened to God's Word. God blessed David and his kingdom.

READER 3: Many other kings came between David and Josiah. Most were evil.

READER 4: They worshiped false gods.

READER 5: They led God's people away from the one true God.

READER 6: They forgot about God's laws and promises.

JOSIAH: They did not listen to God's voice or obey Him. God did not bless them.

READER 1: The Bible says Josiah did what was right in the eyes of the Lord.

READER 2: When he was sixteen years old, King Josiah began to seek the true God.

JOSIAH: I prayed to God. I wanted to learn more about Him. The temple was in bad shape, and I could not worship God there.

READER 3: When he was twenty years old, King Josiah said,

Word Study

Find *Savior* in the Bible Dictionary in the back of this book. Who is our Savior?

_____

JOSIAH: Destroy all the false idols and their altars.

READER 4: It took years, but Josiah tore down the idols and altars. He broke them and beat them into powder.

JOSIAH: I wanted them gone forever.

READER 5: Then Josiah hired workers to repair God's temple.

READER 6: That's when Hilkiah the high priest found a lost treasure.

HILKIAH: I found the Book of the Law in the house of the Lord! It was a scroll of the Bible, God's true Word. I gave it to Josiah's assistant Shaphan to take to the king.

SHAPHAN: I read God's Word to Josiah.

JOSIAH: And when I heard it, I was very sad. I tore my clothes. I knew my people had not kept God's laws. I wanted this to change.

HILKIAH: He knew God did not bless them because they sinned and worshiped idols.

JOSIAH: Hilkiah, how can we find out more about God?

HILKIAH: We can talk to Huldah, a prophetess of God.

READER 1: Huldah's words were hard to hear.

HULDAH: God will punish the people for worshiping false gods. God saw Josiah's sadness. Because Josiah humbled himself, tore his clothing, and wanted to change, God would punish the people later. The king would not have to see it.

HILKIAH: We told the king what Huldah said.

JOSIAH: I called all the people together in the temple.

SHAPHAN: We read the Book of the Law out loud. Josiah made a promise.

JOSIAH: Lord, I will follow You with all of my heart and my soul! I will obey the words written in Your Book!

READER 2: The people made the same promises to God.

READER 3: And as long as King Josiah ruled, the people did not turn away from following the true God.

We Treasure God's Word Too

Use your Bible. Find the Table of Contents. Find two testaments.

One is called __old__. The other is called __new__.

Which testament contains the psalms of King David? Circle the word above.

King Josiah kept the Book of the Law safe. We can read it today in the first five books of the Bible. Fill in the blanks to show their names.

G _en_ nesi _s_   Ex _o_ dus   Le _v_ iti _c_ us

_n_ um _b_ ers   Deu _t_ ero _n_ omy

Bible Words to Remember

From childhood you have been acquainted with the sacred writings, which are able to make you wise for salvation through faith in Christ Jesus. 2 Timothy 3:15

4 God's Promises Kept in Jesus

The Bible is the Word of God. God kept all of the promises in the Bible when He sent Jesus as our Savior.

Jesus said, "I am the way, and the truth, and the life. No one comes to the Father except through Me." John 14:6

Fill in the blanks, using each letter in the list.

a a e e e
i i i i
o o
s t u

God speaks to us in His W _o_ r d,

offering f _o_ r g _i_ v e n _e_ s _s_ ,

l _i_ f _e_ , and s _a_ l v _a_ t _i_ on in J _e_ s _u_ s

C h r _i_ s _t_ .

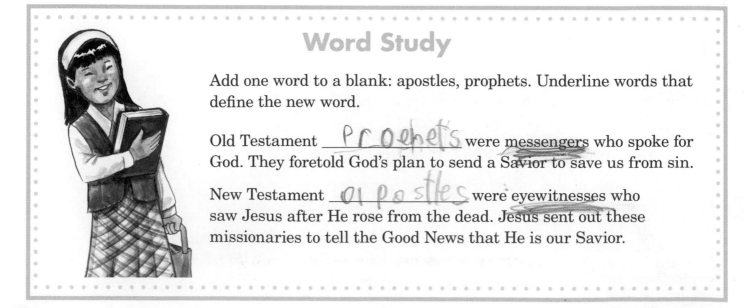

Word Study

Add one word to a blank: apostles, prophets. Underline words that define the new word.

Old Testament _prophets_ were messengers who spoke for God. They foretold God's plan to send a Savior to save us from sin.

New Testament _apostles_ were eyewitnesses who saw Jesus after He rose from the dead. Jesus sent out these missionaries to tell the Good News that He is our Savior.

The Heart of the Bible

For God so loved the world, that He gave His only Son, that whoever believes in Him should not perish but have eternal life. John 3:16

he forgive us
he clean our
sin away

he loved us
he gave his only son Jesus

Bible Words to Remember

All Scripture is breathed out by God and profitable for teaching, for reproof, for correction, and for training in righteousness. 2 Timothy 3:16

One Story

The Bible is important because it tells us the truth about Jesus. It is the source of all that we believe and teach as Christians.

⭐ Turn to the Table of Contents in your Bible.

God's story begins in the Old Testament. It tells how God created the world and promised a Savior.

The New Testament Gospels tell about Jesus, the Savior God promised to send.

The story continues with the story of Jesus' first disciples in the Book of Acts.

Letters to the early Christian churches are called Epistles.

We learn that Jesus promises to come again in Revelation.

Beginning to end, the Bible tells about God's love for His creation and His plan to save us from sin, death, and the devil.

The Story of Jesus

Handwritten labels around circle: Revelation, Old testmant, new testmant, gospels, Acts, epistles

Word Study

Write definitions of these words using the Bible Dictionary in the back of your book.

Testament: _tell about jesus the savior God._

Epistle: _We learn that jesus promises to come again_

God's True Story

Add these words to complete the sentences: **cares**, **saved**, **created**, **calls**.

The Bible tells how God the Father _created_ us, how Jesus _saved_ us, and how the Holy Spirit _calls_ us to faith and _cares_ for us.

The Bible is God's great true story, the most important one ever told.

The events in the Bible are about people and places long ago and far away.

It may seem that these events are not about you, but they are.

God's True Story, for You and about You

Directions: Write the words *I* or *me* in the blanks.

The whole Bible tells about Jesus. It also tells about _me_.

God created the people in the Bible who lived before _me_. God created _me_ and loved _me_, even before _I_ was born.

The people in the Bible who lived before _me_ were sinners. _I_ am a sinner who needs a Savior too.

_I_ hear about my Savior, Jesus, in the Bible. As a member of God's family, _I_ hear the story of my family when _I_ read the Bible.

Bible Words to Remember

These are written so that you may believe that Jesus is the Christ, the Son of God, and that by believing you may have life in His name. John 20:31

6

What Does It Mean to Be a Christian?

Unscramble the letters to find each new word. Write it in the blank.

- Being a Christian means knowing that I am a **ninesr**
  Sinner .

- Being a Christian means that God saved me by grace through faith in Christ **sJuse** _Jesus_ , my Savior. I believe that Jesus paid for my sin with His **ahetd** _death_ and gives me new life through His resurrection.

- Being a Christian means God makes me His **lidch** _child_ and redeems me in Holy **tsmiapB** _Batismap_ .

God's work, not mine, gives me the right and privilege to take Christ's name, *Christian*.

A Child of God

Read the Bible verse, and then use words from it to complete the sentences that follow.

1. In Christ Jesus you are all sons of God, through faith. For as many of you as were baptized into Christ have put on Christ. Galatians 3:26–27

   In Christ Jesus, I am a _Son_ _of_ _god_ through faith.

2. Repent and be baptized every one of you in the name of Jesus Christ for the forgiveness of your sins, and you will receive the gift of the Holy Spirit. Acts 2:38

   Through Baptism in the name of Jesus, God gives _forgiveness_ of your sins and the gift of the _Holy_ _spirit_ .

Word Study

Write definitions of these words using the Bible Dictionary in the back of your book.

Christian: _A follower of and_

repent: _to feel sorry for sin and not want to sin again_

A Story Jesus Told

What did each person in Jesus' story do?

The lost son

he ran off with fahter money spent it all

The father

he gran to meet his son he put a robe, ring, sandel

The older son

feel mad when the lost son came back

Jesus' Story for Me

The father forgave the lost son, welcomed the lost son home, and reclaimed him as his child.

My heavenly Father forgives _____, welcomes _____ home, and reclaims _____ as His child.

Gifts of the Father

Father's Gifts to the Son	God's Gifts to Me
sandel	baptisam
ring	bible
rebe	commantin
feast	famliy
fogireness	chach
hug	friend

Bible Words to Remember

Fear not, for I have redeemed you; I have called you by name, you are Mine. Isaiah 43:1

Study Buddy

- Why do we study?
- How is studying the Bible different from studying history or other subjects?
- What does the Bible do that other books can't do?

Why Should We Study the Bible?

Draw a line to match each picture with the bold word it illustrates.

1. The Bible is the **source** of all we know about Jesus.

2. The Bible is the **authority** on what God wants for our lives.

3. God blesses us with **people** and **tools** to help us **study** the message of **Jesus**.

Word Study

Write definitions of this word from the Bible Dictionary in the back of your book.

respect: _to value to think most highly of to treat as special_

The Good Portion: God's Word

Read Luke 10:38–42. Then circle the correct name and cross out the wrong name.

1. Mary and Martha were sisters. ~~Martha~~ **Martha** Mary welcomed Jesus into her house.

2. ~~Martha~~ **Mary** sat at Jesus' feet and listened to Him teach.

3. **Martha** ~~Mary~~ was upset that her sister didn't help her cook and clean for the guests.

4. Jesus said that ~~Martha~~ **Mary** chose the good portion.

5. Who did the right thing: ~~Martha~~, who cooked and cleaned for her guests, or **Mary**, who stopped to listen to Jesus?

6. How do we know?

read the bible

7. What is the good portion? How can we receive it?

study the bible

Live like Mary

(1) Draw a picture of something that distracts you from learning about God. (2) Then draw a way you can learn more about Jesus.

Bible Words to Remember

Lord, to whom shall we go? You have the words of eternal life. John 6:68

Tools Help Us Work and Learn

Tool: an object that helps to do something.

1. What do these tools help to do?

to build houses or cars.

2. How do these tools help you in school?

learn how to count

learn to write words

to cut paper

to read for understanding

Know Your Bible Tools

Directions: Draw a line from each book to the way it helps us understand God's Word.

1

2

3

a. a list of meanings of Bible words, places, and things

b. a resource with maps of Bible lands

c. a list of Bible words that helps find specific verses

Word Study

Find the definition in the Bible Dictionary in the back of your book. Write it here.

context: setting, situation surrounding words and background

Tools Help Us Understand God's Word

We read the Bible to grow in faith and knowledge of Jesus. The Holy Spirit helps us know and understand God's Word.

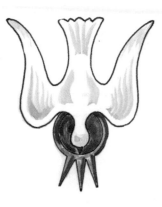

1. **Other Scriptures.** To understand the Bible, let Scripture explain Scripture. Read Matthew 9:1.

Matthew 9:1: And getting into a boat He crossed over and came to His own city.

   • Which town was Jesus' "own city"? Read Matthew 4:13 to find out. Highlight the city name.

Matthew 4:13: Leaving Nazareth [Jesus] went and lived in Capernaum by the sea.

2. **Bible Atlas.** To understand the Bible, learn about the land. The Bible talks about towns and nations, some that no longer exist. A Bible atlas has maps of these places.

Jesus was born in Bethlehem. His family lived in Nazareth in the region of Galilee. He grew up there. He adopted Capernaum as His city when He began His ministry.

   • Turn to the map on page 279. Find and highlight the town of **Bethlehem** in the bottom box. Find and highlight the towns of **Nazareth** and **Capernaum** in the top box. For an extra challenge, find these three cities in the map on page 278.
   • What sea is near Capernaum?

   the sea of galiee

3. **Bible Dictionary.** To understand the Bible, we need to know how people lived over two thousand years ago. People did not have electricity, cars, paved roads, computers, the Internet, refrigerators, and running water. They did not have hospitals, homes, and schools like ours. Jobs and travel were different.

   • What jobs do you think people did around the Sea of Galilee?

   mabye fishing to get fish and bread

   • Find a list of Bible jobs in the box on page 235. Write two jobs you know that people still do today.

   teacher, baker

Bible Words to Remember
The Son of God has come and has given us understanding.
1 John 5:20

What Do We Do with the Bible?

Highlight words that tell what to *do* with the Bible.

We should diligently and reverently read and study the Bible,
listen attentively when it is read and explained, believe it,
and live according to it.

Luther's Small Catechism with Explanation, page 42, from the 1943 edition. © 1943 Concordia Publishing House.

In My Father's House

Find and read Luke 2:41–49 in your Bible. Jesus showed us how to use the Bible. Fill in the blanks to tell what He showed us.

Jesus loved to hear God's Word. I hear God's Word when _I go to the church_

Jesus read Scripture. I read the _bible_.

Jesus talked with teachers about the Scriptures. I discuss the Bible with _family, Teachers and friends_

Do you feel a bit sad after filling in the blanks? Yes, we fail to attend church regularly, we do not listen to God's Word when it is read to us, and we don't read the Bible as much as we should. But God does not give up on you! Jesus loves you and forgives you! He sends the Holy Spirit to encourage and guide you in your study of God's Word so you can know Jesus, your Savior.

Circle the green words or their meaning in the Bible verse.

study

Jesus said, "You search the Scriptures because you think that in them you have eternal life; and it is they that bear witness about Me." John 5:39

listen

Jesus said, "Blessed rather are those who hear the word of God and keep it!" Luke 11:28.

believe

"These are written so that you may believe that Jesus is the Christ, the Son of God, and that by believing you may have life in His name." John 20:31

live

"Be doers of the word, and not hearers only, deceiving yourselves." James 1:22

Word Study

Find the definition in the Bible Dictionary in the back of your book. Write it here.

Passover: _Jewish feast that celebrates Israel's freedom from slavery in egypt. The name reminds that the angels of death passed over their homes during last plague in egypt_

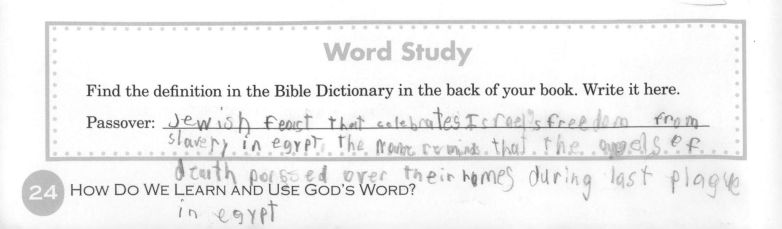

What's Important in Your Life?

You are a detective hired to find out about Noah and Olivia. Study the pictures.

1. List what seems important to each person.

Noah

reads the bibles plays soccer won trophers

Olivia

goes to dance class, plays her dolls plays as cheer- leader

2. If a detective looked in your room, what would he think is important to you?

that i have books i read

3. God's Word tells about blessings God gives us. Write one gift that God gave you.

eternal life

4. What is the most valuable gift God gives us? _love_

5. Write a short prayer, thanking God for His love and blessings.

o God thank you for all the danger away from me

Bible Words to Remember

Blessed rather are those who hear the word of God and keep it!
Luke 11:28

The Painting

Alex's parents gave him a special gift for his birthday, a portrait of him painted by a local artist. The painting was so well done that it looked like a photo. Alex's parents hung it over his desk.

About a week later, Alex noticed changes in the portrait. The nose looked squished. The eyes drooped. The picture turned ugly, bit by bit. Scared, Alex tried to find out why.

One day, Alex noticed the picture changed when his mom sent him to his room for tormenting his sister. A few days later, the picture's smile turned to a frown when Alex cheated on a spelling test, even thought he didn't get caught. Paint dripped from his hair when he disobeyed his dad. His chin line blurred after he argued with his mom about doing chores.

Alex tried to do good things, but the picture didn't change back. Only bad behavior affected it. When he no longer recognized himself, Alex hid the picture in his closet. He looked for new changes every night.

Mirror, Mirror, on the Wall

Alex's painting showed his sin. God's Law is a mirror that shows our sin.

There is not a righteous man on earth who does good and never sins. Ecclesiastes 7:20

Can *anyone* be perfect? Why or why not?

no Because we have all sinned.

For the wages of sin is death, but the free gift of God is eternal life in Christ Jesus our Lord. Romans 6:23

What wage do we earn for our sin?

death

Who can help us? Thank God that Jesus, our Savior, died on the cross to rescue us from sin and death! This is the Gospel.

THE LAW SHOWS OUR SIN AND NEED FOR A SAVIOR.

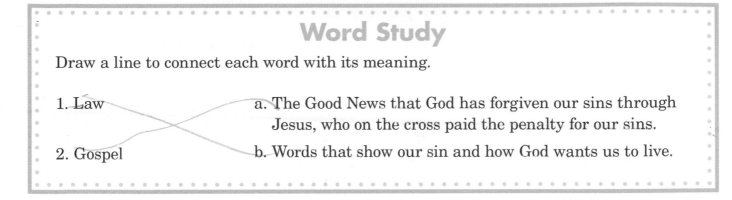

Word Study

Draw a line to connect each word with its meaning.

1. Law

2. Gospel

a. The Good News that God has forgiven our sins through Jesus, who on the cross paid the penalty for our sins.

b. Words that show our sin and how God wants us to live.

In Our Place

Imagine yourself standing in front of a judge in a courtroom, guilty of many crimes. The evidence says so. Guilty!

Just as the judge raises the gavel to announce your punishment, someone asks to take your place. The judge agrees. The person takes your punishment. You go free.

Jesus did this for us! Jesus died on the cross in our place, taking the punishment we deserved. His blood washes away our sin. That is Good News, the Gospel of Jesus.

The Holy Spirit gives us faith in Jesus, our Lord and Savior. In Jesus, we are forgiven. Share this Good News with Alex.

Draw a picture or write Alex a note. Tell him some Good News!

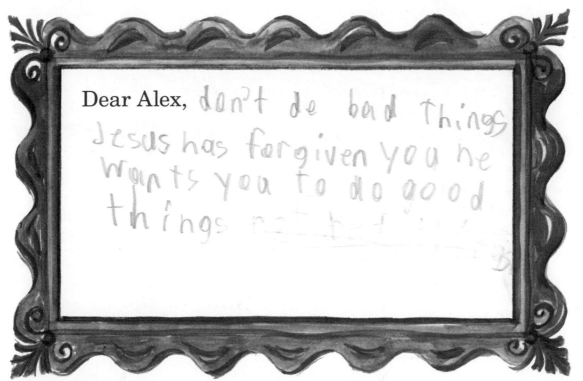

Dear Alex, don't do bad things Jesus has forgiven you he wants you to do good things not bad

Bible Words to Remember

Christ loved us and gave Himself up for us, a fragrant offering and sacrifice to God. Ephesians 5:2

Growing to Know God

God wants us to know Him. There is much to know!

> Now there are also many other things that Jesus did. Were every one of them to be written, I suppose that the world itself could not contain the books that would be written. John 21:25

Let's think about growing. In the leaves on the first plant, write four things plants need to grow. Below the drawing, write things that hurt the plant or stop growth.

The Small Catechism has Six Chief Parts to help us know God and grow in faith in Him. Turn to the Appendix. Find the names of the Six Chief Parts, and write them on the leaves of the second plant. Below the drawing, write things that hurt the plant or stop growth.

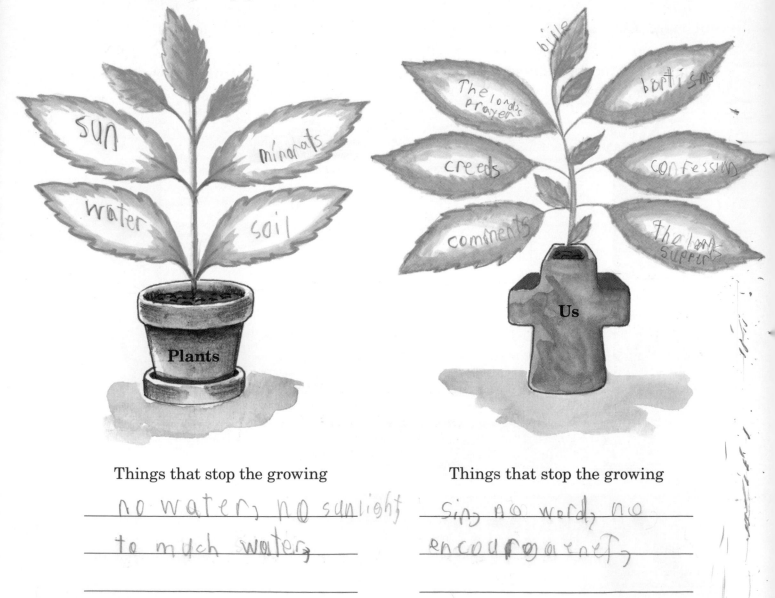

Left plant leaves: sun, minerals, water, soil — labeled **Plants**

Right plant leaves: bible, The lord's prayer, baptism, creeds, confession, comments, The lord's supper — labeled **Us**

Things that stop the growing

no water, no sunlight, to much water

Things that stop the growing

Sin, no word, no encouragarnet,

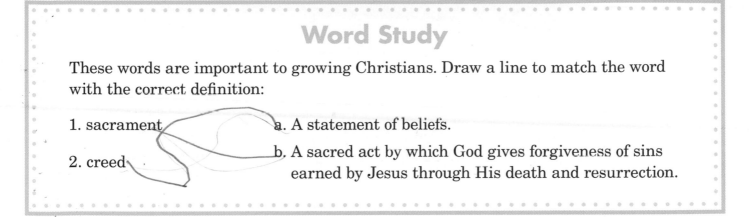

Word Study

These words are important to growing Christians. Draw a line to match the word with the correct definition:

1. sacrament

2. creed

a. A statement of beliefs.

b. A sacred act by which God gives forgiveness of sins earned by Jesus through His death and resurrection.

The Six Chief Parts teach us about God. We can use these tools to help other people know God too. Write specific ways you can help others know God the Father, Son, and Holy Spirit.

reading the bible to them, invite them to church, helping them to read the bible, helping them on there homework.

Helping Others Grow

What is the most important truth that we know about Jesus? Find John 14:6 in your Bible, and add the missing words in the verse below.

[Jesus said,] "I am the __Way__, and the __truth__, and the __life__.

No one comes to the Father except through __me__." John 14:6

Bible Words to Remember

For God so loved the world, that He gave His only Son, that whoever believes in Him should not perish but have eternal life. John 3:16

12

I Love It!

Write the name of something or someone you love in each box.

Jesus The planets	my neighbor	my mom

Each important person or thing competes for time and attention. Should you do homework or play a game? Should you spend time with your family or read a book?

Jesus told us how to decide what's important. Read the Bible Words to Remember. Whom does Jesus say we should love?

love your neighbor, your family and Jesus too.

In the first sentence of the Bible Words to Remember, Jesus summarizes the first three commandments God gave to Moses.

Read Commandments 1–3 and their meanings in Luther's Small Catechism in the Appendix. These commandments are about our relationship with _god_ .

Now look at the second sentence of the Bible Words to Remember where Jesus summarizes commandments 4–10. Read these commandments in the catechism too. These commandments are about our relationship with our _neighbors_ .

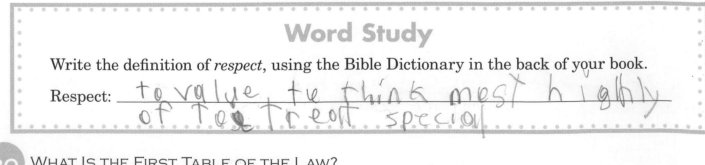

Word Study

Write the definition of *respect*, using the Bible Dictionary in the back of your book.

Respect: *to value, to think most highly of to treat special*

But I Fall Down

Sometimes we don't love God with our whole selves. We love ourselves and what we want more. We love things and other people more than we love God. Sometimes we don't love our neighbor as we love ourselves. When we do, we can pray to God and ask for His forgiveness and help. Do that by completing this prayer.

Dear Jesus,

Sometimes I don't love You as I should. I think about myself too much when I . . .

watch tv play games ride my bike and play and the troimpline too i aways forget about you God.

I'm very sorry and ask that You forgive me for . . .

that i don't listen to you that i forget to read the bible and i'm sorny for all the wrengs i did.

I don't want to sin again, Lord. Please help me to love You and others more and more every day. In Your name I pray. Amen.

Bible Words to Remember

You shall love the Lord your God with all your heart and with all your soul and with all your mind and with all your strength. . . . You shall love your neighbor as yourself. Mark 12:30–31

Holy God

The underlined words tell about the Holy Spirit. Some give His **names**. Some tell what He is like (**characteristics**). Some tell what He does (**works**). Some describe **signs** of His presence. Put the words where they belong in the circle.

Genesis 1:1-2 says the Spirit of God was hovering over the water in the beginning. He is eternal.

Genesis 2:7 tells how God creates man and breathes life into him.

Names — Spirit of god, Holy spirit, Helper

Signs — Wind, Fire

Characteristics — eternal, know all things, fire

Works — holds back evil, creates, power, gives, faith, gives, teaches, produces

Acts 2:1-4, 36-41 tells how the Holy Spirit arrived at Pentecost in wind and fire. He gives power to Jesus' disciples to tell others about Him. Through Baptism, He gives faith to over three thousand people.

John 14:26 calls Him the Helper who teaches us about Jesus.

1 Corinthians 2:10–12 says the Spirit understands God's mind. He knows all things.

Isaiah 59:19 says He holds back evil.

Galatians 5:22–23 says the Spirit produces fruit of faith like love, patience, kindness, goodness, and self-control.

Word Study

Holy Spirit: _____third_____ Person of the Trinity; a real, personal _____being_____, not just the energy of God; the One who gives us _____faith_____ and keeps our faith alive

The Holy Spirit Points to Jesus

Draw a symbol for Jesus. What is the work of the Holy Spirit?

he helps us learn about Jesus and gives us faith to belive in jesus.

The Holy Spirit Breathes Holiness

At Pentecost *gives them power to learn about jesus.*

For me *helps me learn better in class when im learning.*

Bible Words to Remember

No one can say "Jesus is Lord" except in the Holy Spirit.
1 Corinthians 12:3

Called by the Gospel

© CPH/Don Kueker

Jesus shows Saul his sin.

Draw the end of the story.

How does Saul become God's child? hes, Rising te god and batisem too.

Word Study

Match the numbers in the boxes to fill in the correct letters.

While I was BLIND in SIN, the HOLY SPIRIT called me by

the GOSPEL—the Good News that tells me about God's LOVE and

FORGIVENESS in CHRIST JESUS—and made me God's child.

C	O	N	V	E	R	S	I	O	n
1	2	3	4	5	6	7	8	9	10

The Holy Spirit Opens Our Eyes

Color the puzzle. Outline the dove. How does the Holy Spirit bring you to faith in Jesus?

1 = orange	5 = blue
2 = green	6 = yellow
3 = red	7 = purple
4 = brown	

_____

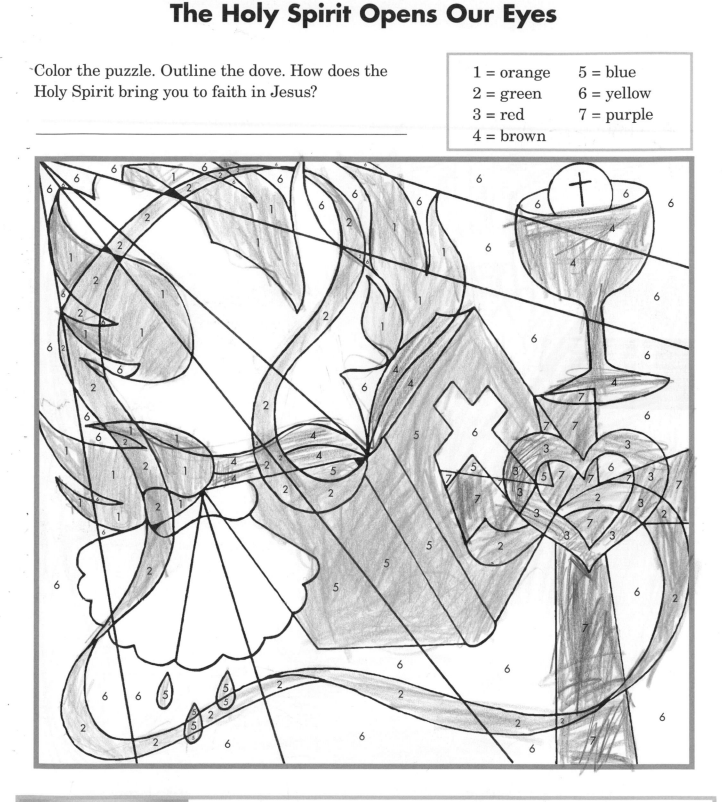

Bible Words to Remember

Repent and be baptized every one of you in the name of Jesus Christ for the forgiveness of your sins, and you will receive the gift of the Holy Spirit. Acts 2:38

What Is Living in You?

God's Spirit dwells in you. 1 Corinthians 3:16

I am born _sinful_ . I cannot _believe_ in Jesus as my Savior on my own. In _batism_, the Holy Spirit comes to live in my _heart_ and helps me _grow_ in _faith_.

sinful
grow
Baptism
heart
believe
faith

How Do You Grow?

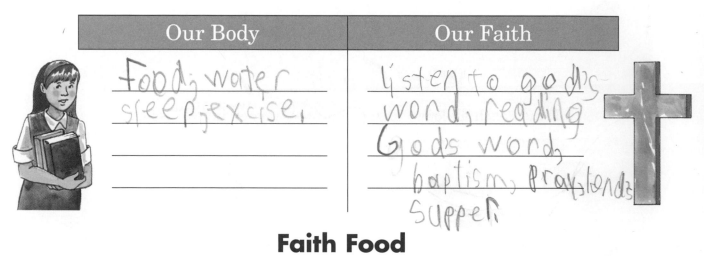

Our Body	Our Faith
Food, water sleep, excise,	listen to gods word, reading Gods word, baptism, prayers lords supper

Faith Food

Your body needs food to live and grow. Your faith needs food too. The Holy Spirit helps your faith grow through God's Word and Sacraments. Fill in the missing words.

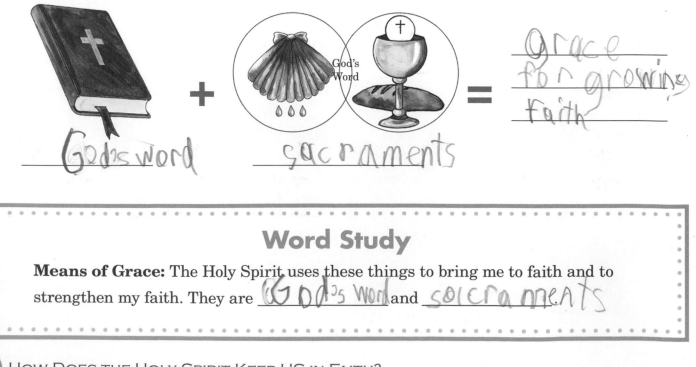

God's word + _sacraments_ = _grace for growing faith_

God's Word

Word Study

Means of Grace: The Holy Spirit uses these things to bring me to faith and to strengthen my faith. They are _God's Word_ and _sacraments_

Life as God's Children

Read Acts 2:42–47. In one box, create a word web about life in the Early Church. In the next, draw a picture to illustrate one thing.

prayer

What Can We Say?

Finish each dialogue using what you learned in the lesson.

Sam: Can you stay overnight at my house Saturday?

Késhaun: Yes, as long as I'm ready when my parents pick me up for church Sunday morning.

Sam: How come you have to go to church every week?

Késhaun: because i want to listen god's word

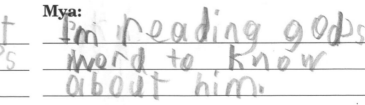

Allie: What are you reading?

Mya: My Bible.

Allie: That sounds boring! Why are you reading that?

Mya: I'm reading gods word to know about him.

Bible Words to Remember

The word of God . . . is at work in you believers.
1 Thessalonians 2:13

A New Creation

If anyone is in Christ, he is a new creation. 2 Corinthians 5:17

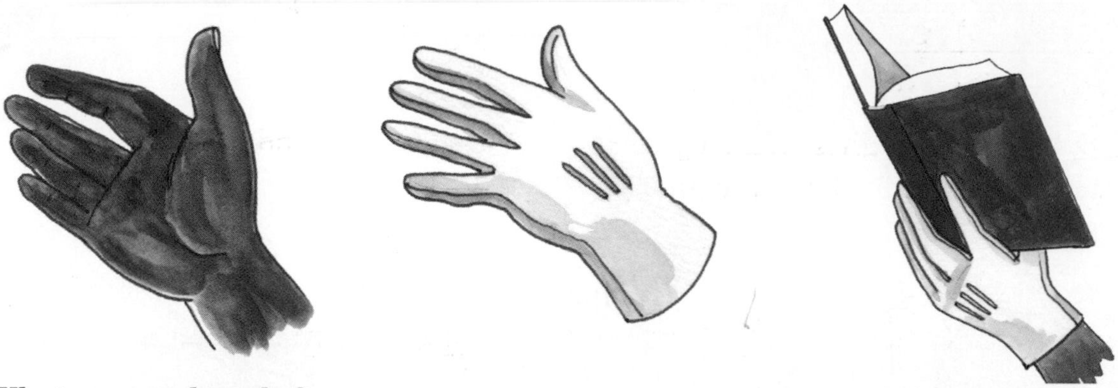

What are good works?

follow the comments to do good deeds

What do the Commandments say?

love eveyone and god too.

How can we do good works?

the holy spirit helps us do good deeds to love god

Word Study

| sanctification |
| justification |

What Jesus did *for us* to save us from our sins.

Justification

What the Holy Spirit does *in us* to make us holy and to change us more and more into people whose lives resemble Christ's.

sanctification

Serving God, Helping Others

Read Acts 9:36–43. What did Dorcas do for others?

she made robes for the poor

What did Peter do?

she brought dorcas to life by god gi

The Holy Spirit gives us gifts. Which gifts do you think Dorcas and Peter had? Put their names on them. Circle the gifts you have.

Living the Spirit-Filled Life

List ways you can use the gifts and abilities the Holy Spirit gives you to help others.

In your family	In your school	In your city	In the world
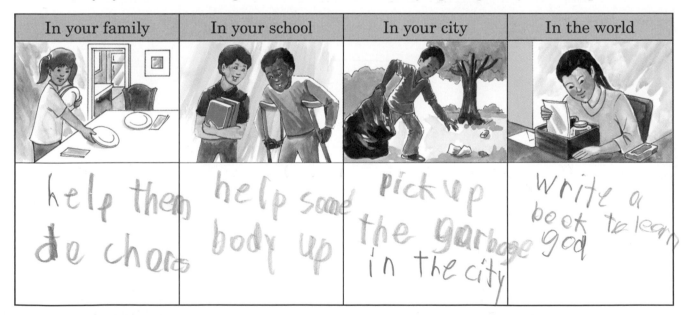			
help them do chores	help some body up	pick up the garbage in the city	write a book to learn god

Bible Words to Remember

For we are His workmanship, created in Christ Jesus for good works, which God prepared beforehand, that we should walk in them. Ephesians 2:10

Here Is the Church . . .

Mark true or false.

[✓] The church is a building for worship.

[✓] The church is a congregation that gathers to worship in one place.

[ ] The church is a group of congregations called a denomination that believes the same things even though the congregations are not in the same place.

[✓] The Church is made up of everyone who believes in Jesus as Savior from all times and places.

I Will Build My Church

Read Matthew 16:13–28 and answer the questions.

1. Who did people say Jesus was?
   the son of man

2. Who did Peter say Jesus was?
   the son of crist

3. Who do you say Jesus is?
   hes the son of god hes our savir

4. Who builds the Church?
   jesus

Word Study

Match the word to the definition.

Communion of saints — A group of congregations in a church body who believe the same things (doctrines)

Denomination — A group of Christians who gather in one place to worship God

Congregation — All who believe in Jesus as their Savior; the Holy Christian Church

We Are the Church Together

God makes us part of His Church through Baptism and His Word. Now we are part of His kingdom. The pictures show ways we can work in His kingdom to share His love in Jesus with others. Draw a way you can use your gifts to serve God.

Bible Words to Remember

We, though many, are one body in Christ. Romans 12:5

Not This . . .

But This!

What does 1 Peter 2:5 say those who believe in Jesus are like? _a living sta_

What does Ephesians 2:19–22 say the household of God (the Church) is built on?

on apostes Draw a picture to illustrate these verses.

Word Study

Unscramble the letters, and fill in the blanks.

estonnercor   rhcuhc

The ___church___ is made up of all those who believe in Jesus as their Savior from sin.

The ___connerstone___ sets the direction for two walls and anchors them together.

Our Life Together

Worksnip

witness

serve

learning

fellowship

Bible Words to Remember

So then you are . . . built on the foundation of the apostles
and prophets, Christ Jesus Himself being the cornerstone.
Ephesians 2:19–20

Martin Luther's Early Years

Fall 1492: Hi, my name is Martin Luther. I'm nine years old. I was born in Eisleben, Germany, on November 10, 1483. The very next day, I was baptized and became a child of God. Now I live in Mansfeld.

A lot is happening in the world. Gutenberg invented a machine with movable type so books can be printed instead of handwritten. And just last month, Christopher Columbus discovered the Bahamas!

I study reading, writing, and Latin. I also sing in the boy's choir at church. My parents love me, but they are very strict. So are my teachers. Once, I was whipped at school with a rod fifteen times. I worry that God is angry with me and will punish me too.

Spring 1501: Hi, I'm seventeen now. I live in Eisenach with the Cotta family. When I first came here, I sang in a men's chorus for my supper. That's how I met Frau Cotta. The Cottas are like a second family to me. I study hard, and I have learned to play an instrument called the lute. When I sing and play music, it helps me feel less afraid.

What about You?

hes like calm and good, that he help me have a good life	a time for everthing.	but on the
Describe how you picture God.	Name a hymn that helps you when you feel bad.	Write a Bible verse that gives you comfort.

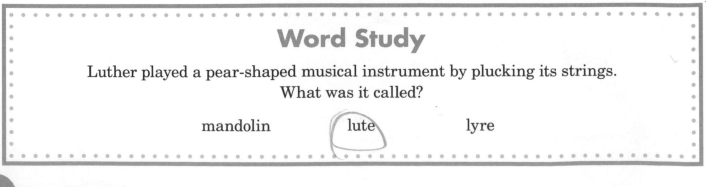

Word Study

Luther played a pear-shaped musical instrument by plucking its strings. What was it called?

mandolin   (lute)   lyre

My Lord and My God

Use the rebus and the words in John 20:19–31 to fill in the blanks. The words in the Bible Word Bank can be used more than once.

On Easter Sunday evening, Jesus appeared to
__the disciples__ . All of them were there, except
__Thomas__

Jesus said, 🫛 🐝 with **U** .
"_peace be with you_ "

He showed them His __hands__ and
__side__ .

A week later, Jesus appeared to __the disciples__ again.
This time, __thomas__ was with them.
Jesus said, 🫛 🐝 with **U** .
"__peace be with you__"

He told __thomas__ to touch His __Hands__ and __side__ .
Finish the story. __Jesus breathed__

Bible Word Bank:
| Thomas | hands |
| the disciples | side |

How Can I Be Sure?

What are some of your fears?
__a spider__

Jesus says, "I will never leave you nor forsake you" (Hebrews 13:5). How does that make you feel?
__it makes me feel safe and joyful__

The Holy Spirit works through God's Word to make your faith strong and help you trust all that Jesus has done for you. Where do you hear God's Word?
__At school or church to listen to gods word.__

Bible Words to Remember

Blessed are those who have not seen and yet have believed. John 20:29

Martin Luther Becomes a Monk

Word Study

Fill in the blanks.

A promise, often one that is made to God: <u>VOW</u>

A man who has promised to spend his life serving God by leaving his family and living with other monks, praying, and working together: <u>Monk</u>

The Light Shines in the Darkness

Look up Isaiah 43:1. Then connect the stepping stones to make the Bible passage.

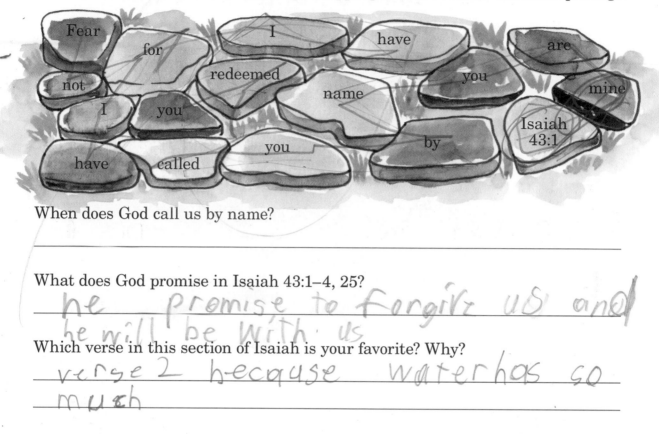

When does God call us by name?

_____

What does God promise in Isaiah 43:1–4, 25?

he promise to forgive us and
he will be with us

Which verse in this section of Isaiah is your favorite? Why?

verse 2 because waterhas so
much

Never Alone

Luther had fears and struggles. But God was with him. What fears do you have?

_____

_____

_____

_____

_____

_____

Bible Words to Remember

[The Lord] has said, "I will never leave you nor forsake you."
Hebrews 13:5

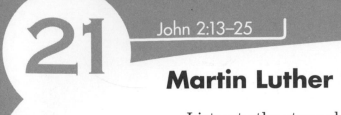

21 John 2:13–25

Martin Luther Shakes Up the Church

Listen to the story about Martin Luther, and use your colored pencils to fill in the mystery pictures below.

Box 1

Purgatory

Box 2

Indulgence

MONEY
POND

Box 3

Jesus paid for all

Box 4

heven

Box 5

Box 6

Word Study

These words from our lesson got their syllables mixed up! Can you put them back in order and write them on the lines below?

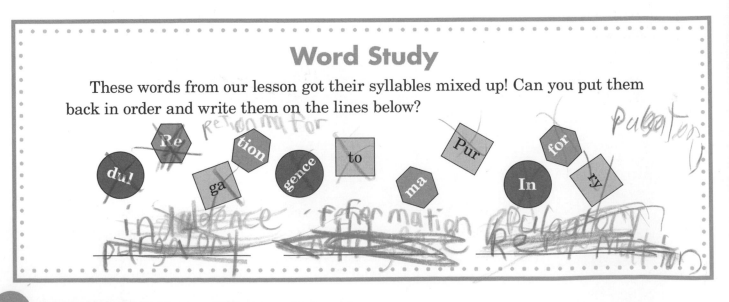

Re tion ma for
dul ga gence to Pur for ty
ma In

indulgence · reformation · Purgatory

Jesus Shakes Up the Temple Courts

Special Report
John 2:13–25

Today, _Jesus came in the Temple and chased out the mechents._

Jesus said, "_do not make this a bad store and this is not gods haase_"

God Shakes Up My Life

True or False?

 F Jesus forgives my sins, but I still have to be a good person to be sure I'll go to heaven.

F I don't have to bother about being good because good works aren't that important.

T I don't *have* to do good works to get into heaven because Jesus paid for all my sins and gives me eternal life.

† The Holy Spirit lives in me because I am God's child and helps me do good works.

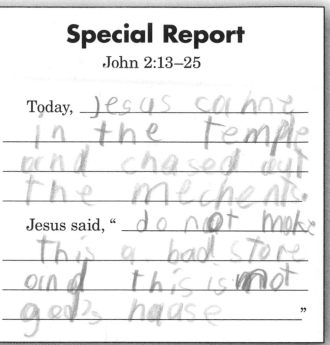

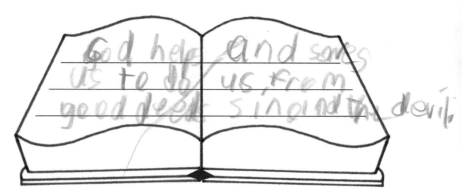

God help and saves us to do us from good deed sin and the devil.

Luther had an "aha" experience. He learned from God's Word that we are saved by grace, not the things we do. Write something in the Bible that you've learned from God's Word.

Bible Words to Remember

He saved us, not because of works done by us . . . but according to His own mercy . . . so that being justified by His grace we might become heirs according to the hope of eternal life. Titus 3:5, 7

22

Standing on God's Word

Chorus 1	Frederick the Wise
Chorus 2	Cardinal Cajetan
Narrator 1	Martin Luther
Narrator 2	Pope Leo X
Narrator 3	Emperor Charles V

Narrator 1: Dr. Martin Luther was a priest and a professor at the University of Wittenberg. By studying God's Word, he learned that we are saved by Faith Alone.

Chorus 1: Faith Alone: Believing in Jesus Christ as our Savior from sin. Doing good works can't save us.

Narrator 2: God sent Jesus to be our Savior. God has saved us by Grace Alone.

Chorus 2: Grace Alone: God saves us because He loves us. It's a gift from God!

Narrator 3: Luther wanted the leaders of the Church to fix their mistakes. He wanted the church to base its teachings on Scripture Alone.

Chorus 1: Scripture Alone: Only God's Word, the Bible, is always correct.

Narrator 1: Pope Leo ordered Luther to go to Rome to defend his work.

Narrator 2: But Prince Frederick the Wise was worried about Luther's safety.

Frederick the Wise: I will write the Pope and ask for the meeting to be in Germany.

Narrator 3: The Pope said okay. He sent

Word Study

Use what you've learned today to fill in this crossword puzzle. Then use the crossword answers to build three pairs of words from our story. There is a color clue if you need it.

DOWN:

2. By yourself

ACROSS:

1. Trust in Jesus as your Savior

3. We read God's _____ in the Bible.

4. God shows His _____ by giving us love when we don't deserve it.

Crossword answers: 1. faith, 2. alone, 3. word, 4. grace

faith alone, word alone, grace alone.

Cardinal Cajetan to the meeting.

Cardinal Cajetan: Dr. Luther, Pope Leo the Tenth says to stop speaking against what the church teaches. Recant—take back what you said! Otherwise, you will be declared a heretic—someone who preaches false ideas. You can be burned at the stake!

Martin Luther: I want to do the right thing. But unless you can show me my mistakes from the Holy Scriptures and good reasoning, I must do what God says.

Narrator 1: The cardinal could not prove Martin wrong, but Pope Leo declared him a heretic anyway.

Pope Leo X: Martin Luther must be punished. My official letter, the Papal Bull, will tell everyone that he is excommunicated from the church.

Chorus 2: Kicked out of the church! Does that mean Martin can't go to heaven?

Narrator 2: Martin knew that faith in Jesus is the only way to heaven. He burned the pope's letter. Then he was ordered to go for questioning again. This time, Emperor Charles the Fifth would be there!

Narrator 3: Again, Martin was asked to recant what he had written or be punished.

Narrator 1: Luther thought and prayed. The next day, he said,

Martin Luther: My teachings are based on God's Word. Unless you can show me my mistakes from the Holy Scriptures and good reasoning, I must teach what God says. I will not recant. God help me.

Charles V: This is an insult! I will make

Martin Luther an outlaw!

Narrator 2: But Frederick the Wise told his men:

Frederick the Wise: Listen, men. Kidnap Dr. Luther on his way home. Take him to Wartburg Castle so nobody can hurt him.

Narrator 3: The plot worked. Luther stayed at the castle.

Narrator 1: He started translating the New Testament into German.

Narrator 2: Then Martin went back to Wittenberg. He taught for many more years. He wrote hymns for the people to sing.

Chorus 1: We've got new songs! This tells us how God is like a strong castle!

Narrator 3: Luther got married and had six children. Many visitors came to hear him tell them about God's love. He always pointed the way to the Savior.

Martin Luther: God's Word tells us the truth: Jesus Christ suffered and died to take away everyone's sins! We are saved through Christ Alone.

Chorus 1 and 2: Christ Alone: God does all the good work that gets us to heaven! Let's thank Him and do things that help point other people to Jesus too!

Bible Words to Remember

For no one can lay a foundation other than that which is laid, which is Jesus Christ. 1 Corinthians 3:11

23 Matthew 19:16–26

Grace Alone—I'll Fix It for You!

Christ Alone—for You!

"I brought you these from home."

"You can take the mist instead of the shot."

"I'll get rid of the spider for you."

"I'm canceling that assignment."

"I'll protect you."

Christ Jesus came into the world to save

_____
(name)

1 Timothy 1:15

Word Study

Match the words with their definition.

Faith   When God gives us forgiveness, life, and salvation as a free gift

Works   Trusting in Jesus alone to give us forgiveness and eternal life

Grace   Anything human beings do; doing good deeds

Faith Alone—What a Relief!

"I feel better."

"I'm so happy!"

"Thank You, Lord!"

"And He did it for you too!"

Scripture Alone—for the Bible Tells Me So!

Bible Words to Remember

For by grace you have been saved through faith. . . . It is the gift of God, not a result of works, so that no one may boast. Ephesians 2:8–9

Who Is a Saint?

- ☐ A really good person
- ☐ Someone who has miraculous powers to help others
- ☑ A believer who has died and gone to heaven
- ☐ Someone who hears your prayers
- ☑ A sinner who believes in Jesus

What Do You See?

Zacchaeus Was . . .

selfish · a cheat · greedy · a thief · not a believer in Jesus

Word Study

Unscramble the letters to complete the definitions.

NIRENS _sinner_ — Someone who thinks, says, and does wrong things, whose heart is against God

NATIS _saints_ — Someone who believes in Jesus as Savior, who has been forgiven and is a new creation

I Am . . . *a saint*

What Does God See?

Write what God sees when He looks at you. *clean, holy,*

How does this make you feel? *happy because it makes me proteced from sins and the devil.*

Bible Words to Remember

Love the LORD, all you His saints! The LORD preserves the faithful.
Psalm 31:23

An Invitation to the Family of God

Fill in the invitation.

You're Invited!

Who: _everyone_

What: be part of God's family and call Him
Father

When: _Now and Forever_

How: Jesus died to take away our sins and make us
Children of God

Why: because _God love us._

God so loved the world, that He gave His only Son, that whoever believes in Him should not perish but have eternal life. John 3:16

Adopted

But when the fullness of time had come, God sent forth His Son, born of woman, born under the law, to redeem those who were under the law, so that we might receive adoption as sons. And because you are sons, God has sent the Spirit of His Son into our hearts, crying, "Abba! Father!" So you are no longer a slave, but a son, and if a son, then an heir through God. Galatians 4:4–7.

Word Study

Highlight the words *redeem* and *heir* in the Galatians 4 verse above.

Define *heir*: _one who inherits possessions property, money or other blessings from someones_

Define *redeem*: _____

God, Our Loving Father

Use what you know and learned today to describe God, our loving Father. Add a word or a phrase by each letter. Make sure the first word begins with the letter.

F: forgiving, _faith_

A: _Abba!_

T: _talant_

H: _elps us_

E: _eternal life porus_

R: _redeem_

Bible Words to Remember

See what kind of love the Father has given to us, that we should be called children of God; and so we are. 1 John 3:1

Why Do We Call God Our Father?

Read God's story about us in these Bible verses. Write the number of the Bible reference under the statement that summarizes it.

Now fill in the face beside each box to show how you feel after reading the Bible verse.

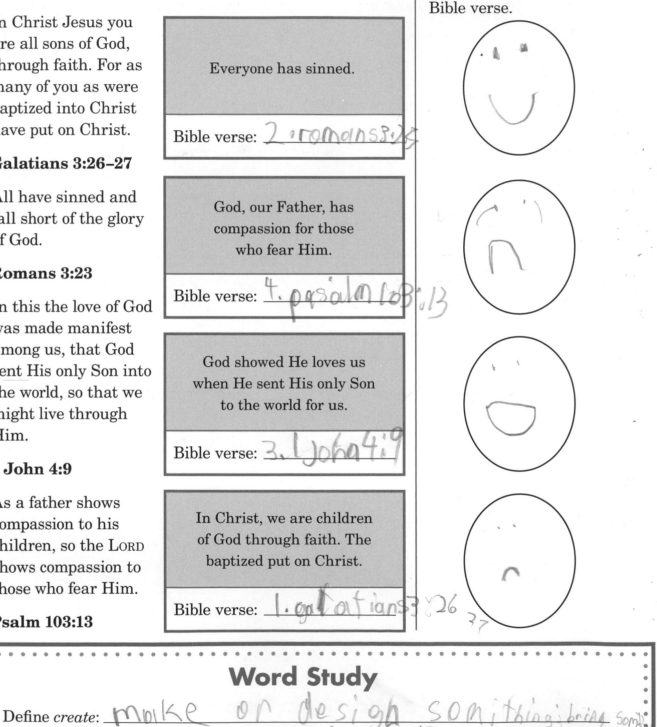

1. In Christ Jesus you are all sons of God, through faith. For as many of you as were baptized into Christ have put on Christ.

   Galatians 3:26–27

2. All have sinned and fall short of the glory of God.

   Romans 3:23

3. In this the love of God was made manifest among us, that God sent His only Son into the world, so that we might live through Him.

   1 John 4:9

4. As a father shows compassion to his children, so the LORD shows compassion to those who fear Him.

   Psalm 103:13

Everyone has sinned.

Bible verse: 2. romans3:23

God, our Father, has compassion for those who fear Him.

Bible verse: 4. psalm 103:13

God showed He loves us when He sent His only Son to the world for us.

Bible verse: 3. John 4:9

In Christ, we are children of God through faith. The baptized put on Christ.

Bible verse: 1. galatians 3:26 27

Word Study

Define *create*: make or design somthing; bring somthing to life

Define *baptize*: the action of sharing God's grace in Christ by aplying water in the Name of the Son and holy spirit; the father

The pastor pours water on our head and says, "I baptize you in the name of the _____ __Father__ and of the __Son__ and of the __holy__ __spirit__ .

2. In Baptism, God makes us His children.

Christ is God the __Son__ . Because of Him, we can call God __Father__ .

At Jesus' Baptism, God said "__this__ __is__ __Myved be roved son__ ." Matthew 3:17

In our Baptism, God says the same thing about us. We are His beloved __sons__ and __daughters__

3. In Baptism, we put on Christ.

When God looks at us, He sees __Jesus__ and His righteousness.

Gifts for God's Children

Parents love to give their children gifts. God loves to give us gifts too. Read Baptism, Section 2 in the Small Catechism (in the Appendix of this book) to find gifts that God gives in Baptism. Write each gift on a box below.

father   son   holy spr

Bible Words to Remember

For in Christ Jesus you are all sons of God, through faith.
Galatians 3:26

The Creation of the World

In the beginning, God created the heavens and the earth. The earth was without form and void, and darkness was over the face of the deep. And the Spirit of God was hovering over the face of the waters. Genesis 1:1–2

And God Said . . .

In the beginning was the Word, and the Word was with God, and the Word was God. He was in the beginning with God. All things were made through Him, and

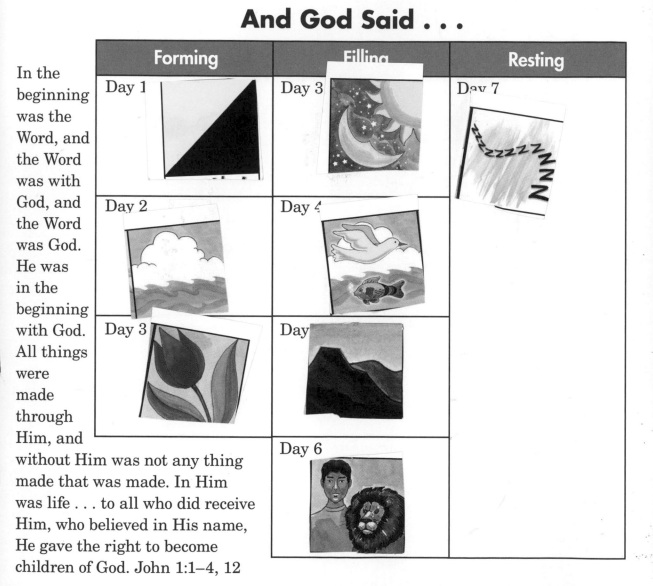

Forming	Filling	Resting
Day 1	Day 3	Day 7
Day 2	Day 4	
Day 3	Day 5	
Day 6		

without Him was not any thing made that was made. In Him was life . . . to all who did receive Him, who believed in His name, He gave the right to become children of God. John 1:1–4, 12

Word Study

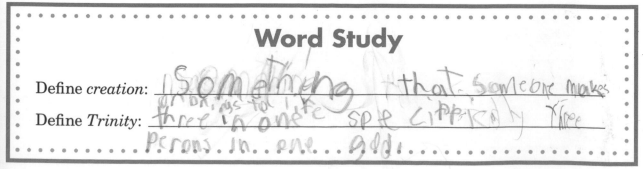

Define *creation*: __something that someone makes and brings to life__

Define *Trinity*: __three in one specifically three persons in one god.__

DID ALL THINGS COME TO BE?

Honoring God by Caring for Creation

Circle pictures that show how we can take care of God's creation. Put an *X* on the pictures that show actions that do not care for God's creation.

Bible Words to Remember

Worthy are You, our Lord and God, to receive glory and honor and power, for You created all things, and by Your will they existed and were created. Revelation 4:11

How Did People Come to Be?

God created people. He formed Adam from the dust of the ground and breathed life into his nostrils. Life is a precious gift from God that we should value and treasure.

God's Gift of Life

Directions: Using a blue crayon, circle gifts that God gives you.

Word Study

Define *Adam*: first man of God creaced disbe
sinned bydisobeyed God thorlory bringotes all peopl

Define *image of God*: _____

Be Fruitful and Multiply

God created all things. He made birds, insects, plants, the stars, animals, and man. God blessed all living creatures and told them to be fruitful, to multiply, and to fill the earth (Genesis 1:22, 28). That means having babies!

Directions: Draw a line to match each child to his or her parent.

Child   **Parent**

Bible Words to Remember

I praise You, for I am fearfully and wonderfully made. Wonderful are Your works; my soul knows it very well. Psalm 139:14

What Do God's Angels Do?

Angels are God's special helpers.

Looks

Actions

the angel anoced the good news to sherpened warh Joseln to flee to egypt they minsten to Jesos

cothing white as snow his appencie like lighting

Joseln menyeb mony sherpebs responded

How people responded

jesus welcomed the angels

Actions

that said the angel to mony that would be a mother of god: giving strength the angels spiten x

---

Word Study

Define *invisible*: not be able to see

Angels in the Life of Jesus

God's angels told about Jesus and cared for Him. Read these verses and write the information on page 64. On the head, write how angels looked. On the wings, write what angels did. On the body, write how people responded to angels. Not all verses have answers for all parts.

1 Before Jesus' birth
Matthew 1:20–21: An angel of the Lord appeared to [Joseph] in a dream, saying, "Joseph, son of David, do not fear to take Mary as your wife, for that which is conceived in her is from the Holy Spirit. She will bear a son, and you shall call his name Jesus, for He will save His people from their sins."

2 When Jesus was born
Luke 2:8–12: And in the same region there were shepherds out in the field, keeping watch over their flock by night. And an angel of the Lord appeared to them, and the glory of the Lord shone around them, and they were filled with fear.
And the angel said to them, "Fear not, for behold, I bring you good news of great joy that will be for all the people. For unto you is born this day in the city of David a Savior, who is Christ the Lord. And this will be a sign for you: you will find a baby wrapped in swaddling cloths and lying in a manger."

3 When Jesus was a baby
Matthew 2:13: An angel of the Lord appeared to Joseph in a dream and said, "Rise, take the child and His mother, and flee to Egypt, and remain there until I tell you, for Herod is about to search for the child, to destroy Him."

4 After the devil tempted Jesus
Matthew 4:11: Then the devil left Him, and behold, angels came and were ministering to Him.

5 When Jesus prayed in the Garden of Gethsemane, before His arrest
Luke 22:43: And there appeared to [Jesus] an angel from heaven, strengthening Him.

6 When Jesus rose from the dead
Matthew 28:2–4: And behold, there was a great earthquake, for an angel of the Lord descended from heaven and came and rolled back the stone and sat on it. His appearance was like lightning, and his clothing white as snow. And for fear of him the guards trembled and became like dead men.

Bible Words to Remember

He will command His angels concerning you to guard you in all your ways. Psalm 91:11

Real Beings and Real Places

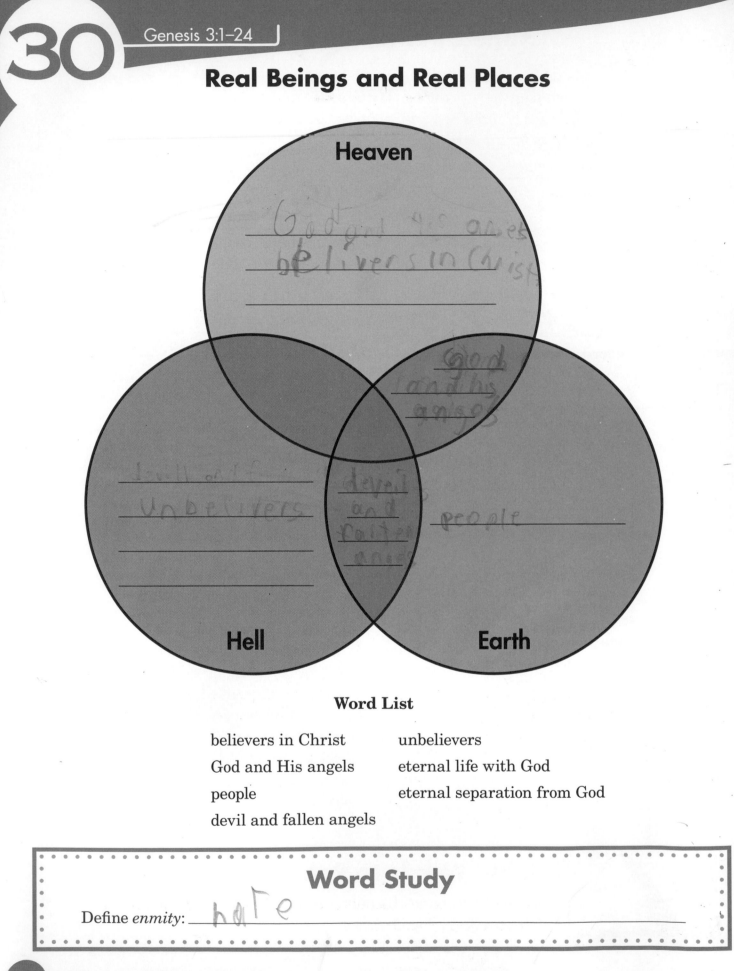

Heaven

God and his anes
belivers in Christ

God
and his
angels

Hell

dull and
unbelivers

devol
and
falten
anes

people

Earth

Word List

believers in Christ   unbelievers

God and His angels   eternal life with God

people   eternal separation from God

devil and fallen angels

Word Study

Define *enmity*: hate

My Prayer

Dear God,

please make me a better person and help those who are dieing from the corona virus and help us to wear a mask and hand santizen so we don't get a virsus too Amen.

Bible Words to Remember

Submit yourselves therefore to God. Resist the devil, and he will flee from you. James 4:7

Ordinary Things, Extraordinary God
God Protected Elijah

 = Ahab   = Elijah   = the widow   = son

King did many **evil** things. married Jezebel, and they worshiped the **FALSE** god Baal. This made the Lord angry.

People believed Baal gave , but Baal was only a statue, not the **TRUE**, **living** God.

God sent His prophet to speak His Word to . said, "The Lord God of Israel is the **TRUE**, **living** God. To show you, there will be no or dew in the next few years."

God told to go hide in a valley near a brook. God sent every morning and evening to bring meat and bread.

The brook dried up. God told to go to the town of Zarephath and stay with . Widows were women whose husbands had died; they were the poorest of the poor.

 saw gathering sticks outside the town gate. asked

 to bring him some water and a piece of bread.

 stopped. "Your **living** God knows I don't have bread, only a handful of flour and a little oil. I'm gathering sticks to make a last meal. Then my and I will die.

 said, "Don't be afraid. Make your food, and also make a small cake for me. The Lord says your flour and oil will not be used up until the Lord gives ."

 did as said. Every day, God provided food. The flour and oil never ran out.

Sometime later, the became ill and died. asked to help. prayed to God. The Lord returned life to the . said, "Now I know that the Word of the Lord from your is true."

God used , oil, and flour to care for , , and her . God cares for us too. When afraid, we can always turn to our God. He protects us from danger and evil.

Define *idol*: _a false god sometimes shows in human form in a staue_

Shepherd and Sheep

Jesus calls Himself our Good Shepherd; we are His sheep. He provides for our needs and protects us from harm and danger. Jesus knows what is best for His sheep and when it is best to give gifts to His flock.

Look up **Psalm 23** and unscramble the bold red words to complete the verses.

The Lord is my **hdrepehs** _sheperhd_; I shall not **twan** _wont_. He makes me lie down in green pastures. He leads me beside **ilstl** _still_ waters. He restores my soul.

He leads me in **thaps** _paths_ of righteousness for His name's sake. Even though I walk through the **yeallv** _valley_ of the shadow of death, I will fear no evil, for You are with me; Your rod and Your **fastf** _staff_, they comfort me.

You prepare a table before me in the presence of my **meneies** _enemies_; You anoint my head with oil; my **puc** _cup_ overflows. Surely goodness and mercy shall follow me all the days of my life, and I shall dwell in the **ouhes** _house_ of the Lord forever.

Bible Words to Remember

For those who love God all things work together for good, for those who are called according to His purpose. Romans 8:28

Wonderfully Made

Just think. God made the earth a perfect place for us to live. The world has just the right amounts of oxygen and water for us. The earth is positioned perfectly from the sun to support life. It spins at just the right speed to keep us aboard. God made this wonderful place for you to live.

God's perfect design extends to plants and animals too. Flowers open at the best time of the day. God made elephants with legs that bend forward to help them rise from the ground easily.

Draw a few of your favorite plants and animals that God wonderfully made.

God made our bodies with amazing abilities too:

- Acid in your stomach that dissolves food is so strong that it can also dissolve metal. Because of that, your body makes a new stomach lining every three days.

- You have over 60,000 miles of blood vessels in your body. That's far enough to travel from New York to San Francisco twenty times!

- The marks on your fingertips are called fingerprints. No one else in the world has the same prints as you. They never change over your lifetime.

Write a prayer to thank God for making our wonderful bodies and planet.

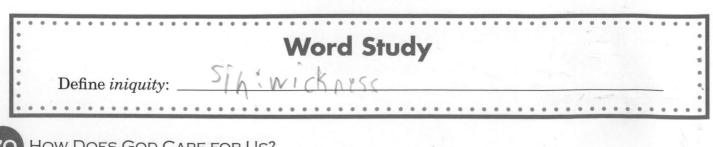

oh god thank you for making us better than animals

Word Study

Define *iniquity*: ___Sin wickness___

God's Great Gifts

Do you remember the greatest present you ever received? Was it on your birthday, or maybe Christmas? How did you feel when you saw it?

God loves you so much that He gave you the greatest gift, His Son, Jesus! And in Jesus, God gives us even more. Open more gifts God offers His children.

Read the verses in Psalm 103 and write the gifts each lists.

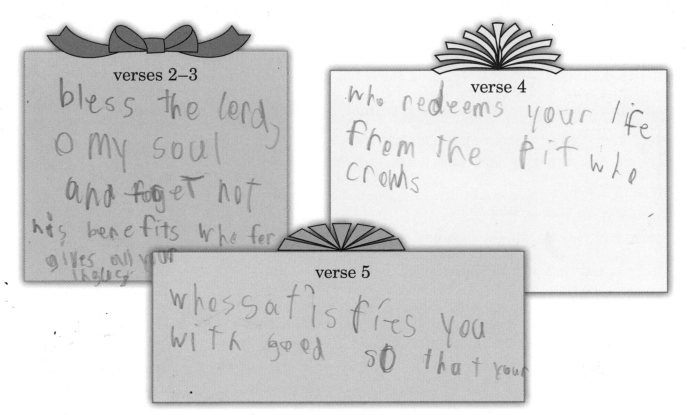

verses 2–3
bless the lord,
o my soul
and forget not
his benefits who for
gives all your
iniqulty

verse 4
who redeems your life
from the pit who
crowns

verse 5
who satisfies you
with good so that your

What kind of God gives these kinds of gifts? Read verse 8.

a God who helps us and Jesus
toke are punisment because of sin

God's mercy, grace, and love are most perfectly shown to us in Jesus. He loved us so much that He died on the cross in our place. He took the punishment we deserved. Those who believe in Him receive forgiveness of sins and eternal life, today and forever!

Bible Words to Remember
I praise You, for I am fearfully and wonderfully made.
Psalm 139:14

Use God's Gifts Wisely

God led the people of Israel out of slavery in Egypt and into the desert on the way to the Promised Land. The Lord told Moses to tell the people of Israel that He would provide meat for them in the evening and bread in the morning. This would show them He is God.

In the evening, quail covered the camp. In the morning, dew fell around the camp. When the dew dried, it left a fine, flaky frost on the ground. The people did not know what it was. They called it manna, which means "What is it?" Moses said, "This is bread from the Lord. Gather as much as you can eat." So the people did. They ground manna and made many different foods from it. The manna was white and tasted like wafers made with honey.

Moses told the people not to keep manna until morning, but some did not listen. When they kept some until morning, it had worms and stank. Moses became angry with them.

1. What did God provide for people to eat in the evening?

   quail

2. What did He provide in the morning?

   manna

3. What manna rules did God give the people through Moses?

   he said get how much you
   can eat and don't keep it,

4. What do we learn from this story about using God's gifts wisely?

   We need to use Gods gifts
   wisly or the gift would go bad
   or conquese

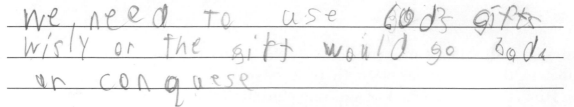

Word Study

Define *steward*: _a person who takes corre of items_
That belongs To someone else.

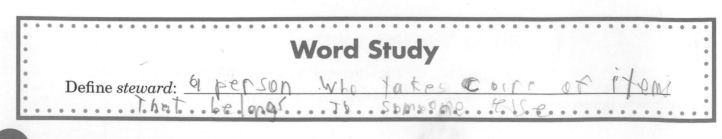

Super Steward or Careless Keeper?

God gave us an awesome gift when He created the earth and all its living things. God made people stewards, or protectors and keepers, of the earth. We honor God when we take good care of the earth and use it well.

Meet Kyle, a third grader, much like you. This morning, Kyle ran the water for ten minutes before getting in to take a shower. He turned off the light when he left his room.

Kyle threw his favorite shirt in the empty washing machine and started the cycle. He got a new paper bag for lunch, the eighth that week.

At school, Kyle tried to hit squirrels with rocks at first recess. He ate a granola bar and put the wrapper in the garbage can. Kyle and a few friends raced to the far fence.

Later, Kyle drew a picture with crayons but didn't like it, so threw the paper in the recycle bin. At home again, Kyle took out the garbage for his mom. Thirsty, he poured a drink of water from the pitcher in the refrigerator.

In the chart, list the things Kyle did or failed to do as a steward or keeper of the earth.

Super Steward	Careless Keeper
helped his mom throw the thrash	he throwed rocks at the squirrels ran the water for ten min and. wrapper in garbage

One way to become a better steward is to become more thankful for the gifts we've been given. In thanks for all God has done, we serve Him and honor Him. How might this Bible verse help Kyle remember to be a Super Steward?

Whether you eat or drink, or whatever you do, do all to the glory of God. 1 Corinthians 10:31

remeber to do it for god.

Bible Words to Remember

Every good gift and every perfect gift is from above, coming down from the Father of lights. James 1:17

Thank and Praise

What kind of prayers do you usually say to God?

Are they mostly GIMME (give me) prayers? Or DOODIS (do this) prayers? It's okay to **request** God's help, but there are also other kinds of prayers to offer God.

• We can **confess** our sins and ask God to forgive us.

• We can **thank** God for His gifts, especially for sending Jesus to forgive our sins.

• We can **praise** the Lord in prayer for His many great qualities and love for us.

Write a prayer to God that has all four types of prayer: confession, request, thanks, praise.

dear God thank you for helping us dodge the corona so we dont get sick also help others as they dodge the corona let us not get sick and others too!

Word Study

Define *praise*: *to tell good things about someone or something*

Serve and Obey

Write down the examples of serving you see in these pictures.

helping a blind man by opening a door

helping some with homework

serving God in chapel.

Feeding a puppy.

Telling what God has done

There are many ways to serve our Lord, including serving and helping others.

We also serve God by doing everyday tasks well and using the gifts God gives us. This is like sending God a thank-You note. Write one thing you will do well today to honor God.

helping someone who falls and hurt themselves

Bible Words to Remember

Jesus said, "If anyone serves Me, he must follow Me; and where I am, there will My servant be also. If anyone serves Me, the Father will honor him." John 12:26

Talent Tune Up

God blessed each of us with talents we can use to glorify Him. You might be good at math, writing, sports, dancing, or even making others laugh. You might already know about your talents, but you may not find some of them until you grow up. What do you dream about doing when you grow up?

I want to be a mechanic so I know how cars are made an parts.

We thank and praise our Lord by using well the gifts He's given us. Tell how people with these gifts could use them to honor God:

writing stories

we can tell how God made everything

playing baseball

how God wins us.

memorizing

so we know what he has done

dancing

honering god

drawing

drawhg pictures of god

Of course, the most excellent gift God has given us is His Son, Jesus Christ! Forgiveness and eternal life are now ours through faith in Jesus. Awesome! Let's use our gifts to praise and thank God for His gifts!

Word Study

Define *talent*: _____

A Variety of Gifts

Look up 1 Corinthians 12:4 to fill in the blanks.

Now there are varieties of __gifts__ , but the same __Spirit__ ; and there are varieties of __service__ , but the same __Lord__ ; and there are varieties of __activities__ but it is the same __God__ who empowers them all in __everyone__.

What do you do well? Draw a picture of yourself using one of your gifts to serve God.

Bible Words to Remember

There are varieties of activities, but it is the same God who empowers them all in everyone. 1 Corinthians 12:6.

36

Your Body Is a Temple of the Holy Spirit

At Baptism, the pastor marks the cross of Christ on your forehead and your chest. God claimed your heart and mind for Jesus. The Holy Spirit now lives in you!

Do you not know that your body is a temple of the Holy Spirit within you, whom you have from God? You are not your own, for you were bought with a price. So glorify God in your body. 1 Corinthians 6:19–20

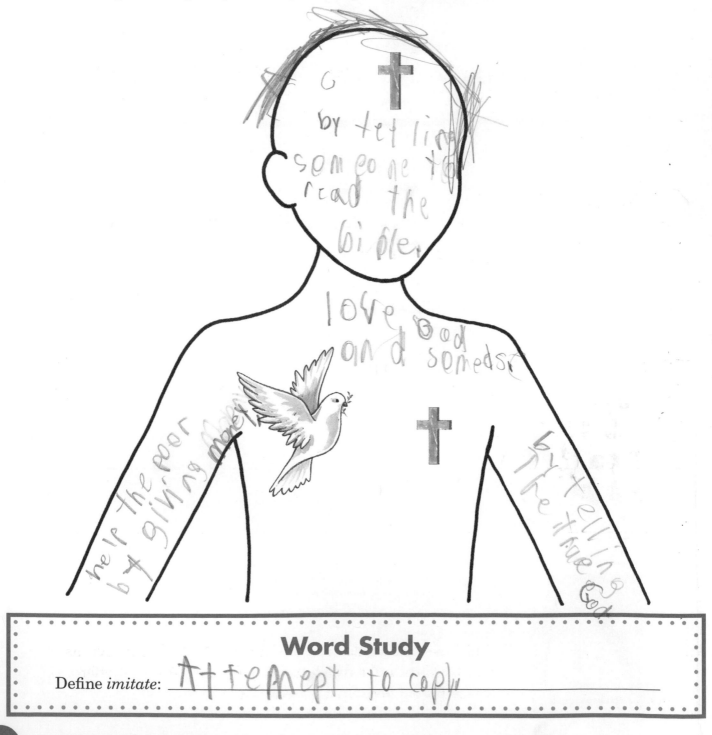

by tel ling
someone to
read the
bible.

love God
and somedse

help the poor
by giving mony

by telling
The true God

Word Study

Define *imitate*: Attemept to copy

Add a few details to make the picture on page 78 look like you, such as hair, clothing, and face. Write words or draw pictures to add this information to your person.

1. How can you use your mind to serve God? Add an idea in the head.

2. How can you serve God with your attitudes? Add one idea on the chest, near the heart.

3. How can you serve God with your actions? Add one idea on each arm.

Imitate God

Have you ever imitated something? Have you ever pretended your hairbrush was a microphone while you sang as your favorite singer? Have you ever tried to talk like your favorite cartoon character?

This is imitating. The Bible tells us to imitate God by doing what God does. Circle the words in the Bible verse that describe God's actions that we want to imitate.

Be kind to one another, tenderhearted, forgiving one another, as God in Christ forgave you. Therefore be imitators of God, as beloved children. And walk in love, as Christ loved us and gave Himself up for us, a fragrant offering and sacrifice to God. Ephesians 4:32–5:2

What motivates us to imitate God by doing these things?

by someone telling us to do something or asking someone and reading the bible to know what to do or when too do it

Bible Words to Remember

Be imitators of God, as beloved children. And walk in love, as Christ loved us and gave Himself up for us, a fragrant offering and sacrifice to God. Ephesians 5:1–2

O Come, Immanuel

Through Adam and Eve, sin entered the world. But God loves us and promised to send a Savior. For many years, God's people waited for the Savior to come. Read the clues and identify the people to whom God promised a Savior.

1. We were the first people to sin, and the first people to hear God's promise to send a Savior.

   Adam and Eve

2. God promised that my descendants would be great in number, as many as the stars in the sky. He said the Savior would come from my family.

   abraham

3. I was king of Israel. God said the Savior would be born in my hometown.

   king david

4. I was one of God's prophets. I told the people that a virgin would have a son and name Him Immanuel.

   Isaiah

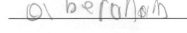

5. I was engaged to Mary. God told me in a dream that she would be the mother of His Son.

   joseph

Word Study

Fill in the blanks with one of these words: *message, love.*

Grace: God's undeserved ___love___ that moved Him to send Jesus to be our Savior, giving us forgiveness, life, and salvation.

Prophet: A person who gave God's ___message___ to people. Messages sometimes included information about the future.

God Loves Me Dearly

Write the circled word *In* on the first blank line on the globe. Going clockwise, write every other word on the lines until they are filled up.

Why did Jesus come? _to clearn_
are sins so we
don't be Dad.

How does Jesus give us life?
by diking on
the cross to
pay for our
sins.

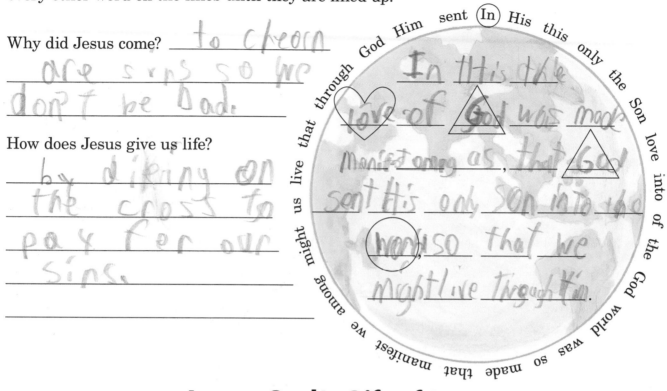

In this the
love of God was made
manifest among us, that God
sent His only Son into the
world, so that we
might live through Him.

Jesus, God's Gift of Love

Write a poem that tells about Jesus to praise God for sending His Son to save us.

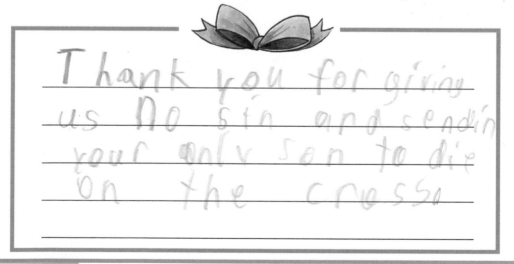

Thank you for giving
us No sin and sendin
your only son to die
on the crosss.

Bible Words to Remember

In this the _love of God_ was made manifest among us,
that God sent _his only Son_ into the world, so that we
might _live_ through Him. 1 John 4:9

What Shall We Name Him?

There are many names for Jesus in the Bible. They tell us who He is and what He has done for us. Write or draw a picture to tell what these names mean.

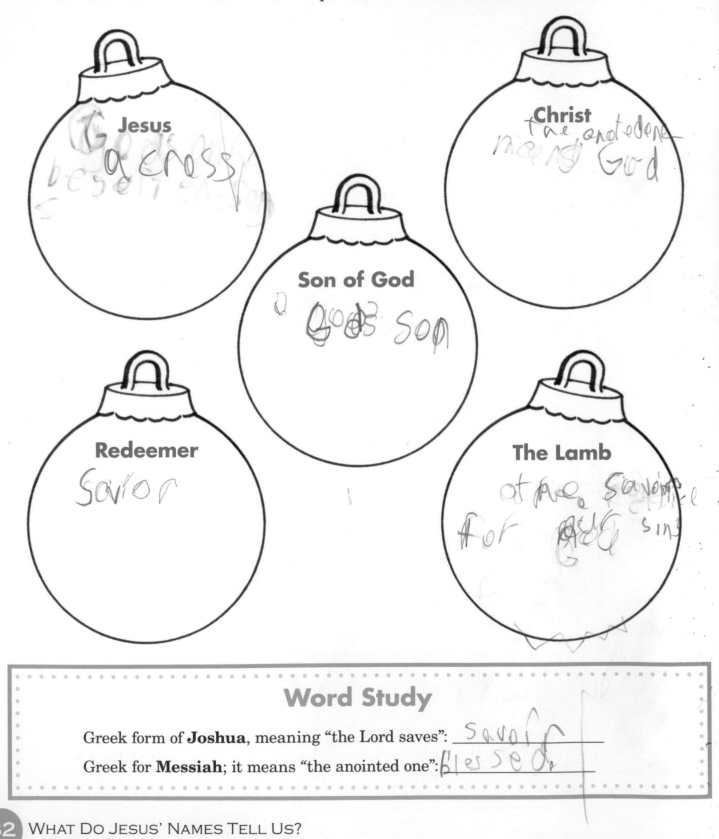

Jesus
a cross

Christ
the anoted one means God

Son of God
a gods son

Redeemer
savior

The Lamb
of the savior for our sins

Word Study

Greek form of **Joshua**, meaning "the Lord saves": savoir

Greek for **Messiah**; it means "the anointed one": blessed

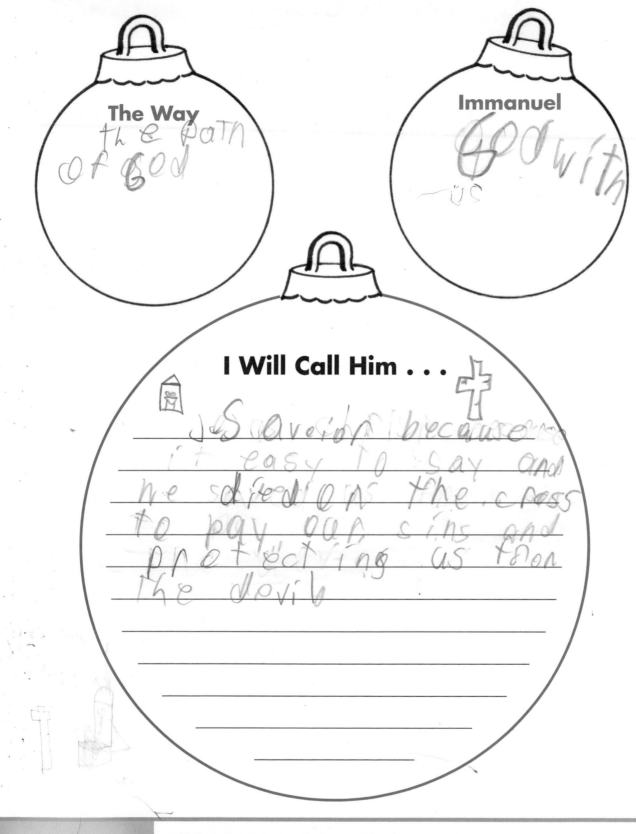

The Way

the path of god

Immanuel

god with us

I Will Call Him . . .

Jesavoior because it easy to say and he died on the cross to pay our sins and protecting us from the devil

Bible Words to Remember

There is salvation in no one else [but Jesus], for there is no other name under heaven given among men by which we must be saved. Acts 4:12

Signs and Wonders

1. Isaiah 9:6 says the Savior will be called **Wonderful Counselor**, **Mighty God**, **Everlasting Father**, **Prince of Peace**. The angel told Mary that Jesus would be called the **Son of God**. Label the first sign to tell what kind of names Jesus has.

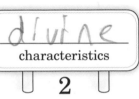

divine
names
1

2. John 1:1 says Jesus was with God from the beginning. He is **eternal**. There are many things we don't know. Even the smartest person in the world doesn't know everything, but John 21:17 says Jesus **knows all things**! This shows He is God because only God knows everything. Label the next sign to tell what kind of characteristics Jesus has.

divine
characteristics
2

divine
works
3

3. John 20:30 says Jesus did many **signs**, or **miracles**, to show people that He was the Son of God who came to save us. Label the third sign to tell what kind of works Jesus did.

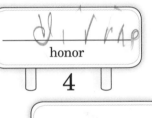

divine
honor
4

4. The Bible says we are to "honor the Son, just as [we] honor the Father" (John 5:23). After Jesus was born, the Wise Men came to bring Him gifts and **worship** Him. Label the fourth sign to show the kind of honor Jesus received.

Jesus is
God

Look at the signs you made. What does the Bible tell us about who Jesus is? Write that on the big sign.

Word Study

A	B	C	D	E	F	G	H	I	J	K	L	M	N	O	P	Q	R	S	T	U	V	W	X	Y	Z
1	2	3	4	5	6	7	8	9	10	11	12	13	14	15	16	17	18	19	20	21	22	23	24	25	26

Use code. What does **sign** mean in John 20? miracle
13 9 18 1 3 12 5

Wind and Waves Obey

What were Jesus' disciples afraid of?

the storm that was mapping

How did Jesus help them?

he calm down the storm

The disciples asked, "Who is this?" How would you answer? J _e s u s_ i _s_ G _o d_ .

Why is it important that Jesus is God? _he saves us with miracles and helps by learning path_

Jesus Is God of My Life Too!

Write some of your troubles on the waves.

grades

sickness

family conflict

bullies

— Help!

loneliness

sickness

I'll help you.

Believe! Pray! Trust!

grades conflict

Bible Words to Remember

He [Jesus] is the true God and eternal life. 1 John 5:20

Announcing . . . God Incarnate

God Becomes Man

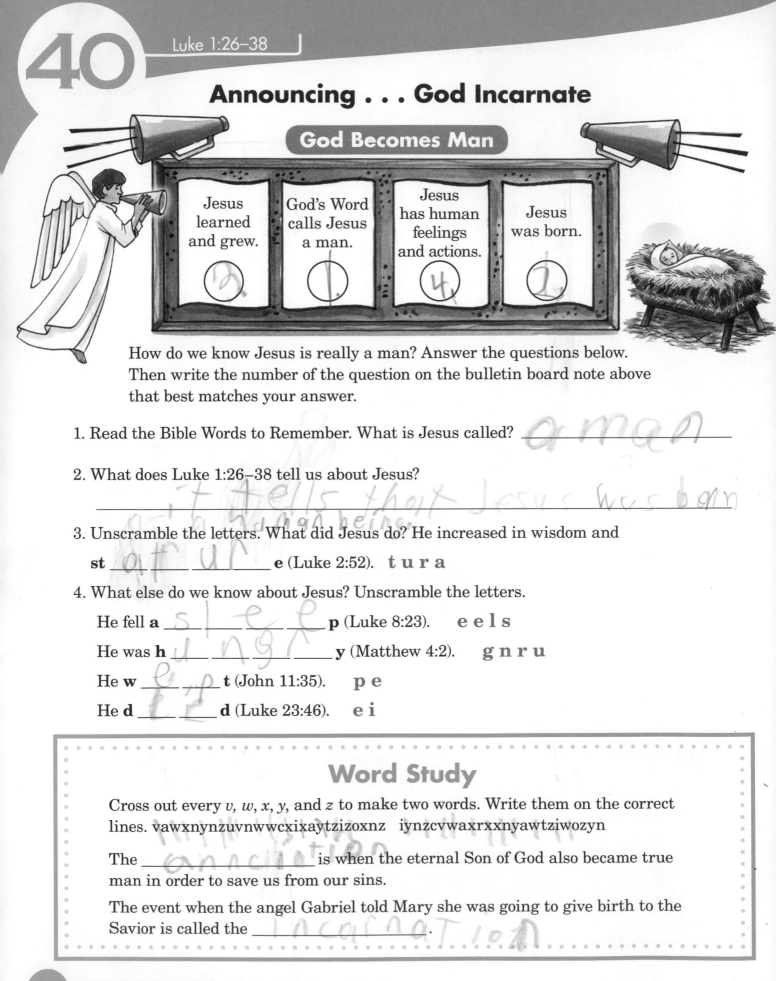

Jesus learned and grew.	God's Word calls Jesus a man.	Jesus has human feelings and actions.	Jesus was born.
③	①	④	②

How do we know Jesus is really a man? Answer the questions below. Then write the number of the question on the bulletin board note above that best matches your answer.

1. Read the Bible Words to Remember. What is Jesus called? _a man_

2. What does Luke 1:26–38 tell us about Jesus?
   it tells that Jesus was born
   as a human being.

3. Unscramble the letters. What did Jesus do? He increased in wisdom and
   st _a_ _t_ _u_ _r_ e (Luke 2:52). **t u r a**

4. What else do we know about Jesus? Unscramble the letters.
   He fell **a** _s_ _l_ _e_ _e_ **p** (Luke 8:23). **e e l s**
   He was **h** _u_ _n_ _g_ _r_ **y** (Matthew 4:2). **g n r u**
   He **w** _e_ _p_ **t** (John 11:35). **p e**
   He **d** _i_ _e_ **d** (Luke 23:46). **e i**

Word Study

Cross out every *v, w, x, y,* and *z* to make two words. Write them on the correct lines. vawxnynzuvnwwcxixaytzizoxnz   iynzcvwaxrxxnyawtziwozyn

The _annunciation_ is when the eternal Son of God also became true man in order to save us from our sins.

The event when the angel Gabriel told Mary she was going to give birth to the Savior is called the _Incarnation_.

Jesus Takes Our Place

Jesus became man to take our place. What two things did He have to do in order to save us?

1. <u>he died on the cross.</u>
2. <u>he did not sin</u>

Thank You, Jesus

Draw a cross over each picture to show that Jesus came to forgive our sins. Describe thankful responses to Jesus' forgiveness.

<u>you should brush your teeth.</u> <u>be happy that it didnt hurt your eyes.</u> <u>stop lying and tell the truth.</u>

Bible Words to Remember

There is one mediator between God and men, the man Christ Jesus, who gave Himself as a ransom for all. 1 Timothy 2:5–6

Jesus, Our Substitute

Complete the graphic organizer to see how Jesus serves as our substitute so that we can have forgiveness, life, and salvation.

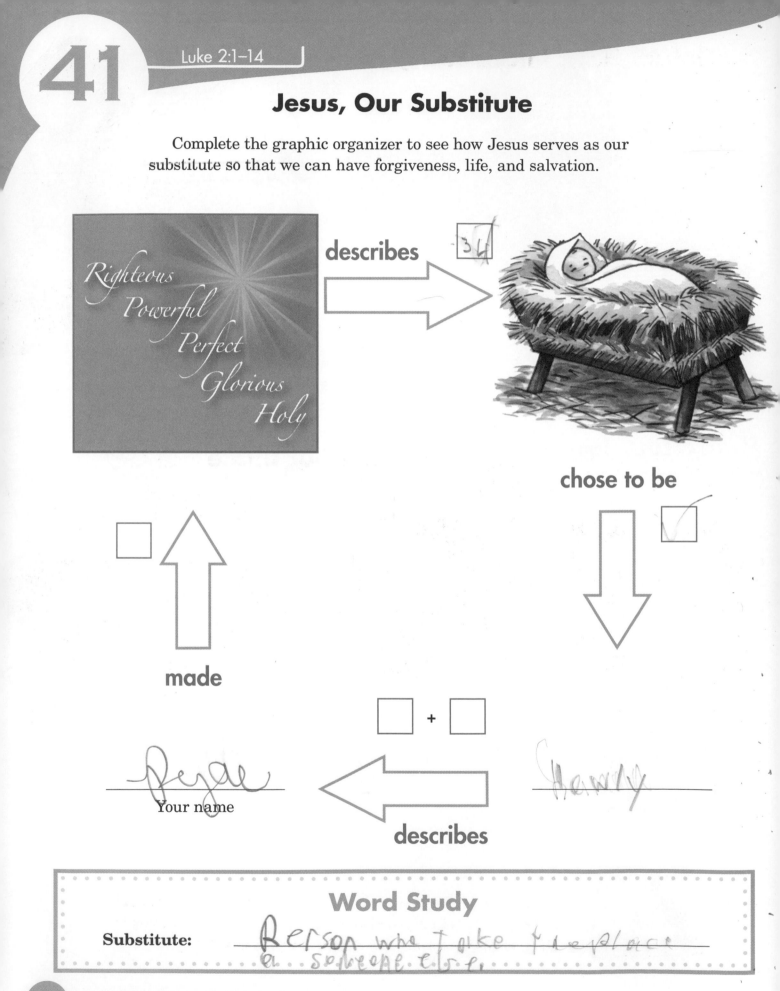

describes [34]

Righteous
Powerful
Perfect
Glorious
Holy

chose to be ✓

made

□ + □

Regae
Your name

lowly

describes

Word Study

Substitute: Person who take the place of someone else.

Infant Holy, Infant Lowly

> Infant holy, Infant lowly, For His bed a cattle stall;
> Oxen lowing, little knowing Christ the child is Lord of all.
> Swiftly winging, Angels singing, Bells are ringing, Tidings bringing:
> Christ the child is Lord of all! Christ the child is Lord of all!
>
> (LSB 393:1)

What does Luke 2:1–14 say about Jesus' birth?

The angels told the
shepeads, 3 wise men.

List other things in Jesus' life that show His humility:

he become a human, sevre
him, eat food

Jesus, our _____

Because Jesus Is Our Substitute

Color the manger beside each statement that shows what having Jesus as our substitute means. Because Jesus is our substitute . . .

- I am God's child. He is pleased with me.
- I can get lots of presents for Christmas.
- I can go to heaven.
- God forgives me, but I still have to do good things if I want to go to heaven.
- My sins are forgiven.

- I get Jesus' righteousness and holiness.
- I get to eat as many Christmas cookies as I want.
- I have Jesus' victory over sin, death, and the devil.
- I tell other people about Jesus, our substitute.
- I don't have to live in a stable.

Bible Words to Remember

For you know the grace of our Lord Jesus Christ, that though He was rich, yet for your sake He became poor, so that you by His poverty might become rich. 2 Corinthians 8:9

The Life of a Slave

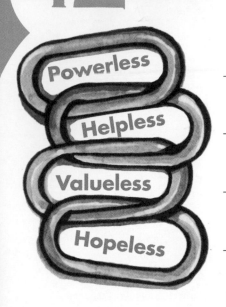

Powerless

Helpless

Valueless

Hopeless

can't quit or have no p____
be___ them weak and tired
not be worth

Held Captive

Draw yourself in jail. Draw bars to show how sin holds you captive.

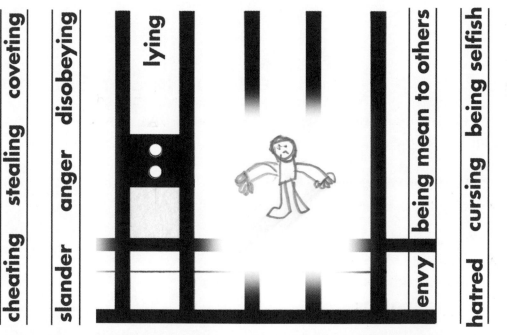

cheating stealing coveting

slander anger disobeying

lying

envy being mean to others

hatred cursing being selfish

Word Study

slavery — free — buy — payment

Redeem: To ___buy___ someone out of ___Slavery___ and set him ___free___

Ransom: The ___payment___ needed to rescue someone

Free

Safe

Valuable

Hope-filled

Redeemed

to be free from slavery

te not be worry about bad stuff.

to be worth some thing.

we have hope that god will save us.

Set Free to Serve

Jesus set you free from the power of sin, death, and the devil by paying for your sins on the cross. Answer the questions to show ways you can live as God's forgiven child.

1. No one will talk with the new student in your class because he has a lisp. What can you say or do?

   talk to the new kid.

2. The kids on your basketball team all use bad language. They are starting to call you a goody two-shoes because you don't. What can you say or do?

   i can say please stop it

3. Your cousin is sleeping over. She wants you to ask if you can skip church in the morning. What will you say or do? i'd say no thanks.

4. Your elderly neighbor needs someone to shovel the snow, but she has no money to pay anyone. What will you say or do? i'd help him shovel the snow

Bible Words to Remember

For you know that it was not with perishable things such as silver or gold that you were redeemed . . . but with the precious blood of Christ, a lamb without blemish or defect. 1 Peter 1:18–19 NIV

Christmas and Easter Connections

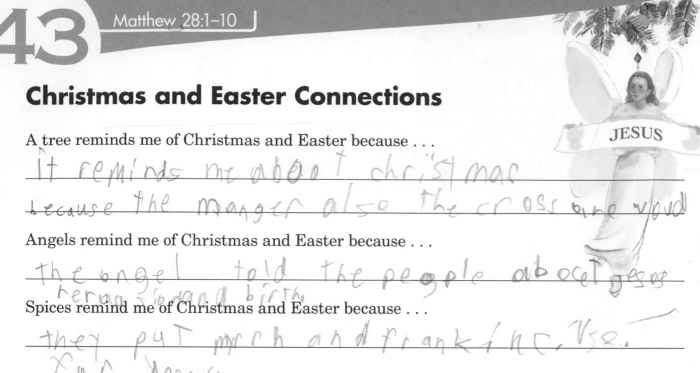

A tree reminds me of Christmas and Easter because . . .

It reminds me aboot christmas because the manger also the cross are wood

Angels remind me of Christmas and Easter because . . .

the angel told the people about jesus heren and birth

Spices remind me of Christmas and Easter because . . .

they put mrrh and frankfinc. Use. For Jesus.

Christmas and Easter are part of the same story—the story of God's plan of salvation. In order to save us, Jesus left heaven and became a real human being while still being God so that He could keep God's Law for us and die on the cross to pay for our sins. He had to come alive again to win the victory over sin, death, and the devil so we could have eternal life with Him.

Now Jesus is both God and man. Jesus as God is always the same. But the Bible describes Jesus as a man in two ways. We call these the states of humiliation and exaltation. Look at the definitions in the Word Study; then answer these questions.

Which state describes Jesus' being born at Christmas?

humiliation

Which state describes Jesus' coming alive at Easter?

exoltation.

Word Study

The state of **humiliation** is when Jesus as a man did not always or fully use His divine powers.

The state of **exaltation** is when Jesus as a man fully and always uses His divine powers.

Easter Surprise!

Find out what surprised the women on Easter. Unscramble the words on the rocks. Then use the numbers to put the words in order.

meht
4
them

aded
10
dead

dlot
3
told

morf
8
from

lenga
2
angel

eht
9
the

na
1
_an_

suseJ
5
Jesus

dah
6
had

nersi
7
risen

an angel told them Jesus had risen from the dead!

Importance of Jesus' Resurrection

Read the statements. Mark statements *T* or *F*.

___T___ Jesus paid for all my sins when He died on the cross.

___T___ Even though Jesus died for me, I still have to be good to be sure I'll go to heaven.

___T___ Jesus' resurrection proves He is really the Son of God, just as He said. That means I can trust Him to keep all His promises.

___T___ Jesus' resurrection means God accepted Jesus' payment on the cross for my sins. Now I can be sure God forgives me.

___F___ Jesus does not want us to tell the Good News of Easter to others.

___T___ When Jesus rose from the dead, it showed He has power over death and will give me eternal life with Him when I die.

Bible Words to Remember

Thanks be to God, who gives us the victory through our Lord Jesus Christ. 1 Corinthians 15:57

Jesus Loves Me, This I Know

How do you know that your parents love you? Write the answers in the heart.

They give me food and water, toy

Jesus loves you even more! Cross out the numbers in the heart. Then write the remaining letters on the lines to find out how you can be sure of this.

B9y2t3h4i5s6w7e8k
9n2o2w4l3o6v5e7t9h8a6
t2J3e4s7u2s9l5a6i7d8
d9o8w7n6H5i4
s3l2i3f9e6f2
o3r8u2s.

You can be sure of God's love and forgiveness! Because Jesus died to wash away your sins, He will proclaim you "not guilty" at the final judgment and take you home to heaven.

by this
we know
love, that
[Jesus] laid
down His
life for us. 1 John 3:16

Word Study

Circle the words that name the day Jesus will come back to earth.

Judgment Day   Second Coming   Last Day   Christ's Return

Write a definition for one of them: *The last day on earth when Jesus return to take his people to heaven*

When Jesus Returns

What does Matthew 25:31–34 tell us about the Last Day? _Come, you who blessed_
by you from the foundation of the world

Who are the sheep? Who are the goats? Write what you decide on each animal.

believers

believers

UA

Read Matthew 25:35–40. When was Jesus hungry, thirsty, sick, or in prison?
On the last day

What does Matthew 25:41–46 say happens to those who do not believe in Jesus?
they will have eternal punishment

Can you be sure you will go to heaven? _no because God choses who_
goes.

Until Jesus Returns

What does the Bible say about the time between now
and Christ's return? Check those that are true.

__✓__ Jesus says troubles in the world will increase—there will be wars,
earthquakes, and false prophets (Matthew 24:3–14).

_____ He told us exactly when He will come back so we can be ready
(Mark 13:32).

__✓__ Jesus wants us to show love for others by caring for their needs
(Matthew 25:40).

_____ Jesus wants us to tell others about Him so they can be saved
(Matthew 28:19).

_____ Jesus left us alone when He returned to heaven (Matthew 28:20).

Bible Words to Remember

So Christ, having been offered once to bear the sins of
many, will appear a second time . . . to save those who are
eagerly waiting for Him. Hebrews 9:28

Messages from God

Road signs give messages to drivers. If these messages came from God, what might they mean? Draw lines to match each sign with its possible meaning.

Slow down your busy life and pay attention to God.

Expect difficulties in your life, but I'll be with you.

I am making you new in Jesus!

Stop doing evil.

Turn from your wicked ways.

Yield yourself to God.

Jesus is the only way to heaven.

Messengers from God

What do we call messengers from God? _prophets_

Check the things prophets did.

☒ Prophets spoke for God on His authority.

☐ Prophets *only* gave people messages from God about future events.

☒ Some prophets told people about how God was sending a Savior so people would recognize Jesus when He came.

☒ Some prophets told people about the "right now." They said they needed to repent and listen to God so He would forgive them; otherwise, bad things would happen.

☐ People always listened to the prophets and did what they said.

Word Study

Fill in the missing words.

Prophecy: A _message_ from God, usually intended to bring people to _repent_ and _faith_.

Messianic prophecy: A message from God about _Jesus_, even before He was born.

Pointing to Jesus

Read Luke 1:57–80. Who was just born? *John the baptist*

According to Zechariah, who was about to be born? _____

What would John do when he grew up? *be a prophet*

What picture language does Zechariah use to describe Jesus?

_____

_____

Why is this Good News?

so we can be saved

_____

Isaiah

The Greatest Prophet

Circle the best answer. The greatest prophet is:

Isaiah   John the Baptist   (Jesus)

Tell why you think this. *he wasn't born with sin*

_____

_____

John the Baptist

Jesus

God's Messengers Today

☐ Missionaries

☐ Pastor

☐ *ygae*

As prophet, Jesus still works through the Gospel to proclaim Himself the Son of God and Savior. Put a check by those who share God's Word today. Draw yourself in the empty frame. You are God's messenger too! Write the name of someone you can tell about Jesus: *my brother*

Bible Words to Remember

We are ambassadors for Christ, God making His appeal through us. 2 Corinthians 5:20

Jesus, Our Priest and Sacrifice

Use a brown pencil to outline the words *priest* and *sacrifice*.

What do these words make? _____

Jesus is our _PRIEST_. He is a real human being, but He is perfect. He never sinned but kept the Law perfectly for us. He can face God when we can't.

Jesus is also the perfect _sacrifice_.
What did Jesus sacrifice? _himself on the cross_

What other words do you see in the puzzle a lot?
death and _sin_

Color all the letters in the puzzle black except those in *sacrifice* and *priest*.

When Jesus sacrificed Himself on the cross, He rescued us from sin and death. Now we are _forgived_ and have life with Him forever.

Jesus, Our Mediator

Fill in the letters. Jesus is our _mediator_. He stands between us and God as an everlasting reminder of how He paid for our sins on the cross. He intercedes, or _talking_, for us. Draw yourself beside the child.

Word Study

Intercede: _To pray to God on behalf of some one else_

Sacrifice: _To offer something to God for his use_

Who Is This Baby?

What does Luke 2:21–40 say Simeon did?

he preised god

What did Anna say?

she todd everyone of Jesus and praise god

How will you respond to knowing Jesus came to save you?

i feel That we will nave eternal life

Because Jesus Is Our Priest . . .

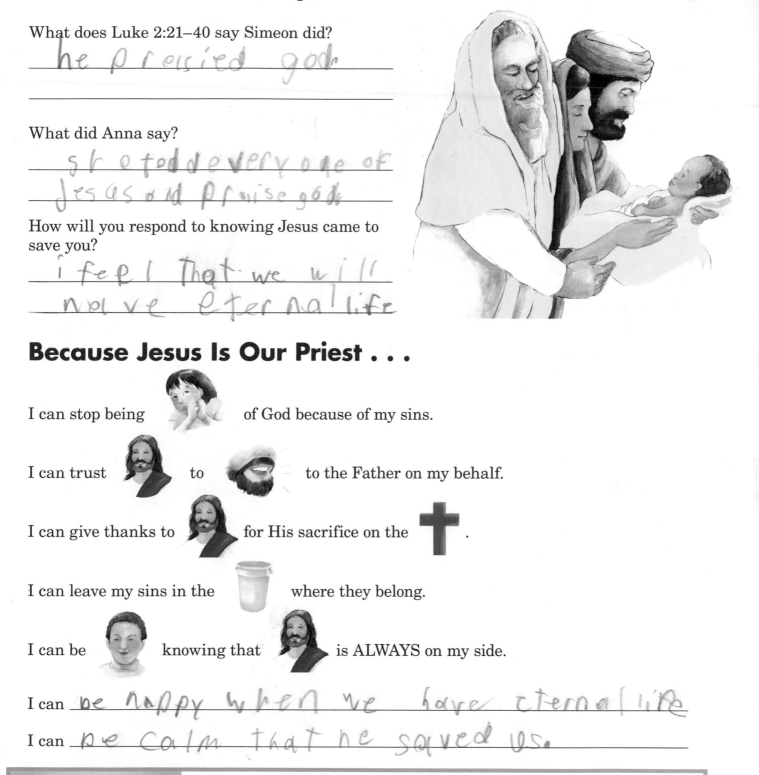

I can stop being  of God because of my sins.

I can trust  to  to the Father on my behalf.

I can give thanks to  for His sacrifice on the .

I can leave my sins in the  where they belong.

I can be  knowing that  is ALWAYS on my side.

I can be nappy when ve have eternal life

I can be calm that ne saved us.

Bible Words to Remember

But if anybody does sin, we have one who speaks to the Father in our defense—Jesus Christ, the Righteous One. He is the atoning sacrifice for our sins. 1 John 2:1–2 NIV

Recipe for a King

On the recipe card, write qualities that make a good king.

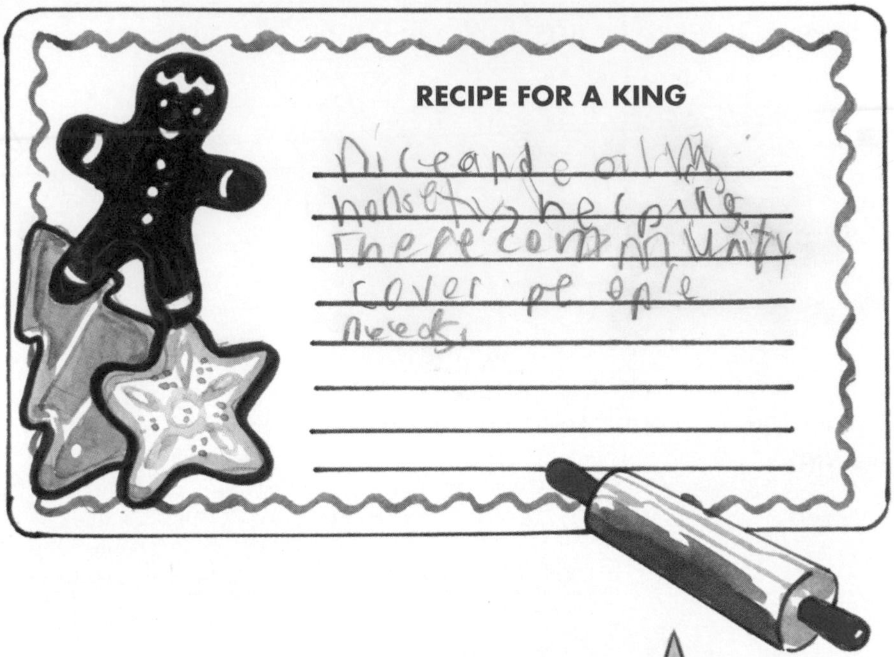

RECIPE FOR A KING

nice and caring, honesty, helping there community, cover people needs.

We Three Kings

Read Matthew 2:1–11. Fill in the blanks.

king   ruler
Wise Men   worshiped
Bethlehem   gifts

Wise men from the East came to find Jesus after He was born. They asked, "Where is He who has been born _king_ of the Jews?" The priests told them that God's Word said a _ruler_ would be born in _bethlehem_. This was the hometown of Joseph's ancestor, King David. When the Wise Men found Jesus, they fell down and _worshiped_ Him. They gave Him _gifts_ of gold, frankincense, and myrrh.

Word Study

Fill in the blanks with one of these words: **kingdom**, **believers**, **creation**.

Kingdom of power: Christ's rule with almighty power over all _creation_.

Kingdom of grace: Christ's rule over and care for all _believers_.

Kingdom of glory: Christ's heavenly _kingdom_ that lasts forever.

Three Kingdoms

In the three crowns, tell about Jesus' power, grace, and glory.

Power

he has power over earth.

Jesus said, "All authority in heaven and on earth has been given to Me." Matthew 28:18

Grace

he cares for all beilevers

Jesus said, "My kingdom is not of this world . . . I have come into the world—to bear witness to the truth." John 18:36–37

Glory

he rescue us from the devil

The Lord will rescue me from every evil deed and bring me safely into His heavenly kingdom. 2 Timothy 4:18

Jesus is your King! Describe what this means to you.

it means he has power and saves us from the devil.

Bible Words to Remember

The Lord will rescue me from every evil deed and bring me safely into His heavenly kingdom. To Him be the glory forever and ever. Amen. 2 Timothy 4:18

Lost and Alone

Find your way through the maze
to rescue the puppy.

Why would you rescue this puppy and take it home? _its probly sad and cate._

Why did God rescue you and make you His own? _god love us._

Word Study

Match the words to their definitions.

Adoption: When someone chooses you to be his or her child

Heir: An Aramaic word that means "Daddy" or "Father"

Abba: A person who inherits possessions, property, money, or other blessings from someone else

---

How Much Is That Person in the Window?

Draw yourself in the window.

How much does Jesus love you?

he became my savior

How do you know? _he died on the_
cross

How much did you cost?

death on the cross

What does it mean to belong to Jesus?

we are his children,
eternal life

How does belonging to God's family affect your actions?

Forever Loved

Dear Abba, Father,

thank you for
forgiving with my
sins,

Your Child,

ryal

Bible Words to Remember

We are children of God, and if children, then heirs—heirs of
God and fellow heirs with Christ. Romans 8:16–17

God Hears and Answers Our Prayers

Number the pictures from 1 to 9 to show the correct order of the Bible events.

__8__ God sent a fire.

__1__ Queen Jezebel said she'd kill Elijah.

__5__ Elijah felt alone.

__2__ Elijah ran away.

__3__ In the desert, God's angel brought food and water.

__6__ God sent a strong wind.

Word Study

Highlight the bold words in the story captions above.

God was not in the **fire**. God was not in the **earthquake**. God was not in the **strong wind**. God told Elijah, **"Go!"** God had work for Elijah to do.

Earthquake!

Go!

___4___ Elijah hid in a cave.

___7___ God sent an earthquake.

_____ Elijah heard a whisper. He went to the door. God spoke.

Thy Will Be Done

Read the Lord's Prayer in the Appendix.

Write a phrase from the Lord's Prayer that reminds you of God's work in Elijah's life. Why did you choose it?

"The ferth petition becouse an angel gave him bread like The Forth petition soud.

Write a phrase from the Lord's Prayer that reminds you of God's work in your life. Why did you choose it?

The senvith petition becouse we are always into

Bible Words to Remember

Call upon Me and come and pray to Me, and I will hear you.
Jeremiah 29:12

Praying for Many Reasons

1. To ask God for help
2. To praise God
3. To thank God
4. To ask God to protect

5. To tell God about events or feelings
6. To ask God for guidance or wisdom
7. To confess sin and ask God for forgiveness

Directions: Look at the pictures and think of what kind of prayer to say for each. Write numbers from the list above to show which kind of prayer to say. For example, for the first one, the person could thank God, number 3.

thankful
_3_

sick
_1_

storm
_4 5, 6_

Word Study

Use these words to fill in the blanks in this sentence: **Samaritan, believed, leprosy**

Ten people had a disease called _leprosy_. They _believed_ in Jesus and asked Him to heal them. One _Samaritam_ came back to say thank You to Jesus.

meals

3, 2.

sin

7,

failures

1, 6, 5, 7,

family and friends

3, 2, 7, 4, Munk
5, 6, 7,

church

1, 2, 3, 4,
5, 6, 7

morning and night

1, 2, 3, 4,
5, 6, 7,

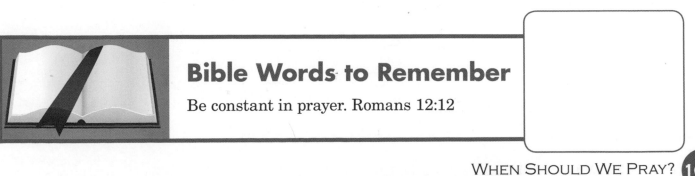

Bible Words to Remember

Be constant in prayer. Romans 12:12

God Speaks; We Listen

"Long ago, at many times and in many ways, God spoke to our fathers by the prophets, but in these last days He has spoken to us by His Son." Hebrews 1:1–2

God speaks to us by His Son,

Jesus.

"These are written so that you may believe that Jesus is the Christ, the Son of God, and that by believing you may have life in His name." John 20:31

Word of
God

Jesus said, "Go therefore and make disciples of all nations,

Baptizing

them in the name of the Father and of the Son and of the Holy Spirit." Matthew 28:19

Jesus said, "Take, eat; this is My body." Then He took the cup and said, "Drink of it . . . this is My blood of the covenant, which is poured out for many for the forgiveness of

sins." Matthew 26:26–28

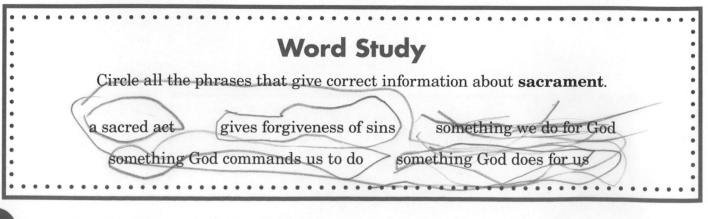

Word Study

Circle all the phrases that give correct information about **sacrament**.

a sacred act   gives forgiveness of sins   something we do for God

something God commands us to do   something God does for us

Jesus said, "If you __forgive__ the sins of any, they are forgiven them; if you withhold forgiveness from any, it is withheld." John 20:23

"Let the __word__ of Christ dwell in you richly, __teaching__ and admonishing one another in all wisdom, __singing__ psalms and hymns and spiritual songs." Colossians 3:16

__word__
of God

Dear God,
__Can you speak and forgive me for my sins.__

In Jesus' name. Amen.

We speak God's Word when we say and sing Scripture, and when we forgive others in Jesus' name.

Bible Words to Remember

Cast all your anxiety on Him because He cares for you. 1 Peter 5:7 NIV

Return to the Lord

The Call

If you **return to the Lord** with your whole , then put away your , and direct your ♥ to the L a R R. Believe in Him only, He will **deliver** you from your enemies.

The Response

So the people **repented**, put away their and **believed** in God only. They did not eat all day to show they were sorry for their sins.

Samuel sacrificed a lamb for the people's sins.

The Result

The Lord forgave their sins and kept His promise. He **delivered** them from their ~~enemies~~.

The Lord ♥ the people and cared for them. The people served the Lord only.

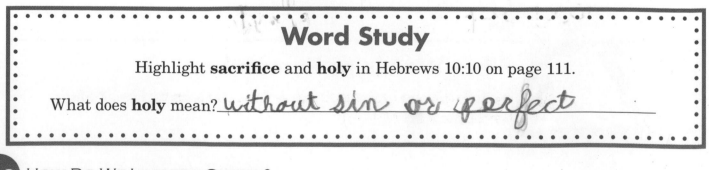

Word Study

Highlight **sacrifice** and **holy** in Hebrews 10:10 on page 111.

What does **holy** mean? _without sin or perfect_

The Call

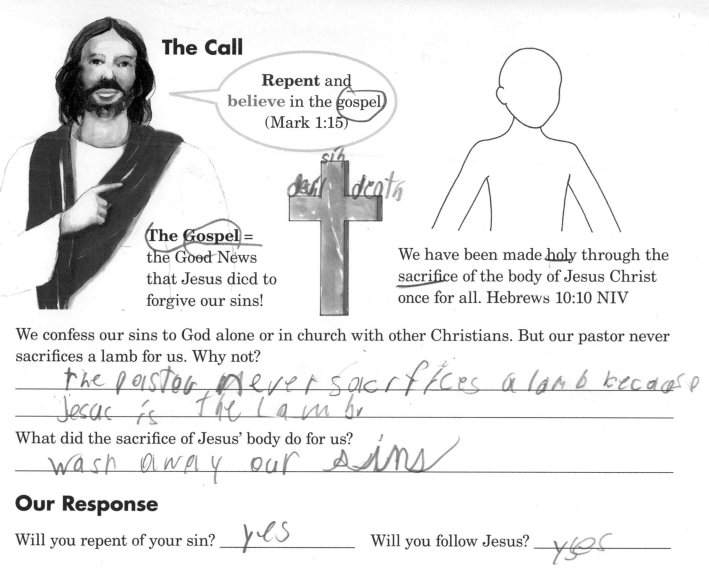

Repent and **believe** in the gospel. (Mark 1:15)

The Gospel = the Good News that Jesus died to forgive our sins!

We have been made holy through the sacrifice of the body of Jesus Christ once for all. Hebrews 10:10 NIV

We confess our sins to God alone or in church with other Christians. But our pastor never sacrifices a lamb for us. Why not?

The pastor never sacrffices a lamb becaose Jesus is the lamb.

What did the sacrifice of Jesus' body do for us?

wash away our sins

Our Response

Will you repent of your sin? *yes*   Will you follow Jesus? *yes*

The Result

Jesus **delivers** us from **sin**, **death**, and the **devil**. Write these **enemies** on the cross above.

Forgiven, we are free to live as Jesus' disciples. In Box 1, show one way you can live for Jesus now. In Box 2, show a way you can live for Jesus in your home or your career when you are an adult.

1. *being baptize*

2. *praynte god*

Bible Words to Remember

[Jesus] loves us and has freed us from our sins by His blood. Revelations 1:5 NIV

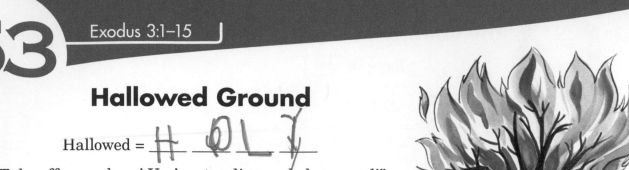

Hallowed Ground

Hallowed = H O L Y

"Take off your shoes! You're standing on holy ground!"

More Holy Things

God's WORD

The Holy SPIRT

Holy Communion

Yahweh

God's holy yahweh

God's holy people

Word Study

God's name is I am who i am

Keeping God's Name Holy

How do we hallow God's name?

God's name is kept holy when the Word of God is taught in its truth and purity, and we, as the children of God, also lead holy lives according to it.

Luther's Small Catechism, The Lord's Prayer, and Explanation of the First Petition.

1. In the sentence above, circle a word that describes God's name.
2. Highlight words that show how to teach God's Holy Word.
3. Underline the word that describes the lives children of God should live.

God's Word Taught in Truth and Purity

Circle words in the Bible verse that show how to teach God's Word.

Let Him who has My word speak My word faithfully. Jeremiah 23:28

Lead Holy Lives According to God's Word

Circle words in the Bible verse that describe how to lead holy lives for God.

Walk in a manner worthy of the Lord, fully pleasing to Him, bearing fruit in every good work and increasing in the knowledge of God. Colossians 1:10

Bible Words to Remember

Teach me Your way, O LORD, that I may walk in Your truth; unite my heart to fear Your name. Psalm 86:11

The Power of a Name

Knowing this name

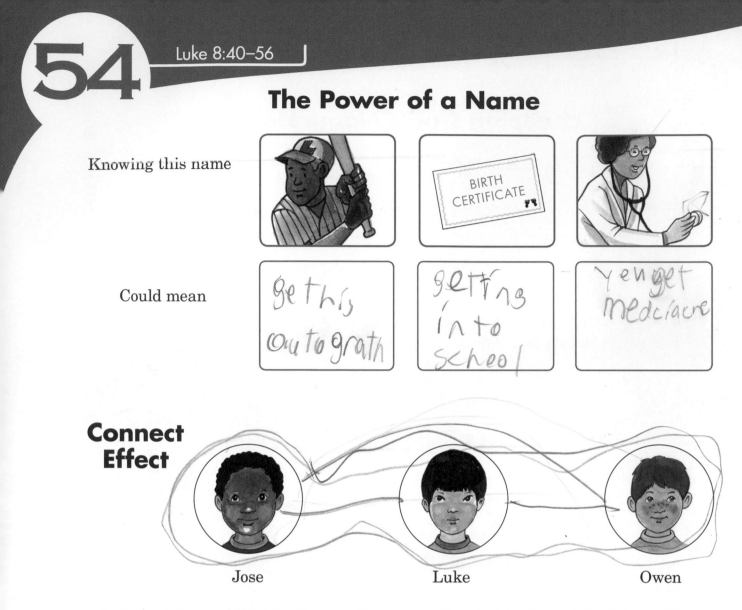

Could mean

ge this
ou to grath

getting
into
scheol

yen get
medciace

Connect Effect

Jose   Luke   Owen

Luke and Jose are friends. Draw a line to connect them.

Luke joined a baseball team. Jose knew his friend Owen was on the same team. Draw a line to connect them.

Jose told Luke to tell Owen "Hi from Jose" to introduce himself. Draw a line to show a new friendship between Luke and Owen.

Jose is friends with both boys. He helped them become friends too. Draw a circle around all three boys.

We often help friends connect to other friends. We say: Tell them I sent you. Mention my name. Tell them you know me. Say "Hi" for me.

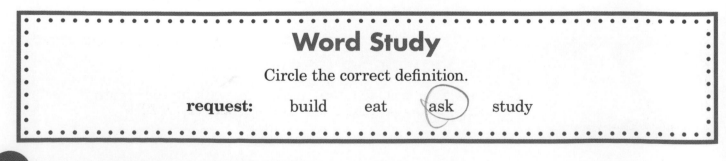

Word Study

Circle the correct definition.

request: build   eat   (ask)   study

Jesus' Name Has Power

Jesus said, "I am the **door**." John 10:9

We go through Jesus to get to _heaven_.

Jesus said, "I am the **way**." John 14:6

Jesus is the way, the road to _hevan_.

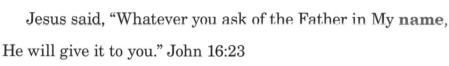

Jesus said, "Whatever you ask of the Father in My **name**, He will give it to you." John 16:23

Jesus connects us to God the Father. He says to pray in His _Name_.

God loves His children and hears our prayers.

To all who received [Jesus], to those who believed in His **name**, He gave the right to become children of God. John 1:12 NIV

When we believe in Jesus, we are _children_ of God.

Bible Words to Remember

Call upon My name, and I will answer. Zechariah 13:9

There's a Kingdom Coming

Elijah and the Baal Prophets at Mount Carmel

Narrator: King Ahab and Queen Jezebel did evil in the eyes of the Lord. They worshiped the false god Baal. Jezebel had many prophets killed. So God stopped the rain and dew for three years to show He was the true God, not Baal. God's prophet Elijah hid until God sent him to see King Ahab.

Ahab: Is that you, you troublemaker of Israel?

Elijah: I'm not the troublemaker. You and your family are. You turned away from the Lord and followed Baal, so, let's settle this. Meet me at Mount Carmel with the people of Israel and Baal's prophets.

Narrator: So Ahab sent word. The people, 450 of Baal's prophets, and Ahab met Elijah at Mount Carmel.

Elijah: People, how long are you going to serve God and Baal? If God is the true God, follow Him. If Baal is, follow him. Make up your minds!

Narrator: The people said nothing.

Elijah: I am the only one of the Lord's prophets left, but there are 450 prophets of Baal here. Let them bring up two bulls to sacrifice, one for them and one for me. Neither of us will set it on fire. Instead, we'll pray. The true God will answer with fire.

People: Good plan! Do it!

Narrator: Baal's prophets prayed and made a lot of noise, but Baal did not answer.

Elijah: Shout louder! Maybe your God is thinking, or going to the bathroom, or traveling. Maybe he's sleeping and you need to wake him up!

Narrator: Hours passed. Still, Baal did not answer.

Elijah: Okay, enough. Now, it's my turn.

Narrator: Elijah found twelve stones, one for each tribe of Israel. He made an altar dedicated to the name of the Lord. He dug a wide trench around it. He put wood and the dead bull on the altar.

Elijah: Fill four buckets with water and pour it on the offering and wood.

People: Okay, Elijah.

Elijah: Do it again.

People: Okay, Elijah.

Elijah: Do it a third time.

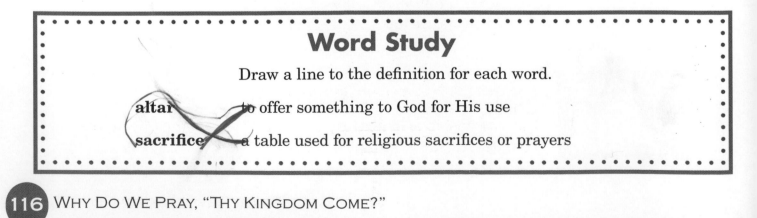

Word Study

Draw a line to the definition for each word.

altar — to offer something to God for His use

sacrifice — a table used for religious sacrifices or prayers

People: Okay, Elijah.

Narrator: The altar was drenched. The trench was full of water. The people probably thought God's prophet Elijah was crazy. They listened as Elijah prayed.

Elijah: LORD, let it be known that you are God and I am your servant who did these things at Your word. Answer me and show the people that You are the true and living God and that You have turned their hearts back to You.

Narrator: Immediately, the Lord sent fire from heaven. It burned up the bull, the wood, stones, dust, and even the water in the trench. When the people saw this, they fell on their faces and worshiped the Lord.

People: The LORD is the true God! There is only one God, our living LORD.

Elijah: We killed all of Baal's prophets and before the day was over, God sent a great rain storm too. I ran in front of Ahab's chariot all the way back to Jezreel, about twenty miles away where the king had a home.

Narrator: God's kingdom came that day when God showed He was the true God and the people believed in Him.

People: God's kingdom comes to each of us when our heavenly Father gives us His Holy Spirit so that by His grace we believe His Holy Word and lead godly lives here and in eternity.

CHILD OF GOD

The Holy Spirit gives me faith to believe His Holy Word.

I believe in Jesus.

I belong to God's kingdom.

The Holy Spirit helps me live for God now and forever.

_____
Name

Bible Words to Remember

Our citizenship is in heaven, and from it we await a Savior, the Lord Jesus Christ. Philippians 3:20

My Will, My Way

Will you or won't you? How do you show your *will* at home and school?

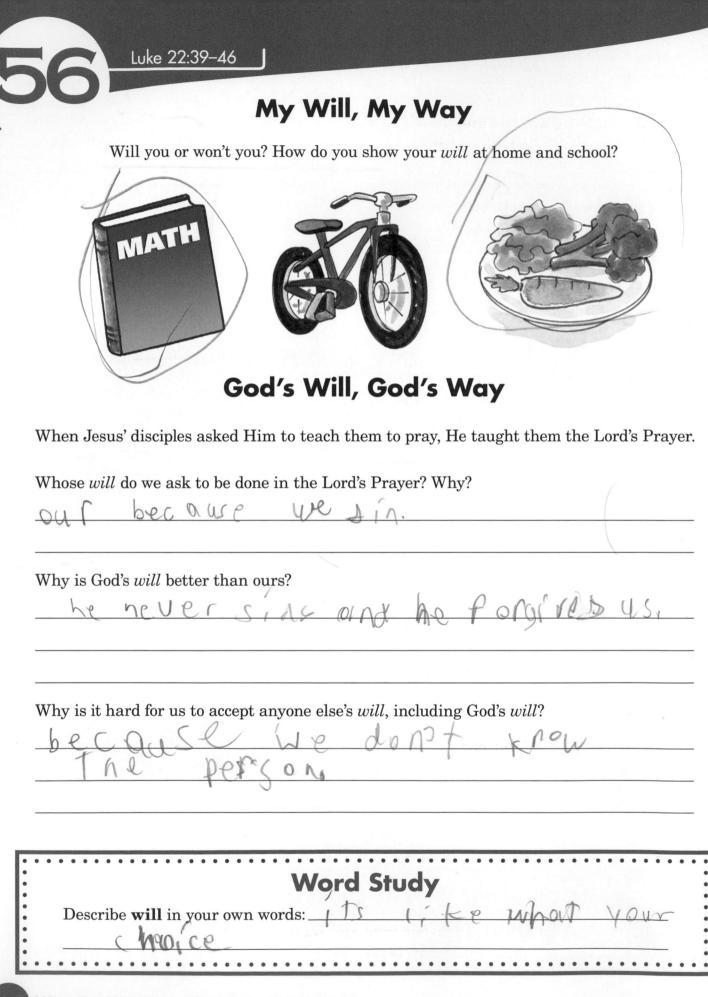

God's Will, God's Way

When Jesus' disciples asked Him to teach them to pray, He taught them the Lord's Prayer.

Whose *will* do we ask to be done in the Lord's Prayer? Why?

our becaure we sin.

Why is God's *will* better than ours?

he never sins and he forgives us.

Why is it hard for us to accept anyone else's *will*, including God's *will*?

because we don't know the person.

Word Study

Describe **will** in your own words: its like what your choice

---

Jesus Prayed in Gethsemane

On the night He was betrayed, Jesus prayed to His Father in the Garden of Gethsemane.

Jesus knew He would die on the cross to pay for our sins. He knew He would rise again from the dead. But Jesus knew it wouldn't be easy. He asked God to reconsider, but prayed "God's will be done."

Why do you think God willed that Jesus die for our sins?

That he would be saved

Why was Jesus the only one whose death would pay for our sins?

god sent his son to die

Did Jesus accept God's will? Do you think this was easy or hard for Jesus?

yes and it was hard

Why do you think Jesus accepted God's will? _he love his little children_

Where would we be if Jesus had not died for our sin and rose from the dead to give us new life? _in hell_

Bible Words to Remember

Jesus said, "Abba, Father, all things are possible for You. Remove this cup from Me. Yet not what I will, but what You will." Mark 14:36

Counting Blessings

Think about the many blessings God gives you.

Circle a blessing God gives you 1–5 times a year.

Draw a line to a blessing God gives you 1 or more times a week.

Draw a square around a blessing God gives you every day.

Write your name by a blessing God gives you every second.

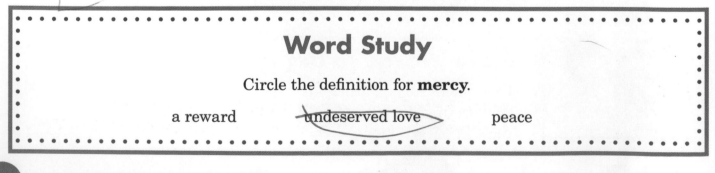

daily bread = everything we need for daily life and health

Word Study

Circle the definition for **mercy**.

a reward   ~~undeserved love~~   peace

SPR

What does each letter mean?

S _say it_

P. _pray it_

R _replay it_

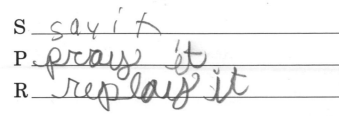

Before SPR
messed-up heart

After SPR
mercy-filled heart

Practice SPR

1. At lunch, Josh felt antsy. He poked Lauren, interrupting her conversation with Jocelyn. When she frowned, Josh snickered. Lauren said, "Stop it," but Josh kept poking her. Finally Lauren moved her chair away. Then Josh knocked over her milk.

2. It was Bella's turn for the recess ball. Sam wanted it, but Bella kept it for her game. Sam grabbed the ball and booted it into the field.

3. The girls were jumping rope. Each took a turn swinging the rope. Trace asked to play but left without swinging the rope. He did it again later. The third time, the girls said he couldn't play. After that he repeatedly ran through the rope to tangle it.

4. Nick got in trouble for talking to Allison. So in math class, he drew a witch picture of her. Later in the day, he showed it to a friend and both boys giggled. Allison saw the picture and her feelings were hurt.

5. Jack and Nate goofed off on the way to music. The teacher reminded them to walk properly. They didn't listen and fell against Bea, pushing her forward. She banged her chin hard.

6. Chris forgot to spit out his gum. When the teacher asked him if he was chewing gum, he lied. When the teacher turned her back, he swallowed it.

7. Jacob couldn't read well. Sometimes he left class for reading help. One day, Destiny whispered, "You're going to the baby class," because he called her a name at recess.

8. Edwin, new to school, often told whoppers. Whenever the teacher talked about a new place, Edwin had always been there. Edwin thought his new class would think he was important. One day, Zack said loudly, "Yeah, and if we talk about the moon, Edwin's been there too." Edwin's face turned red.

Bible Words to Remember

He who conceals his sins does not prosper, but whoever confesses and renounces them finds mercy. Proverbs 28:13 NIV

Jesus Resisted Temptation

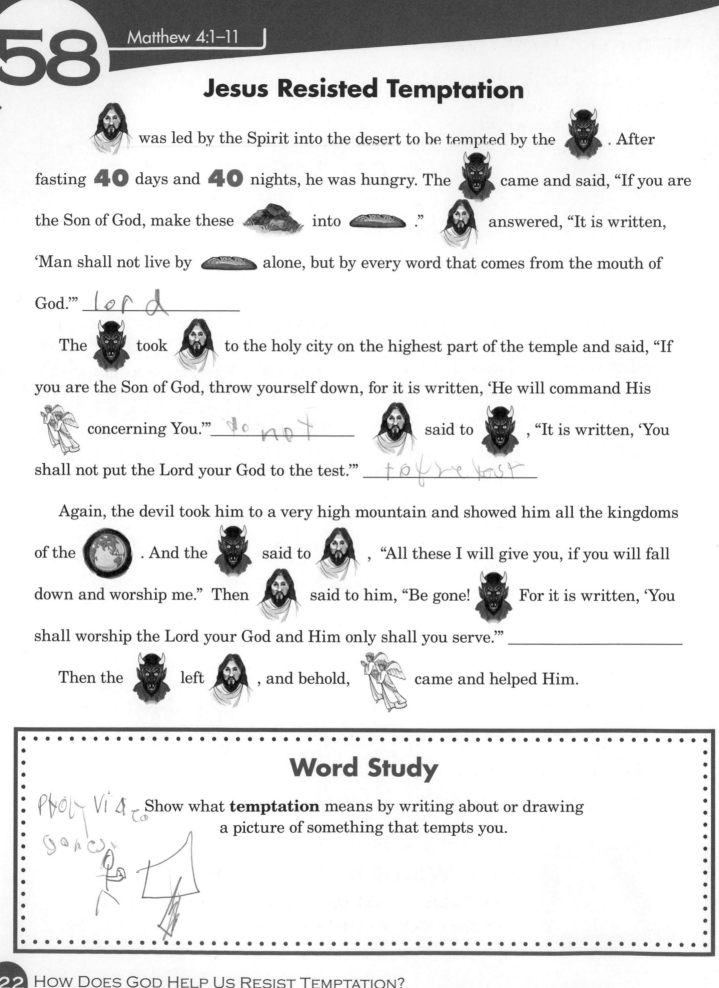

was led by the Spirit into the desert to be tempted by the . After

fasting **40** days and **40** nights, he was hungry. The came and said, "If you are

the Son of God, make these into ." answered, "It is written,

'Man shall not live by alone, but by every word that comes from the mouth of

God.'" _lord_

The took to the holy city on the highest part of the temple and said, "If

you are the Son of God, throw yourself down, for it is written, 'He will command His

concerning You.'" _do not_ said to , "It is written, 'You

shall not put the Lord your God to the test.'" _to the test_

Again, the devil took him to a very high mountain and showed him all the kingdoms

of the . And the said to , "All these I will give you, if you will fall

down and worship me." Then said to him, "Be gone! For it is written, 'You

shall worship the Lord your God and Him only shall you serve.'" _____

Then the left , and behold, came and helped Him.

Word Study

Show what **temptation** means by writing about or drawing
a picture of something that tempts you.

Pholy via to gonc

Help from God's Word

God's Word can help us resist temptation. Write the number of the Bible verse that helps the situation.

_4_ Everybody lies once in awhile.

_3_ Mom's always telling me what to do. I'm not doing it!

_1_ No one will see you and besides, the store has lots.

_2_ I don't need to help with chores. Somebody else can do it.

_5_ Church is boring. Pretend to be sick and stay home to watch cartoons.

1. You shall not steal. Deuteronomy 5:19

2. Whatever you wish that others would do to you, do also to them. Matthew 7:12

3. Honor your father and your mother. Deuteronomy 5:16

4. Speak the truth in love. Ephesians 4:15

5. Observe the Sabbath day to keep it holy. Deuteronomy 5:12

Bible Words to Remember

God is faithful . . . with the temptation He will also provide the way of escape. 1 Corinthians 10:13

Lord, Deliver Me from Evil

Word Study

The devil's name even has the word **evil** in it. Circle **evil** in his name:

d e v i l

1. God protects us. On page 124, write *Lord, deliver me from evil* on the barriers between the boy and the lions, one word per barrier.

2. The devil is our enemy. Read these Bible verses. Write words that describe the devil or his actions on or near the lions on page 124.

- Be sober-minded; be watchful. Your adversary the devil prowls around like a roaring lion, seeking someone to devour. 1 Peter 5:8

- Jesus said, "[The devil] was a murderer from the beginning . . . there is no truth in him. When he lies, he speaks out of his own character, for he is a liar and the father of lies. John 8:44

God, Help Me

Write a prayer asking Jesus to protect you from evil.
Use it when you feel afraid or are in danger.

Dear Jesus,

portect me from every and sin

_____

_____

_____

In Your name. Amen.

Bible Words to Remember

I was rescued from the lion's mouth. The Lord will rescue me from every evil deed and bring me safely into His heavenly kingdom. 2 Timothy 4:17–18

Walking with the King

If you could go for a walk with anyone in the world, whom would you choose? Why?

Mom because i love her

What would you talk about?

The exied things in my life

Following Jesus is walking with our King. We stay close to Him and enjoy talking to Him. God promises some special blessings for those who walk with Him. Underline three blessings in the verse below.

> Walk in all the way that the LORD your God has commanded you, that you may live, and that it may go well with you, and that you may live long in the land that you shall possess. Deuteronomy 5:33

Word Study

We end prayers by saying **Amen**. What does this word mean? Check the Bible Dictionary.

So be it or we agree

Pray with Confidence

We memorize some prayers to say at certain times of that day, such as at meals and bedtime. We also memorize the Lord's Prayer because Jesus taught it to His disciples. We say it in worship and at many other times.

We also can pray to God like we're talking to a friend. We can tell God our worries, concerns, things we're thankful for, and things we need.

Sometimes it is hard to pray. Sin can keep us from talking to God. It can make us feel awkward or embarrassed. We need to remember we can always talk to God. The Holy Spirit is at work to help us confess our sins, trust God, and grow in faith.

Learning to Pray

Match the first and last part of the following well-known prayers. If you don't know them, ask your friends.

A Come Lord Jesus be our guest.

C Jesus, Savior, wash away all that has been wrong today.

b Now I lay me down to sleep, I pray the Lord my soul to keep.

A. If I should die before I wake, I pray the Lord my soul to take. Amen.

B. And help me every day to be kind and gentle more like Thee. Amen.

C. Let these gifts to us be blessed. Amen.

Write a prayer to God in your own words here.

o lord please wash me from all evil

Bible Words to Remember

Blessed be God, because He has not rejected my prayer or removed His steadfast love from me! Psalms 66:20

Weight of Sin

Write some sins on two of the bricks. Now think of how you feel when you have done something wrong. Worried? Ashamed? Scared? Write how you feel on the other two bricks.

Getting It Off Your Chest

The heavy load of sin weighs us down. We can't deal with it by ourselves. Only Jesus can bear the weight of sin, and He did that on the cross. Draw a cross between these students, making the horizontal bar go under the bricks.

In the worship service, we begin with Confession and Absolution in order to get our sins "off our chest." When we tell God we are sorry for our sins, He forgives us. We don't have to worry or feel guilty about our sins because Jesus took all our sins to the cross and paid for every last one of them there. Knowing we are forgiven, we can pray, praise, and give thanks to God for His great big love for us.

Word Study

Fill in the missing letters. Use the words in sentences.

C ____ ____ fe ____ s ____ on: Telling God about our sins and how sorry we are for them

Ab ____ olu ____ ion: Getting a guarantee that our sins are forgiven for Jesus' sake

Peter's Sin

Read Matthew 26:30–35, 69–75. What clues in the Bible story tell you that Peter loved Jesus?

_____

_____

What sin did Peter commit? _____

_____

How do you know that Peter was sorry for his sin?

_____

Jesus Reinstates Peter

Read John 21:1–19. What did Jesus ask Peter?

_____

Why did Jesus ask Peter this so many times?

_____

_____

_____

Thanks and Praise

Jesus forgave Peter and called him to serve Him. In the worship service, after we confess our sins and receive forgiveness in the Absolution, the weight of our sin is lifted. We respond in thanks, prayer, and praise, and then go out to serve God.

Finish the following sentences.

Jesus, thank You for _____

Jesus, I praise You for _____

Jesus, help me this week to _____

Bible Words to Remember

As far as the east is from the west, so far has He removed our transgressions from us. Psalm 103:12 NIV

62

Rules, Rules, Rules

Are rules good or bad? What would your school be like without rules?

_____

God's Rules (Law)

God's Law is good. It tells how God wants us to live as His children. The problem is that we cannot keep the Law. We sin. Write a sentence to describe how you feel when you've sinned. Draw how you feel on the first face.

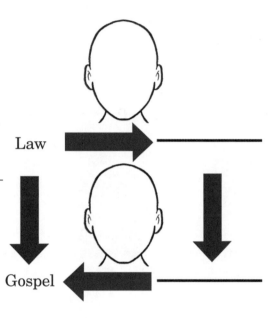

_____

The Law cannot give us hope or comfort. It just makes us feel bad because it shows us our sin and tells us that we deserve to be punished. But God loves us. He wants us to be sorry for our sins and tell Him about them. That is called confession.

God's Good News (Gospel)

Write a sentence to describe how you feel when you own up to what you did (confess) and receive forgiveness (absolution). Draw how you feel on the second face.

_____

When we confess our sins, God forgives us for the sake of His Son, Jesus, who paid for our sins on the cross. God's forgiveness is called absolution. It is the Good News of the Gospel.

Word Study

The Law tells us that we did something wrong. It shows us our _____.

The Gospel tells us that our sins are forgiven because Jesus died on the cross for us. It shows us our _____.

Set Free to Serve

Read John 21:1–19. What did Jesus do that made the disciples realize who He was? _____

_____

Jesus made breakfast for the disciples. List two things this shows us about Jesus.

    1. _____

    2. _____

How do you know Jesus forgave Peter? _____

_____

What did Jesus ask Peter to do? _____

Fruit of Repentance

When we repent and confess our sins, God forgives our sins for Jesus' sake. He works in our hearts and lives through the Gospel to help us share His love with others. The Bible calls this the fruit of repentance. Color all the fruit that show God's love at work in you.

 Sharing your video game with a friend

 Ignoring your neighbor when she says hi

 Leaving your plate on the table after dinner

 Making your bed before your mom asks you

 Singing in a nursing home

Sending a card to someone who is hurting

 Letting your little sister play outside with you

Making fun of a classmate behind his back

Inviting a friend to church

Bible Words to Remember

You shall love the Lord your God with all your heart and with all your soul and with all your mind. This is the great and first commandment. And a second is like it: You shall love your neighbor as yourself. Matthew 22:37–39

What Is Sin?

Romans 3:23 says, "All have sinned." Put a check mark by the sins.

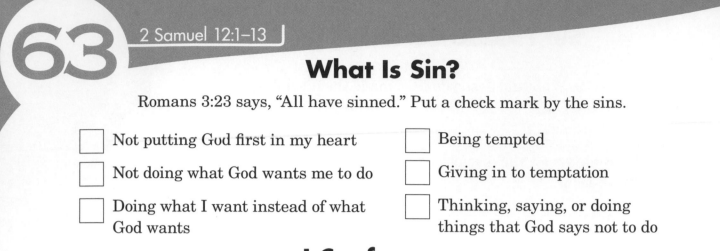

☐ Not putting God first in my heart

☐ Not doing what God wants me to do

☐ Doing what I want instead of what God wants

☐ Being tempted

☐ Giving in to temptation

☐ Thinking, saying, or doing things that God says not to do

I Confess . . .

God's Law shows us our sin. Read the Ten Commandments. In the thought balloon, write examples of ways we sin by not keeping the Commandments.

_____

_____

_____

_____ sins to God

Sins _____

Sins _____

Confession doesn't just mean saying "I've been bad." It should name the sin you did. "Mom, I'm sorry I cut up my sister's homework" is an example. You can use private confession with friends, parents, or your pastor.

You don't always know about all of your sins, though. That's why you confess all your sins to God. You're telling God, "I'm sorry for **all** my sins, even the ones I don't know about." When does this happen at church?

_____

Word Study

Use **sin of commission** or **sin of omission** to complete the definitions.

A _____ is when we fail to do what God commands.

A _____ is when we do what God forbids.

Acknowledging Sin

Read 2 Samuel 12:1–13.

1. Was David's sin one of commission or omission?

   _____

2. How was David convicted about his sin?

   _____

   _____

3. What did David do after he knew he sinned?

   _____

   _____

4. To whom did David confess his sin?

   _____

My Psalm of Confession and Praise

In Psalm 51, David confesses his sin and asks for forgiveness. He promises to teach others God's Word and sing His praise. Write your own psalm to God.

Have pity on me, God, and wash away my sin.

Be merciful and forgive me for _____ .

Then I will sing about your power to save.

I will tell others that You are an awesome God who

_____ .

Bible Words to Remember

If we confess our sins, He is faithful and just to forgive us our sins and to cleanse us from all unrighteousness. 1 John 1:9

What Is Repentance?

Everyone sins. But how do we get rid of our sins? Read the Bible Words to Remember. Then to find out what it means to repent, follow the arrows and discuss the steps.

A   B   C

I sin. ⟶ I am sorry. ⟶ I ask to be forgiven. ⟶ I am forgiven.

God works repentance in our hearts. It is being truly sorry for our sin so we want to change (A) and also trusting God to forgive us for Jesus' sake (B). God "wipes out our sin" (C).

Read the story and use the pictogram to answer the questions.

Grayson was spitting mad at his older sister. She had taken his new video game and thrown it in the trash. It was already crushed, in the garbage truck, and on its way to the landfill. Yet, Grayson couldn't tell on Claire. His parents had warned him against playing games with so much killing. It didn't matter that he had used his own money to buy it; he had disobeyed his parents. But shouldn't Claire be punished too?

What should Grayson and Claire do? How will they know they are forgiven?

1. Which step on the pictogram should Grayson and Claire follow first?_____

2. Will they really be sorry and tell the truth? _____

_____

3. After they are sorry and admit their sin, which step comes next? _____

4. Will the other person willingly forgive? _____

5. Will they be forgiven? Which step shows this? _____

_____

Word Study

Fill in the blanks using either **repentance** or **contrition**.

_____ Being truly sorry for my sin

_____ Being sorry for my sin and trusting God to forgive me for Jesus' sake, leading to changed behavior

Forgiven

Who forgave David? _____

In the words of forgiveness, what did the Lord put away? _____

Why did David receive absolution? _____

A Change of Heart

My heart is repentant when . . .

I am truly _____ for grieving God with my sins.

I am willing to _____ my sins to God.

I trust God to _____ me for Jesus' sake.

I want to _____, not continue to sin.

When we are sorry for our sins and ask God to forgive us, He does. Being sorry also means we don't want to go on sinning, but want to change. The Holy Spirit will help us live as God wants. Color the hearts that show the changed behavior that comes from being forgiven. On the blank line, write a way you want to change. Ask God to help you.

♡ The next time Kass wants to wear Dora's things, she asks permission.

♡ Grayson goes to his friend's house to play a war video game.

♡ Kass takes one of Dora's DVDs to watch without asking Dora, but puts it back before Dora gets home, so she won't miss it.

♡ Instead of bossing Grayson around, Claire helps him clean up his room.

♡ Grayson stops playing games and watching movies his parents don't approve of.

♡ _____

Bible Words to Remember

Repent, then, and turn to God, so that your sins may be wiped out, that times of refreshing may come from the Lord. Acts 3:19 NIV

The Job of Shepherding

B	B	A	P	T	I	Z	I	N	G
C	R	R	O	T	S	A	P	O	C
O	B	X	N	T	S	P	S	S	A
M	V	I	S	I	T	R	I	I	L
F	O	R	G	I	V	E	N	C	S
O	B	S	O	V	M	A	S	K	K
R	P	P	R	A	Y	C	A	P	T
T	G	T	E	A	C	H	I	N	G

Your pastor cares for God's people on earth. He is God's servant. The word *pastor* means shepherd. Servant and shepherd have almost the same meaning. Both help and care for others. Jesus is my Shepherd, and so is my pastor.

The word search has some jobs Jesus gave pastors. Work with a partner to find out what the jobs are by filling in the Bible verses. Then find and circle the words in the word search.

___ ___ ___ ___ ___ ___ the word. 2 Timothy 4:2

I was ___ ___ ___ ___ and you ___ ___ ___ ___ ___ed me. Matthew 25:36

___ ___ ___ ___ then like this. Matthew 6:9

___ ___ ___ ___ ___ ___ ___ those who are in any affliction. 2 Corinthians 1:4

Even so I am sending you. . . . If you ___ ___ ___ ___ ___ ___ ___ the

___ ___ ___ ___ of any, they are forgiven. John 20:21–23

Make disciples of all nations, ___ ___ ___ ___ ___ ___ ___ ___ ___ them . . . and

___ ___ ___ ___ ___ ___ ___ ___ them. Matthew 28:19

Pastors serve us. Thank God for your pastor!

Bonus: Find the word in the word search that means shepherd.

___ ___ ___ ___ ___ ___

Word Study

Use the Bible dictionary in your book to find the meaning for these words.

Servant:_____

Shepherd:_____

My Pastor as Shepherd

A pastor works hard at leading and caring for the people in his congregation just like a shepherd works hard at caring for his sheep. Read and check the items below that you think your pastor does each week.

- [ ] Studies the Bible readings
- [ ] Writes a sermon
- [ ] Chooses hymns
- [ ] Visits members in hospitals and nursing homes
- [ ] Attends meetings
- [ ] Plans and does chapel services at school
- [ ] Makes time for people who want to talk to him

- [ ] Makes sure the Sunday bulletin is correct
- [ ] Teaches confirmation class
- [ ] Keeps records of everything he does
- [ ] Plans funerals, weddings, and Baptisms
- [ ] Keeps in touch with people who don't come to church anymore
- [ ] Prays for people and with them
- [ ] Other:_____

My Attitude

God wants us to have a special attitude toward our pastor. Color the shapes that have even numbers to see what that attitude is. Use the letters to make the word.

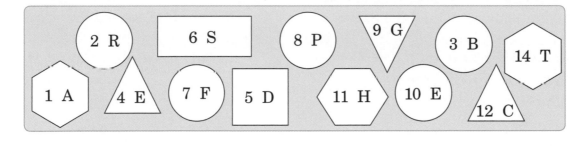

2 R   6 S   8 P   9 G   3 B   14 T
1 A   4 E   7 F   5 D   11 H   10 E   12 C

___ ___ ___ ___ ___ ___ ___

We show respect to God because He is so great and awesome. Our pastor serves us here on earth as God's shepherd. God wants us to respect him too. Talk about how you can do that.

Bible Words to Remember

We ask you, brothers, to respect those who labor among you and are over you in the Lord . . . and to esteem them very highly in love because of their work. 1 Thessalonians 5:12–13

Make a Joyful Noise to the Lord

The sentence by each instrument give reasons why God is worthy of our worship and praise. Find the Bible verses they come from, and write the letter beside the verse.

A. He gives eternal life.

C. He forgives us.

B. He sent Jesus to save us.

D. He is our Creator.

F. He loves us.

E. He is our God.

G. He answers our prayers.

_____ He is our God, and we are the people of His pasture. Psalm 95:7

_____ He is faithful and just to forgive us our sins and to cleanse us from all unrighteousness. 1 John 1:8–9

_____ Oh give thanks to the LORD, for He is good, for His steadfast loves endures forever! Psalm 107:1

_____ Behold, the Lamb of God, who takes away the sin of the world! John 1:29

_____ Our help is in the name of the LORD, who made heaven and earth. Psalm 124:8

_____ Lord, to whom shall we go? You have the words of eternal life. John 6:68

_____ Let my prayer be counted as incense before You, and the lifting up of my hands as the evening sacrifice! Psalm 141:2

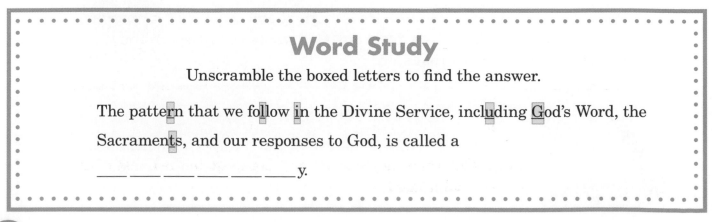

Word Study

Unscramble the boxed letters to find the answer.

The pattern that we follow in the Divine Service, including God's Word, the Sacraments, and our responses to God, is called a

___ ___ ___ ___ ___ ___ y.

The Liturgy Story

The liturgy tells a story. It is about God's gifts to us and our response in prayer and praise. Take a walk through part of the Divine Service, and you will discover the story that congregations all around the world are telling. After you discover what each item means, fill in the blanks under the picture to put it into words.

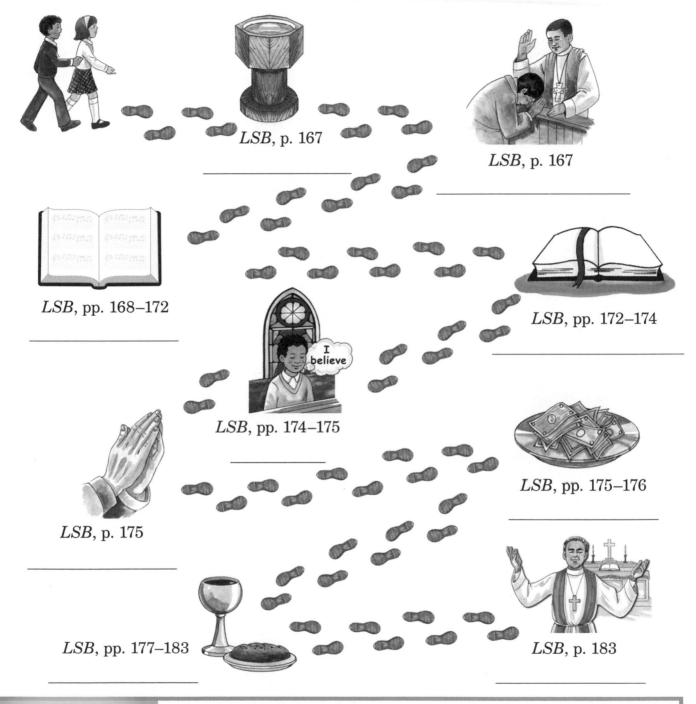

LSB, p. 167

_____

LSB, p. 167

_____

LSB, pp. 168–172

_____

LSB, pp. 172–174

_____

LSB, pp. 174–175

_____

LSB, p. 175

_____

LSB, pp. 175–176

_____

LSB, pp. 177–183

_____

LSB, p. 183

_____

Bible Words to Remember

I was glad when they said to me, "Let us go to the house of the Lord!" Psalm 122:1

We Worship Together

We worship the true God—Father, Son, and Holy Spirit. But did you know your worship service includes more people than just your congregation? Look who is joining you! Draw yourself in the congregation below. Label who the people are by each picture.

Word Study

Fill in the blanks, using one of these words: **prayers**, **praise**, **gifts**, **thanks**.

Worship: When we gather as God's children to receive His _____ and to give Him our _____, _____, and _____

Worship in the Temple

Solomon built a beautiful temple. Read 2 Chronicles 6:40–7:6. Describe the event in your own words.

_____

_____

_____

What things are similar to our worship today? _____

_____

My Faith Story

I became part of God's family of believers when

_____

My earliest memory of worshiping in God's house is

_____

My favorite part of worship is _____

My favorite hymn about Jesus is _____

The part of the church service that helps me remember I am part of God's family from all over the world and all time is _____

Someone who reminds me of Jesus is _____

because _____

One way I'd like to help in worship is _____

_____

One way I can show I am connected to believers around the world is _____

_____

Bible Words to Remember

Oh give thanks to the LORD, for He is good; for His steadfast love endures forever! 1 Chronicles 16:34

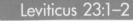

Hero Worship

When someone is our hero, we talk a lot about the person and try to act like him or her. We might say we "worship" the person. In the blank boxes, sketch pictures of things people do when they "worship" someone. Discuss this with your classmates to get ideas.

Jesus, Our All in All

For Christians, Jesus is our hero. Why?

_____

Jesus is the focus of our attention, both in church and in our daily lives. Read the stanzas of the hymn "Chief of Sinners Though I Be" (*LSB* 611). On the lines below, list four reasons the hymnwriter gives for why Jesus is "all in all" to him.

1. _____

2. _____

3. _____

4. _____

Word Study

Place the letter of the correct definition on the line in front of each term.

_____ Ordinary Time

_____ Church Year

_____ Liturgical colors

A. Church's calendar organized to observe the events in the life of Christ and the Church

B. Colors used to show seasons of the Church Year

C. Part of the Church Year after Pentecost until Advent where Sundays are numbered and counted

A Life of Worship

What do we learn from Leviticus 23:1–2? _____

On feast days, God's people celebrated God's forgiveness and blessings. Jesus is the center of our worship now. The church has a new calendar for worship too. During the first half of the year, we focus on the *life of Christ*. The second half of the year tells about our *life in Christ*. It is called the Time of the Church or Ordinary Time.

Worshiping Christ All Year

The **Time of Christmas** includes Advent, Christmas, and Epiphany. The **Time of Easter** includes Lent, Holy Week, Easter, and the Day of Pentecost. The **Time of the Church** starts with Trinity Sunday and includes the season after Pentecost.

Use these terms to label the Church Year circle. Colors are used to designate days or seasons of the Church Year. Color the seasons of the Church Year. What season of the Church Year is it now? _____

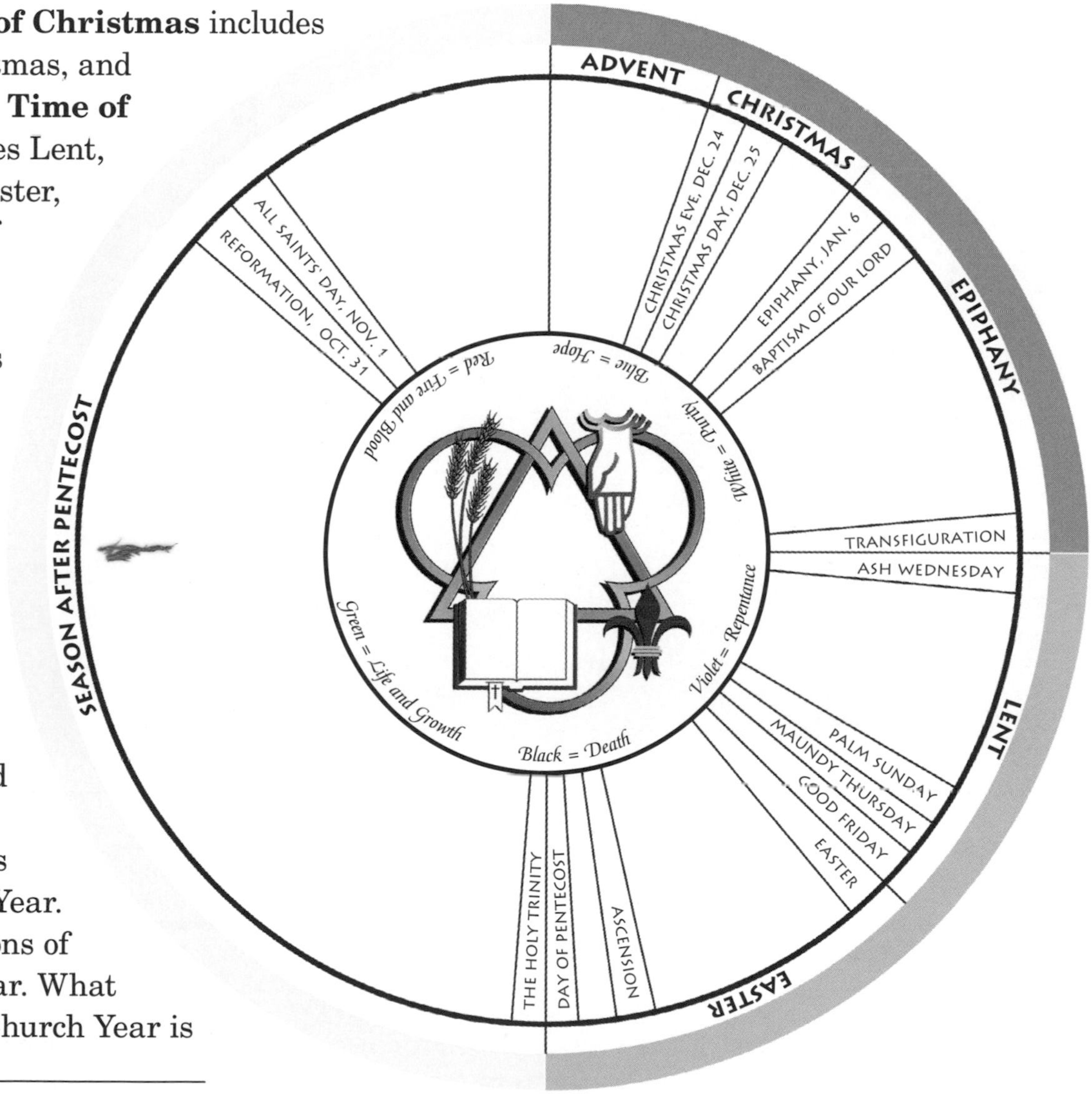

The Church Year circle contains the following labels:

ADVENT · CHRISTMAS · CHRISTMAS EVE, DEC. 24 · CHRISTMAS DAY, DEC. 25 · EPIPHANY, JAN. 6 · BAPTISM OF OUR LORD · EPIPHANY · TRANSFIGURATION · ASH WEDNESDAY · LENT · PALM SUNDAY · MAUNDY THURSDAY · GOOD FRIDAY · EASTER · EASTER · ASCENSION · DAY OF PENTECOST · THE HOLY TRINITY · SEASON AFTER PENTECOST · REFORMATION. OCT. 31 · ALL SAINTS' DAY, NOV. 1

Color key in center: *Blue = Hope* · *Red = Fire and Blood* · *White = Purity* · *Violet = Repentance* · *Green = Life and Growth* · *Black = Death*

Bible Words to Remember

Let us fix our eyes on Jesus, the author and perfecter of our faith, who for the joy set before Him endured the cross, scorning its shame, and sat down at the right hand of the throne of God. Hebrews 12:2 NIV

Where's the Word?

Check the places in the Divine Service where you find God's Word.

- [ ] In the readings
- [ ] In the sermon
- [ ] In hymns that talk about Jesus
- [ ] In the liturgy
- [ ] In Christian art that pictures what Scripture says
- [ ] In Baptism
- [ ] In the Lord's Supper

Nothing Hidden from Its Heat

Think about how God's Word is like the sun. _____

Word Study

These words got their letters mixed up. Unscramble them and match the words to the correct definitions.

pelsoG   fpuiyr

_____: The Good News of salvation in Jesus Christ

_____: To make someone clean, good, and wholesome

Sweeter Than Honey

What Makes My Mouth Happy

What Makes My Heart Happy

Great Reward

God's Word is more desirable than gold. Write a prayer of thanks for it.

_____

_____

_____

Bible Words to Remember

Sanctify them in the truth; Your word is truth. John 17:17

What's There to Sing About?

David was strong and brave. He killed the giant Goliath. Later, God chose David as the king of Israel. Jesus came from David's lineage. David also liked to write, sing, and play music. Discuss why you think he might have liked to do this.

Around the notes, write some reasons why we sing today.

A, B, C, D, E, F, G...

Word Study

psalm: a sacred song or poem
lyre: a stringed instrument like a harp
praise: to tell good things about someone, to glorify

These three words fit together in a sentence. Can you put them in the right order?

David sang _____ to God in a _____ with his _____.

So Many Songs!

David wrote psalms to worship God. His psalms show some of the reasons we go to church to worship God. The bookshelf lists some of these reasons. Help the palace librarian put the scrolls away. Draw a line from each scroll to the shelf where it should go. **Hint:** Look up the psalms on the scrolls to match them to the reasons on the shelves.

To confess

To learn

To praise

To pray

To thank

To be encouraged

Psalm 5:2

Psalm 8:1

Psalm 119:105

Psalm 32:5

Psalm 9:1

Psalm 23:4

Bible Words to Remember

Even though I walk through the valley of the shadow of death, I will fear no evil, for You are with me. Psalm 23:4

That We May See Jesus

Christians from all over the world have written the words and music of the hymns and songs we use in worship. What do these hymns teach us about our Savior? How does each one help us thank Jesus?

"When I Behold Jesus Christ" (*LSB* 542)

Photo: LCMS World Relief and Human Care

Could this girl be Almaz Belhu, the writer and composer of this hymn?

_____

_____

"Christ, the Word of God Incarnate" (*LSB* 540)

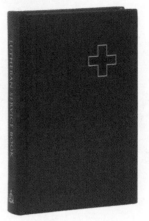

What hymns would you include if you were going to make your own hymnbook?

_____

_____

Word Study

Match each word with its meaning by writing the correct letter on the line in front of the word.

_____ stanza

_____ chorale

_____ incarnate

A. Religious song, originally intended for singing in the Lutheran Church

B. Part of a religious song, made up of a group of lines that often rhyme

C. God existing as a human being

"Lamb of God" (*LSB* 550)

On her album *Small Sacrifice,* Twila Paris said that anything we do is a small sacrifice compared to what Jesus did. What do you think she meant?

_____

_____

_____

_____

How does the picture illustrate the words to this hymn?

_____

_____

_____

"O Jesus So Sweet" (*LSB* 546)

The words to hymns are poems. Here's a challenge: try writing your own hymn or poem about Jesus.

Bible Words to Remember

Let the word of Christ dwell in you richly, teaching and admonishing one another in all wisdom, singing psalms and hymns and spiritual songs, with thankfulness in your hearts to God. Colossians 3:16

Praise in the Wilderness

Read Exodus 14:13–15:21. What did God do for the Israelites?

_____

_____

How did the children of Israel respond (v. 31)?

_____

_____

Where did Miriam and the others sing their song of praise?

_____

What part of their song do you like the best? Why?

_____

God's Gifts to Us

When we gather with other believers in worship, we hear how God has saved us by sending Jesus to die on the cross for us. God forgives us and gives us power to go and serve Him.

Think about your church worship service. What gifts does God give you there? Write them on the gift bag.

Word Study

Think of an example of each word that would be pleasing to God.

Attitude: How you look at things, your viewpoint or feeling about something

Behavior: How you act, what you do in response to something

God's Love Leads Me to Respond in Love

At the end of the church service, the pastor says to go and serve the Lord. Look at the offering plates below. Check the things that show ways you can praise and thank God during the week, wherever you are, for all He's done for you. Then, think of two things you will do.

Things I do

Check things you can do that show honor to God.

- [ ] Pray
- [ ] Sing
- [ ] Help others
- [ ] Use my talents to serve others
- [ ] Disobey
- [ ] Show kindness
- [ ] Fight
- [ ] Be lazy
- [ ] Cheat
- [ ] Cooperate

Things I say

Check things you say that honor God.

- [ ] Use bad language
- [ ] Speak well of others
- [ ] Gossip
- [ ] Tell the truth
- [ ] Tell someone about Jesus

How I think about things

Check attitudes that honor God.

- [ ] Thankfulness
- [ ] Worry
- [ ] Grumbling
- [ ] Praise
- [ ] Haughtiness
- [ ] Whining
- [ ] Patience

Bible Words to Remember

Sing to the Lord, all the earth; proclaim His salvation day after day. 1 Chronicles 16:23 NIV

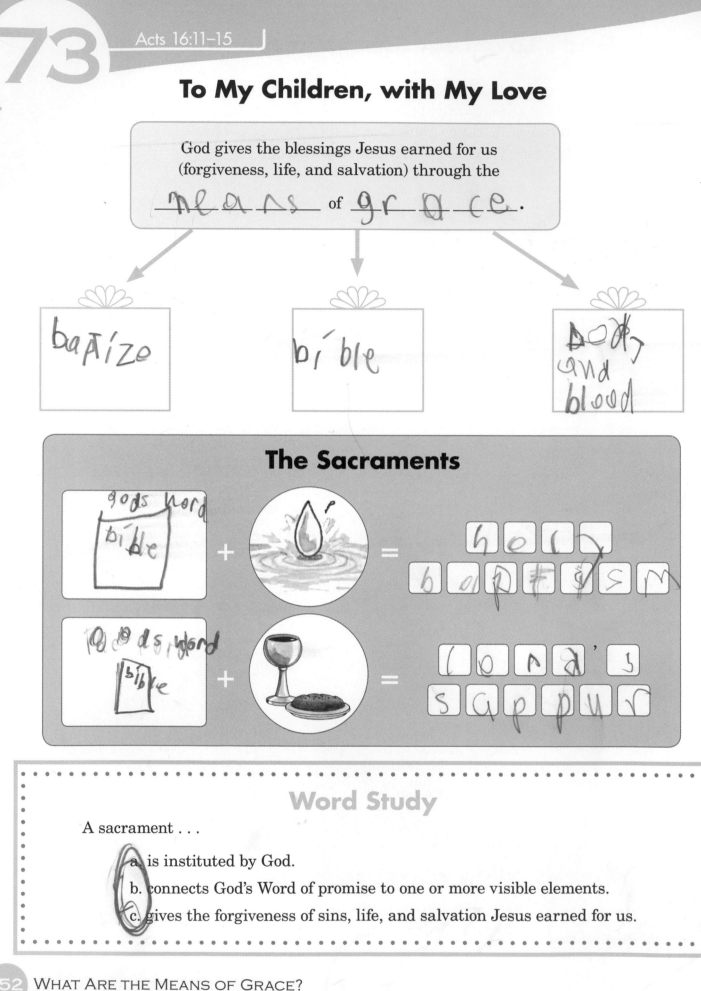

To My Children, with My Love

God gives the blessings Jesus earned for us
(forgiveness, life, and salvation) through the
___means___ of ___grace___.

baTize

bible

body and blood

The Sacraments

gods word bible + = her baptism

gods word bible + = lord's sapur

Word Study

A sacrament . . .

a. is instituted by God.

b. connects God's Word of promise to one or more visible elements.

c. gives the forgiveness of sins, life, and salvation Jesus earned for us.

An Open Heart

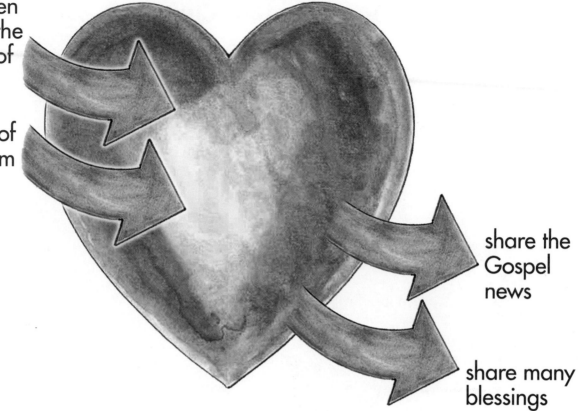

faith given through the Means of Grace

blessings of Baptism

share the Gospel news

share many blessings

Go, My Children, with My Blessing

Look at the hymn "Go, My Children, with My Blessing." Write words from the stanzas that refer to these gifts from God.

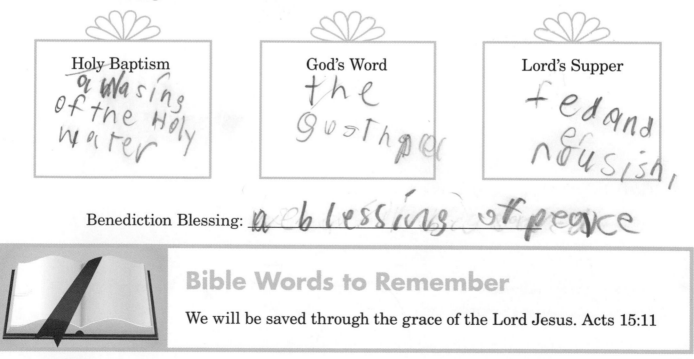

Holy Baptism	God's Word	Lord's Supper
a wasing of the Holy water	the gospher	fed and nousish,

Benediction Blessing: a eb blessing of peace

Bible Words to Remember

We will be saved through the grace of the Lord Jesus. Acts 15:11

Baptized into Christ

Reborn

Life

In the name of . . .

Adopted into God's family

Child of God

Salvation

Forgiveness

Sins washed away

Word Study

God's Love + Undeserved Gift = *grace*

God's Love + Undeserved Gift + God's Word + God's Command + Visible Element = *Holy spirit*

God's Love + Undeserved Gift + God's Word + God's Command + Water = *baptize*

Remembering Our Baptism

Landon's class had an art contest. Everyone was supposed to put one vote in the box to pick the best drawing. Landon voted for himself twice. He didn't win, but he feels guilty that he voted more than once. As a baptized child of God, what could he do?

he could go to the teacher and tell

Kylie's dad left the family when she was two years old. Kylie hasn't seen much of him since. She feels rejected by her father. As a baptized child of God, she still has a father. Who is He? How does she know God is her true and faithful Father?

he got married?

Carrie made friends with a new student, named Amy. When Carrie went to the store with Amy and her mother, the two girls got to shop by themselves for a few minutes. Amy asked Carrie to steal some candy with her. As a baptized child of God, what could Carrie say to Amy? What could Carrie do?

we don't do that

Tanner and his sister seem to fight about one thing or another all the time. He is tired of all the arguing. He wants to get along with her better, but doesn't know where to start. As a baptized child of God, what could Tanner say? What could he do?

im sorry

Bible Words to Remember

And now why do you wait? Rise and be baptized and wash away your sins, calling on His name. Acts 22:16

To Whom Do You Belong?

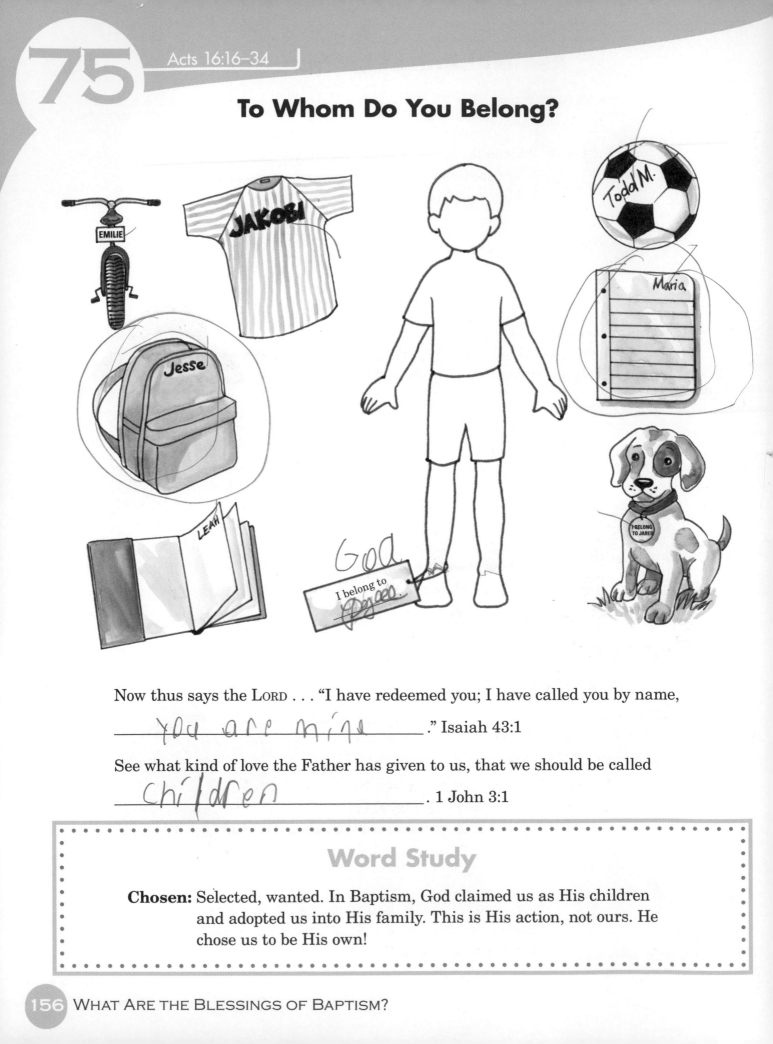

Now thus says the LORD . . . "I have redeemed you; I have called you by name,

___you are mine___." Isaiah 43:1

See what kind of love the Father has given to us, that we should be called

___children___. 1 John 3:1

Word Study

Chosen: Selected, wanted. In Baptism, God claimed us as His children and adopted us into His family. This is His action, not ours. He chose us to be His own!

An Amazing Day

Read the story in Acts 16:16–34. Pretend you are the jailer. Complete the letter telling about that amazing day.

Dear Atticus,

What a terrible, horrible, frightening day I had yesterday! An angry mob beat up two guys named Paul and Silas. The magistrates had them beaten even more and ordered me to put them in jail. It doesn't make sense to me—locking up the victims. But that's my job! It's a crummy job, but somebody's got to do it.

Then about midnight, these two guys who should have been moaning about their aches and pains began singing. They praised their God, but He didn't seem to be paying attention to them—at least, that's what I thought. Then, the earthquake struck. What else could go wrong? I soon found out! All the prison doors unlocked, and all the chains fell off the prisoners. I figured I would soon be dead—either the prisoners would kill me or that angry crowd would come back to finish me off for letting the prisoners escape. Then amazingly, the whole day changed from terrible and horrible to great and glorious!

i did survive ne one was was angry at me and theysaid belive in god.

Your own Baptism day is an amazing day that you can celebrate now or anticipate in the future. You have been chosen by God through His Word or through His Word in Baptism. What is your life like when you live as God's own chosen ones? Read together the Bible Words to Remember from Colossians 3:12.

Bible Words to Remember
Put on then, as God's chosen ones, holy and beloved, compassionate hearts, kindness, humility, meekness, and patience. Colossians 3:12

That's a Good Question!

We know that Baptism offers the promise of forgiveness, life, and salvation. Now the question is: How can the waters of Baptism do such great things? Let's see Martin Luther's answer to that question.

> *How can water do such great things?* Certainly not just water, but the word of God in and with the water does these things, along with the faith which trusts this word of God in the water. For without God's word the water is plain water and no Baptism. But with the word of God it is a Baptism, that is, a life-giving water, rich in grace, and a washing of the new birth in the Holy Spirit.
>
> From *Luther's Small Catechism with Explanation*

What Can Water Do?

Ordinary Water

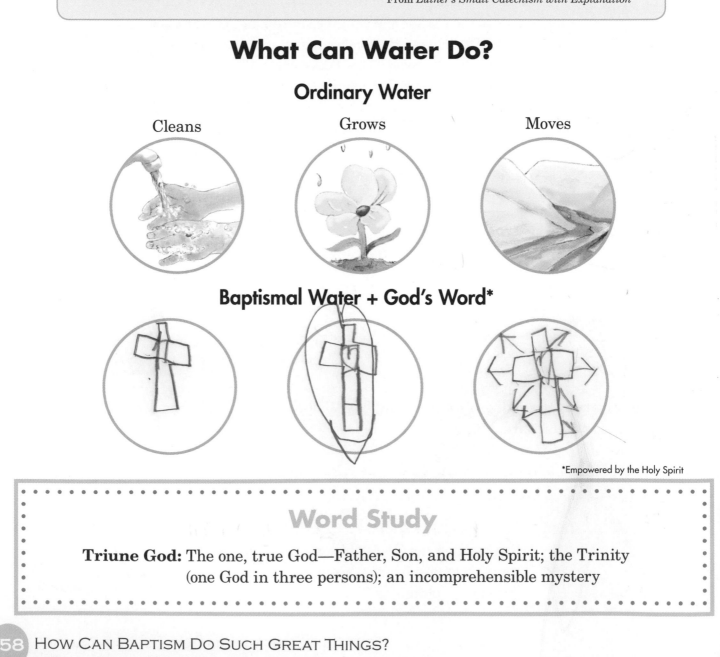

Cleans   Grows   Moves

Baptismal Water + God's Word*

*Empowered by the Holy Spirit

Word Study

Triune God: The one, true God—Father, Son, and Holy Spirit; the Trinity (one God in three persons); an incomprehensible mystery

What Happened?

| What was added? | What changed? | Before | After |

Bible Words to Remember

Tell what you think each part of this Bible verse means.

He saved us through the washing of rebirth and renewal by the Holy Spirit,

We are made new in the washing of rebirth

whom He poured out on us generously through Jesus Christ our Savior,

as the water is poured the bleessiags come down

so that, having been justified by His grace,

by the grace of god our sins are washed away

we might become heirs having the hope of eternal life.

as children of god we might have eternal life

This is a trustworthy saying.

its true because Jesesrose ana gives us the sami vicctory

Titus 3:5–8 NIV

Needed—Today and Every Day

There are some things you have needed every day since you were born. List some of those in the first column. There are also things you need spiritually every day since you were reborn in faith through God's Word and in Baptism. List those daily needs in the second column.

Daily Since Birth	Daily Since Rebirth
food, water air and cloths home	gods love Gods word Trinty, baptism

Baptism is not something that just happened long ago. It is not just a single event. Baptism is lifelong. God's blessings through Baptism pour on us each day. "Being baptized" is a heart condition that tells who you are!

Why Be Baptized?

Here are the ABCs of Baptism that tell why Baptism is important.

All the blessings. (Read Acts 2:38–39.)

Be imitators of Jesus. (Read Matthew 3:13–17 and Ephesians 5:1-2.)

Christ's command. (Matthew 28:18–20.)

Word Study

Use the Bible Dictionary in your book to find the meanings.

Confession: amitting we have done something wrong

Repentance: being sorrey for ones sins

(Martin Luther suggests that we daily remember our Baptism in contrition and repentance. The Holy Spirit leads us through this process. Contrition is the first step, but true repentance has faith in God's promises, and results in changes in behavior.)

Share the Baptism Message

This little story has many important lessons about Baptism—underline or highlight words and phrases that teach Bible truths. Then act it out, or use puppets to tell this story to a group of younger children.

(Jenna passes by, quietly holding a small pitcher or glass of water.)

Jake: Hey Jenna, where are you going with that water?

Jenna: I'm going to baptize my dolls.

Jake: Hold on there! Wait just a minute! Baptism is not a game to play. It is a very important gift from God. The Bible tells us that Jesus said, "Go and make disciples of all nations, baptizing them in the name of the Father and of the Son and of the Holy Spirit."

Jenna: Okay, I'll be careful when I baptize my dolls.

Jake: You still don't get it, Jenna. Baptism isn't for dolls. It's for people! It's for people because we need the forgiveness of our sins that Jesus offers.

Jenna: It's just a little bit of water.

Jake: Wrong again. Baptism is not just water; Baptism is water that is connected with God's Word by God's command and promise. That's why most of the time a Baptism is done in church by the pastor.

Jenna: I think I understand now. Baptism is a special gift from God, so I'll honor and thank God rather than play in a silly way.

Jake: Now you get it! In Baptism, God makes us His children. Even Jesus was baptized.

Jenna: He was? Why? Jesus didn't have any sins to wash away.

Jake: That's exactly what John the Baptist said to Him. But Jesus wanted to fulfill all of God's commands as He lived a perfect life in our place. Once again, Jesus shows us God's will for our lives. God wants to give us forgiveness, life, and salvation through Jesus!

(Jenna walks off, carrying the water.)

Jake: Now where are you going?

Jenna: I'm going to use this to water some plants. And then I'm going to say a prayer thanking God for His many gifts to us like the blessings of Baptism.

(From *Bible Stories with Jake and Jenna*, © 2005, CPH.)

Bible Words to Remember

Whoever believes and is baptized will be saved. Mark 16:16

Growing in Our Faith

AMEN

The words *confirmation* and *amen* have similar meanings. Some people think both words mean "The End." But they really mean "Yes, I believe this."

Reaffirmation of Baptism

The sentences below tell about confirmation. They have many "re" words. Read the sentences, and highlight the words beginning with "re." Look up their definitions in a dictionary, and be ready to explain what each "re" word tells about confirmation.

1. Confirmation instruction is a time of study in which you recall what you have learned about God's Word, reflect on what it means for your life, and reaffirm what you believe in faith.

2. The Rite (or celebration) of Confirmation is usually held in a church worship service in which all confirmands remember the blessings of their Baptisms and renew the promises made at that time. Confirmands publicly restate what they believe, and they recommit to faithfully live as people of God.

3. This is a special time for families, baptismal sponsors, and the whole church as they are reminded of the faith that they share. All in faith are reassured of the promises of God and pray that God will guide them to remain faithful all their lives.

4. We pray that God will daily lead us to realize we are sinners whom He has called to repentance so that we may continue to receive the reward our Redeemer Jesus has won for us—the blessings of forgiveness, life, and salvation. We rejoice in all that God has done for us!

Word Study

Confirmation: A special celebration of faith in which a person states publicly what he or she believes about God and salvation in Christ Jesus

Who Do People Say I Am?

A public statement of faith is simply saying what you believe about God. Read about Peter's statement of faith in Matthew 16:13–16.

Who did Peter say Jesus was?

you are the christ the son of the living God

Write your statement of faith here:

a Redeemer son of God.

A Symbol of a Faith Statement

Peter's faith statement is similar to "Jesus Christ, God's Son, Savior." The first letter of each word in this phrase makes the Greek word for fish (below). Use colored pencils to copy the phrase inside the other fish. Fill up the space so the letters look like fish scales.

Early Christians used the fish as a symbol of their faith in Jesus. Luther's rose is a picture of his faith statement. In the box, draw a symbol to show what you believe.

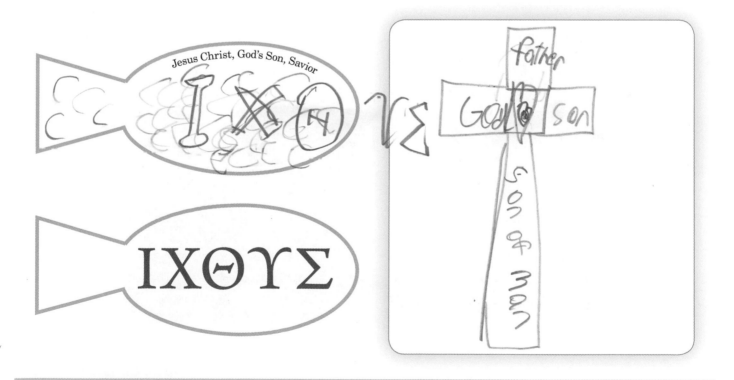

Jesus Christ, God's Son, Savior

ΙΧΘΥΣ

Jesus Gives a Special Meal

Take, eat; this is My __lody__, which is __givin__ for you.
This do in __given__ of Me.

Drink of it, all of you; This cup is the new testament in My __blood__,
which is shed for __you__ for the __forginies__ of sins. This do, as
often as you drink it, in remembrance of Me.

Word Study

Lord's Supper: __holy cemunion the sacrament of The altar__

Reasons to Eat a Meal

Tasty

Grow healthy

Have energy

Reasons to Eat a Meal Together

Friendship

Caring Concern

Community

Reasons to Eat and Drink the Lord's Meal

F

L

S

It's a Miracle Because . . .

In

With

Under

. . . the *bread* and *wine* is Jesus' *body* and *blood*

Bible Words to Remember

Jesus said, "This is My body. . . . This is My blood."
Matthew 26:26, 28

The Blame Game

Sometimes little children invent imaginary friends. The friend might be another child. It might be an animal. It might be an alien from outer space. Have you ever created an imaginary friend?

Little children talk to their imaginary friends. They play with their imaginary friends. Sometimes they blame their imaginary friends. In the picture, Mom asks, "Who broke the lamp?"

Three-year-old Arthur answers, "My friend, Zimbo!"

Mom knows Zimbo isn't a real person. Arthur has to go sit in time-out.

We may be age 4 or 10 or 14 or 40, but most of us still blame other people for our sins—at least, part of the time. Why do you think this is?

We fool ourselves by blaming others. We also fool ourselves by thinking we don't sin all that much or that our sins aren't really too bad. Here's a way to think about sin that helps us see the truth. There are two kinds of sin—doing bad things and failing to do good things. Put examples of each on the lines below.

Sins of Commission	**Sins of Omission**
(Doing Wrong)	(Not Doing Good)
I hit my sister.	I didn't take out the trash for Mom.
not going to church breaking stuff	_stealing my drinks not playing with my brother_

Word Study

Sins of Commission are _when we do what God forbids_

Sins of Omission are _when we fail what God command_

Forgiveness for You!

In Lesson 79, we learned what Matthew wrote about the night Jesus instituted the Lord's Supper. Today, read about it from Paul's letter to the believers in Corinth:

"For I received from the Lord what I also delivered to you, that the Lord Jesus on the night when He was betrayed took bread, and when He had given thanks, He broke it, and said, "This is My body which is for you. Do this in remembrance of Me." In the same way also He took the cup, after supper, saying, "This cup is the new covenant in My blood. Do this, as often as you drink it, in remembrance of Me." For as often as you eat this bread and drink the cup, you proclaim the Lord's death until He comes." 1 Corinthians 11:23–26

1. Underline the words that tell where Paul got this information.
2. Circle the words **This is**. What do these words tell us about the bread and wine?
3. Highlight the words **in remembrance of Me**. What does this mean?

Turning Sin Upsy-Daisy

Upsy-daisy is a word we say when a child falls down and we lift him up again. It has the sense of making things right again. In Acts 17:6, people said that the disciples had "turned the world upside down" with the Gospel. Sin makes us fall down. But Jesus makes our lives right again through His death on the cross for our sins. Now the Holy Spirit lives in us and works through His Word to help us to love others. How can you, with God's power, turn the sins you named earlier upside down, to show Jesus' love?

Loving by Commission	**Loving by Omission**
(Doing Good and Being Kind)	(Not Doing Bad Things)
I take out the trash without being asked.	I no longer hit and hurt others, even when I'm angry.

Loving by Commission: helping my mom sharing taking care

Loving by Omission: not breaking rases keeping my roon clean

Bible Words to Remember

As often as you eat this bread and drink the cup, you proclaim the Lord's death until He comes. 1 Corinthians 11:26

Jesus Prepares a Special Meal

The Lord's Supper is a very special meal Jesus Himself gave to us. The meal has bread and wine, but it has much more than that. The meal also has Jesus' true ___*body*___ and His true ___*blood*___ . It is a miracle—but miracles are never too hard for Jesus because He is true ___*God*___ . Jesus says that this meal gives ___*forgiveness*___ of sins, which also brings ___*life*___ and ___*salvation*___ with it.

Jesus won these blessings for us by giving His body and blood on the cross to pay for our sins. Draw a large cross around the elements of the Lord's Supper to show this.

Jesus completed everything for us in His victory at Easter. Draw orange rays of sunlight surrounding the cross to show this.

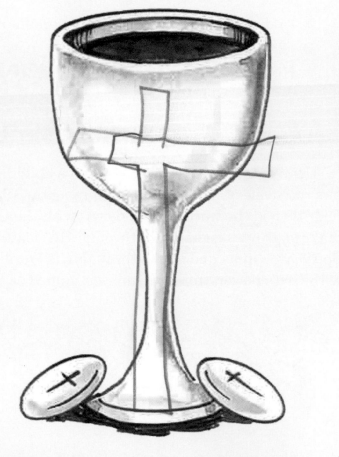

Word Study

Worthy: Deserving something. No one is worthy of taking the Lord's Supper because we are all sinners. But Jesus makes us worthy by giving us His righteousness. The Holy Spirit calls us to repentance and gives us faith to believe in Jesus as our Savior. He makes us able to live as God's people. It is all the work of the Lord, working in our hearts through the message of the Gospel in God's Word.

We Prepare for a Special Meal

Haley prepared for a special meal with Grandma and Grandpa by setting the table. We will use a modern-day place setting like Haley's as we think about how we prepare for the special meal called the Lord's Supper. Keep in mind that Jesus has done all things to prepare the Lord's Supper. We come to the meal with hearts prepared—through the Holy Spirit working in us!

Believe
(Ephesians 2:8)

for who Jesus died

Be Faithful
(Ephesians 4:32–5:2)

for God

Be Thankful
(Psalm 136:3)

belive Jesus is presnt

Be Sorry
(Psalm 38:18)

for my someone sins

Bible Words to Remember

This is love: not that we loved God, but that He loved us and sent His Son as an atoning sacrifice for our sins. 1 John 4:10 NIV

Five Good Reasons

Many churches offer the Lord's Supper every Sunday in worship services. Why do we take the Lord's Supper often? Here are five answers to that question.

1. Jesus tells us to do that.
2. It is one of the ways God says "I love you."
3. Who would refuse a gift?
4. We need constant reminders of God's grace.
5. Remembrance honors Jesus and all He did for us.

A Closer Look

Communion Wafers

Individual Communion Cups

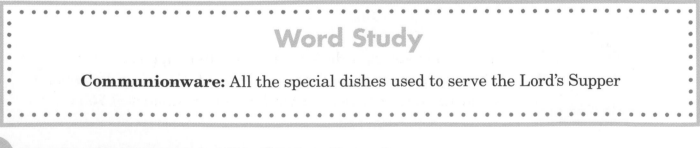

Word Study

Communionware: All the special dishes used to serve the Lord's Supper

Tableware

There are many styles of communionware. Most often, it is made of silver. Sometimes it is gold. The originals used at the first Lord's Supper were probably made of pottery, which was common in that day. This diagram names and tells the purpose of the pieces that are often used.

Flagon
The pitcher that supplies more wine.

Chalice
The long-stemmed cup that holds the wine.

Ciborium
A lidded-chalice that holds extra bread (wafers).

Paten
The plate from which the bread is distributed.

Host Box
A container that is used to hold bread instead of a ciborium.

Portable Communion Set

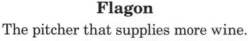

Bible Words to Remember

In the same way also He took the cup, after supper, saying, "This cup is the new covenant in My blood. Do this, as often as you drink it, in remembrance of Me." 1 Corinthians 11:25

The Old Covenant

Celebrating the Passover

1. The rescue, with blood on wooden ___doorpost___

2. Saved from slavery in ___Egypt___ and from ___death___

3. Remembrance celebration every ___passover___

4. The ___lamb___ with no stain or blemish

5. The meal—unleavened bread, wine, and more

6. The promise: "I shall be your God and you shall be My people."

Word Study

Use the Bible Dictionary in your book to find the meanings.

Covenant: ___a prasimise___

Testament: ___a stanent of trath___

The New Covenant

On the night before Jesus was crucified on the cross, He and His disciples celebrated the Passover meal. Then Jesus told them about a new celebration and a new promise. Replacing the Passover of the Old Testament is the Lord's Supper of the New Testament.

Celebrating the Lord's Supper

1. The rescue, with blood on a wooden _cross_

2. Saved from slavery to _sin_ and from eternal _death_

3. Remembrance celebration every _Sunday_

4. The _lamb_ is _Jesus_, who is pure and holy.

5. The meal—bread, wine, and much, much more

6. The promise: forgiveness, life, and salvation through Jesus' body and blood

Bible Words to Remember

Behold, the Lamb of God, who takes away the sin of the world! John 1:29

The Ark of the Covenant

1. Circle what was made of acacia wood then covered in pure gold.
2. Draw a box around the cherubim.
3. Draw arrows to point to the acacia poles, covered in gold.
4. Draw a triangle above the Mercy Seat, but below the wings of the cherubim.

Now fill in the blanks with your teacher's help.

The ark of the covenant showed God's ___throne___.

The ark of the covenant showed the need for ___forgiveness___.

The ark of the covenant showed the need for a ___sacrifice___.

Word Study

Liturgical Arts: Artwork with a spiritual purpose to guide our understanding of God's Word, to focus our attention in worship, and to remind us of the grace and greatness of God.

Liturgical Arts All around Us

You may be starting to notice all the artwork around your church and school. As you work through this lesson, think about noticing it more often and letting it remind you of what it means.

Connect the images to the Bible verses on the right:

The eternal God is your dwelling place, and underneath are the everlasting arms. Deuteronomy 33:27

[Jesus said,] "I am the light of the world." John 8:12

Go therefore and make disciples of all nations, baptizing them in the name of the Father and of the Son and of the Holy Spirit. Matthew 28:19

[Jesus said,] "I am the good shepherd. The good shepherd lays down His life for the sheep." John 10:11

[John said,] "I saw the Spirit descend from heaven like a dove, and it remained on [Jesus]." John 1:32

[Jesus said,] "Be faithful unto death, and I will give you the crown of life." Revelation 2:10

Search your school, church, and home for these symbols. Every time you see one of the symbols, tell someone what it means. Then, remember your relationship with God. You are His child, welcomed in His kingdom forever!

Did you know . . .

Baptism and Holy Communion aren't just reminders! They are Sacraments. God has connected His Word to them. They convey (bring) God's forgiveness and strength to us.

Bible Words to Remember

I will remember the deeds of the LORD; yes, I will remember Your wonders of old. Psalm 77:11

Who Is Your Neighbor?

The Second Table of the Law talks about how we treat our neighbor. "You shall love your neighbor as yourself" is a summary of the Second Table of the Law.

Work with a few friends, and use the illustration to draw a square in the middle of a piece of paper. Without discussion, each person in your group should use a different side of the paper to answer the question, "Who is your neighbor?" Discuss your answer as a group; then write it in the center section (Group Ideas).

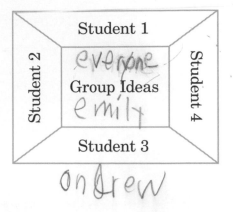

Student 1

Student 2

everyone

Group Ideas

emily

Student 4

Student 3

andrew

Being a Good Samaritan

Write or show thoughts and feelings.

Make a portrait of the priest, the Levite, the Samaritan, or the injured man from the story of the Good Samaritan in Luke 10:25–37. Attach three pieces of drawing paper with a fastener.

1. On the top piece, draw and color a large portrait of the head and neck of the character.

2. Cut around the portrait through all three thicknesses.

3. Lift the portrait, and draw or write about the character's thoughts at key points in the story on the thinking pages.

4. Share your portraits with classmates, and talk about the words and pictures you chose to include on the thinking pages.

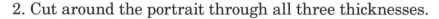

Word Study

Fill in the blanks with the correct word: **Samaritan**   **Levite**   **priest**

An assistant to the priests _____ *Levitan* _____

A person who offered sacrifices for God's people _____ *priest* _____

A person most Jewish people disliked, even hated _____ *samaritana* _____

What Is Compassion?

Compassion is when you feel bad for someone who is suffering or has troubles and want to help the person. The Good Samaritan showed compassion for the hurt man.

Describe how someone with compassion acts when

1. A new student at Sunday School seems nervous. _help him_

2. A young child is crying. _heal him_

3. A bully falls off his bike. _help him_

We Love Because . . .

It must have been hard for the Good Samaritan to show love to the stranger. Write two or more types of neighbors you might find it hard to love or serve. _people who doesnt listen to directions people_

Jesus told this parable to show that God wants us to love our neighbor. But we can never do this on our own.

Read the Bible Words to Remember. Draw a heart around the word *love*. Underline words that show why we can love others.

The Good Samaritan in the story is a picture of Jesus and what He does for us. We can only love others because Jesus first loved us and came to rescue us from our troubles—sin, death, and the devil—by dying on the cross for us. By faith, we are His children. The Holy Spirit helps us to be like the Good Samaritan. He helps us share Jesus' love with our neighbor.

What neighbor can you show love to this week? In the heart, write or draw what you will do.

Bible Words to Remember

We love because He first loved us. 1 John 4:19

What Does God Want?

"Aw, do I have to? I don't want to do it now!" Have you ever said this to your mom or dad or to your teacher? Maybe you have just thought it or grumbled as you unwillingly obeyed. Turn to a friend and share a time you acted like this. Talk about why you did it.

With your partner, read the Bible Words to Remember and do the Word Study. Now use God's Word to talk about what you should have done in the situation you shared. Which of the following responses is God's choice for you? Underline it.

1. Whine, complain, or grumble either out loud or silently as you grudgingly do the task

2. Happily obey right away without arguing or complaining

3. Avoid, delay, or just plain not do what you were asked to do

Obeying and honoring are hard to do. Paul said in Romans 7:19, **"I do not do the good I want, but the evil I do not want is what I keep on doing."** Do you ever feel that way? To find out where to get strength to help you obey and honor your parents and teachers, unscramble the letters in each square and fill in the blanks in the Bible verses.

For it is ___God___ who works in you, both to ___will___ and to ___work___ for His good pleasure. Philippians 2:13

I can do all things through ___him___ who ___strengthens___ me.
Philippians 4:13

Word Study

Look up the Bible Dictionary definition for each word. Write it here.

obey: _follow comands_

honor: _to respect_

Joseph Honors and Obeys

In the Fourth Commandment, God says to honor your father and mother. Read Genesis 46:26–34. How did Joseph show respect and love for his father, Jacob?

The Fourth Commandment also includes honoring those God puts in charge over us. Read the verses again. How did Joseph also respect his ruler, the Pharaoh?

Jacob, Joseph's Father	Pharaoh, Joseph's Ruler
gave him a color of a rainbow	*he helped him a respect.*

I Will Honor and Obey

Honor and obey: little words attached to a BIG promise! Choose one of the words, and create an acrostic poem to describe how you will obey and honor your parents or someone else in authority. Write your poem beside the example below.

H elp before being asked. *like open the door*

O bey without complaining. _____

N ever talk back. _____

O pen the door for Mom. _____

R espect my parents. _____

Hiding God's Word in My Heart

Singing the Bible is a great way to hide God's Word in your heart! Sing the first part of the Bible Words to Remember to the tune of "Jesus in the Morning" to help you remember it.

> Honor, honor, honor your father,
> Honor your mother.
> Ephesians, Ephesians, Ephesians six, verse two.

Bible Words to Remember

Honor your father and mother (this is the first commandment with a promise), that it may go well with you and that you may live long in the land. Ephesians 6:2–3

Honoring God by Honoring Others

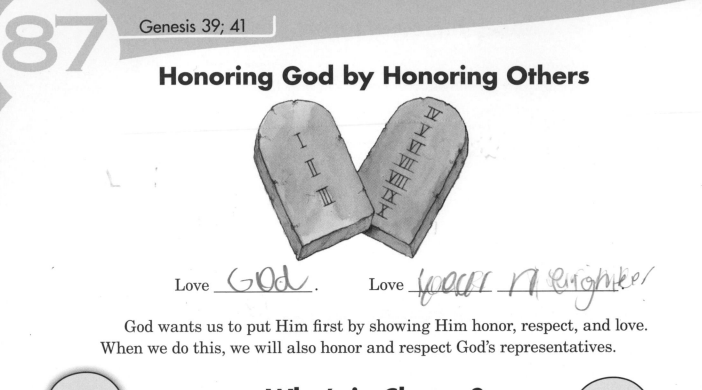

Love __God__ .   Love __your neighbor__

God wants us to put Him first by showing Him honor, respect, and love.
When we do this, we will also honor and respect God's representatives.

Who's in Charge?

__G O D__

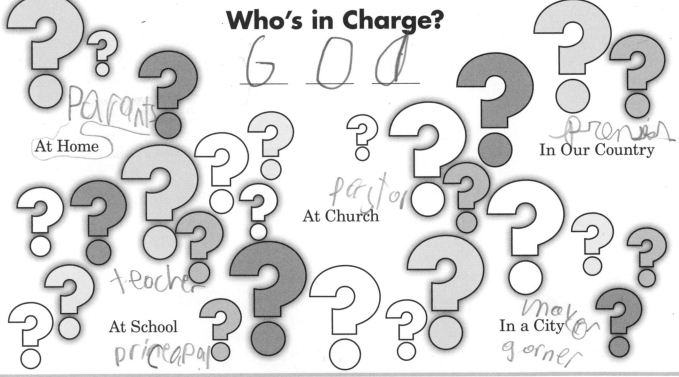

At Home — parents

At School — teacher, principal

At Church — pastor

In Our Country — president

In a City — mayor, governor

Word Study

Draw a line to match the word with its definition.

prosper   the person in charge of the prisoners

overseer   a person who directs the work of others

keeper of the prison   to succeed or do well

God's Idea—Not Joseph's

Genesis 39:1–6: Joseph was working for an Egyptian official named _Poterph_ in Egypt (v. 1). God blessed Joseph and made him succeed at everything he did (v. 2). Potiphar made Joseph the _overseer_ of his house (v. 4).

Genesis 39:20–23: Joseph was put into _prison_ (v. 20). _God_ watched over Joseph (v. 21). The _keeper of the prison_ put Joseph in charge of all the other prisoners (v. 22).

Genesis 41:1–16: The leader of Egypt, named _pharaoh_, had a dream (v. 1). _seven_ lean cows ate _seven_ fat cows (v. 4), and _ugly_ thin heads of grain swallowed _seven_ healthy heads of grain (v. 7). Pharaoh's magicians didn't know what it meant, so Pharaoh sent for _Joseph_ (v. 14). Joseph let Pharaoh know that _God_ would tell him about his dreams (v. 16).

God's Helping Hands

On the lines below, write a way in which you can show your love for the Lord by giving honor and respect to those in authority over you in these places:

At Home _a parment would help me_

At School _a teecher_

In the Community _mayer or govener_

What Should They Do?

Juan and Julio had a fight. Hurtful words were said. What should they do about that? Use the key to fill in the blanks.

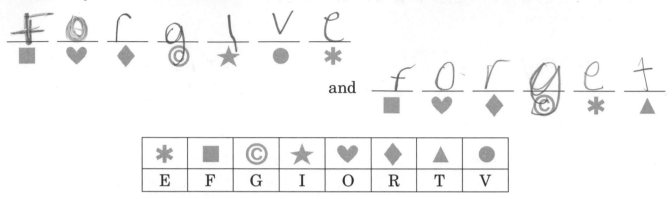

F O r g i v e

and f o r g e t

✳	■	©	★	♥	◆	▲	●
E	F	G	I	O	R	T	V

The Fifth Commandment: You shall not murder.

What does this mean? We should fear and love God so that we do not hurt or harm our neighbor in his body, but help and support him in every physical need.

Brotherly Love?

Israel is another name for Jacob. Jacob was the father of twelve sons. His favorite was Joseph. Jacob gave Joseph a coat of many colors to show how much he loved him.

Jacob's other sons felt jealous of Joseph. One day, Jacob asked Joseph to go and check on his sons to see how they were doing while they watched over the flocks in the field.

Read **Genesis 37:12–36.**

How did Joseph's brothers treat him?

badly

How did the sons of Jacob disobey the Fifth Commandment?

named him and lied

Word Study

Find these words in your Bible Dictionary and write their meanings.

reconcile: _____

persecute: _when someone say god idty_

What Would You Do?

Jesus loves us—so much that He died for us. He told His disciples, "A new commandment I give to you, that you love one another: just as I have loved you, you also are to love one another" (John 13:34).

How do we show others that we love them? Find out what Jesus said. Jot down what He said in these verses.

Matthew 5:21–24 _solve problems_

Matthew 5:43–44 _love your enemays_

Matthew 25:37–45 _help the homeless people_

How can we live our lives in His grace and forgiveness? Think about ways you could respond in a God-pleasing way to the following situations. Who helps you do these things?

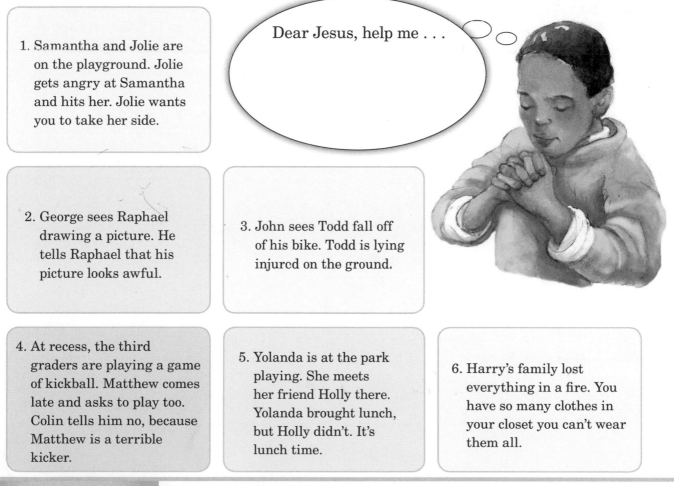

1. Samantha and Jolie are on the playground. Jolie gets angry at Samantha and hits her. Jolie wants you to take her side.

Dear Jesus, help me . . .

2. George sees Raphael drawing a picture. He tells Raphael that his picture looks awful.

3. John sees Todd fall off of his bike. Todd is lying injured on the ground.

4. At recess, the third graders are playing a game of kickball. Matthew comes late and asks to play too. Colin tells him no, because Matthew is a terrible kicker.

5. Yolanda is at the park playing. She meets her friend Holly there. Yolanda brought lunch, but Holly didn't. It's lunch time.

6. Harry's family lost everything in a fire. You have so many clothes in your closet you can't wear them all.

Bible Words to Remember

Love your enemies and pray for those who persecute you.
Matthew 5:44

How Are We Tempted?

How does a mousetrap work? How does a fishing lure work?

To a hungry mouse, a piece of cheese looks like a treat! To a fish, a lure looks like a nice dinner! But they have deadly consequences.

In **2 Corinthians 11:14**, Paul says, "Satan disguises himself as an

angel of _light_."
The devil's disguises are like lures or traps. He uses them to trick us into sinning. His temptations may look like fun, but they are against God's will for us.

Satan's Tricky Traps

While Joseph worked for an Egyptian officer named Potiphar, Satan tried to lure Joseph into sin. Potiphar's wife wanted Joseph to be with her in a way that only a husband should be. Joseph knew this was wrong. God made marriage to be a covenant between one man and one woman. Joseph would sin against God if he treated Potiphar's wife as a husband does. He knew God wants His people to live pure and decent lives. He said, "No!"

Joseph was tempted to sin. Write his answer in the speech bubble.

With God's power, we can say, "No!" when tempted. Draw yourself saying, "No!" to sin.

Word Study

Look up these words in the Bible Dictionary. Write definitions here.

disguise: _to change your appearence_

purity: _the quality of being pure free from evil and sin_

God's Commandments

Write the Sixth Commandment on the scroll.

This Commandment says marriage and families are gifts from God. We are also part of God's family through faith in Jesus, who paid for our sins on the cross. God forgives us. He helps us to love and forgive others.

You shall not comst Aoldtrv

Read **2 Corinthians 6:18** to fill in this verse:

And I will be a _____*Father*_____ to you, and you

shall be _____*sons*_____ and _____*dauter*_____

to Me, says the Lord Almighty.

See, Hear, and Speak No Evil

God was with Joseph, and He is with us too! Our bodies are temples of the Holy Spirit (1 Corinthians 6:19). Because we belong to God, we do not want to misuse our bodies

Read the Bible verses and decide if the verse guides us to guard the **heart**, **eyes**, **ears**, or **mouth**. Draw a line connecting each verse to the correct picture.

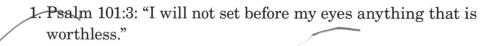

1. Psalm 101:3: "I will not set before my eyes anything that is worthless."

2. Hebrews 10:22: "Let us draw near with a true heart in full assurance of faith, with our hearts sprinkled clean from an evil conscience."

3. Ephesians 4:29 (NIV): "Do not let any unwholesome talk come out of your mouths, but only what is helpful for building others up . . . that it may benefit those who listen."

4. James 1:22: "But be doers of the word, and not hearers only."

5. Psalm 19:14: "Let the words of my mouth and the meditation of my heart be acceptable in Your sight, O Lord."

Bible Words to Remember

Blessed are the pure in heart, for they shall see God. Matthew 5:8

To Steal or Not to Steal?

 -K + L

<u>thall shall not steal</u>

Sometimes it is hard to tell if something is being stolen. Look at these three pictures with a partner. Decide if someone is stealing or not. Be ready to explain your answer.

 "Finders keepers!"

God Works for Good

Read Genesis 44:1–13. Benjamin did not steal the silver cup, but it was in his grain bag. Circle the consequences the servant gave for stealing the silver cup.

Being sent home   Death   Jail   Slavery   Physical punishment

The brothers felt afraid. They did not know God was working to restore their family.

It is often easy to *want* to take what is not ours. But God gives us power through the Holy Spirit to resist these temptations. When we do sin, "If we confess our sins, He is <u>faith</u> and just to <u>forgive</u> us our sins" (1 John 1:9). God promises, "I will remember [your] sins <u>no more</u>" (Hebrews 8:12).

Word Study

Read the definitions. Use both words in one sentence.

temptation: something that lures us to do something that God says is wrong
consequences: the results of a behavior or decision

<u>temptaiton leads us to consequences</u>

Through the Cross

In the Ten Commandments, God tells us how He wants us to love and treat one another. Our sinful attitudes of selfishness and greed get in the way. But Jesus came to keep God's Law perfectly for us, and then He died on the cross to pay for our sins. Through Him, we have forgiveness. Now we are "a new creation" (2 Corinthians 5:17).

The Holy Spirit changes our attitudes and gives us the power to love and serve others. Read the situations on the left. Then draw a line "through the cross" to match each temptation with a Christ-like response on the right.

When tempted to . . .

Take a pencil from a classmate without asking

Copy someone else's homework, instead of doing it myself

Keep a video game I borrowed from a friend

Use offering money to buy candy

Destroy something that isn't mine

Be jealous of someone's belongings

Stay angry at someone who hurt me

I Can . . .

Do my own work, asking for help if I need it.

Ask a friend to borrow one.

Give to God with a cheerful heart.

Return it; then offer one of mine.

Thank God for the gifts He has given me.

Help others take care of their things.

Say, "I forgive you because Jesus forgave me!"

Thank You, Lord!

Write a prayer asking God to help you have actions and attitudes towards others that are pleasing to Him.

oh God please help me to be gooder to others and be good amen

Bible Words to Remember

[Jesus said,] "These things I command you, so that you will love one another." John 15:17

91

Power of Life and Death

"The tongue has the power of life and death" (Proverbs 18:21 NIV). It can do more harm or good than any muscle in your body. Read these Bible verses to find out what your tongue can do.

Psalm 34:13 *keep our toung flon evil*

Psalm 126:2 *shout for joy*

Proverbs 12:18–19 *there words the con hert people*

Stick and Stones

Listen to situations your teacher reads to you.

How might words hurt Elizabeth?

the could get a detention

How might words hurt Joe?

he might

How might words hurt Max?

he gets punish for things he dindt do

What's in a Word?

Underline or circle the sentence that helps explain each word.

Verbal

a. I hit my friend.
b. I talk to my friend.
c. I used words to hurt.

Slander

a. I told a lie.
b. I made someone feel good with my words.
c. I said something nice.

Word Study

Write a sentence with **slander** or **verbal.** Find a classmate who wrote a sentence using the other word. Share your sentences.

jack him told a lie about Joe laghing at him when he fell

Words Can Hurt Us

These pictures show lies that Joseph's brothers and Potiphar's wife told about Joseph. Beside each picture, write or draw a picture that shows the result of those lies.

Lie: Genesis 37:31–32

lie about Joseph being dead.

Result of Lie: Genesis 37:33–35

Lie: Genesis 39:16–18

Result of Lie: Genesis 39:19–20

Build One Another Up

Built on Lies

Built on Truth

What Is a Lie?

What do you think? When I don't say anything, is that lying?

It's Not Always What You Say

Listen to stories your teacher reads. Discuss what happened when the people did not say anything. Then think of God-pleasing responses. Write them in the speech bubbles.

Word Study

omission: _____

Failing to Speak Up

Speaking in a Kind Way

Choosing God-pleasing words is important too.

How are these towers like us and the words we use?

Bible Words to Remember

Above all, keep loving one another earnestly, since love covers a multitude of sins. 1 Peter 4:8

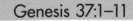

Recipe for Jealousy

Use the code to figure out the recipe for jealousy that Joseph's brothers had for him.

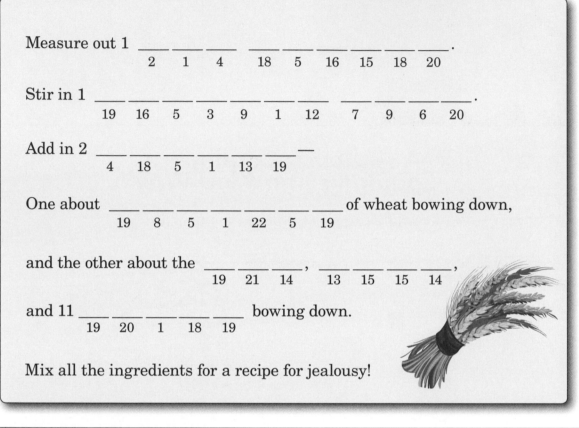

Measure out 1 __B__ __A__ __D__ __R__ __E__ __P__ __O__ __R__ __T__.
               2   1   4   18 5 16 15 18 20

Stir in 1 __S__ __P__ __E__ __C__ __I__ __A__ __L__ __G__ __I__ __F__ __T__.
      19 16 5 3 9 1 12   7 9 6 20

Add in 2 __D__ __R__ __E__ __A__ __M__ __S__—
      4 18 5 1 13 19

One about __S__ __H__ __E__ __A__ __V__ __E__ __S__ of wheat bowing down,
            19 8 5 1 22 5 19

and the other about the __S__ __U__ __N__, __M__ __O__ __O__ __N__,
                   19 21 14   13 15 15 14

and 11 __S__ __T__ __A__ __R__ __S__ bowing down.
       19 20 1 18 19

Mix all the ingredients for a recipe for jealousy!

A	B	C	D	E	F	G	H	I	J	K	L	M	N	O	P	Q	R	S	T	U	V	W	X	Y	Z
1	2	3	4	5	6	7	8	9	10	11	12	13	14	15	16	17	18	19	20	21	22	23	24	25	26

What Does Jealousy Look Like?

Read Genesis 37:4–11. Put the letter beside the verse that shows the jealous action.

_____ Verse 4   a. Hated him, could not speak peacefully to him.

_____ Verse 8   b. Were jealous of him.

_____ Verse 11   c. Hated him even more.

Word Study

jealousy: _____

Results of Jealousy

The brothers' jealousy had bad results for Joseph. Read Genesis 37:23–28. Show the order of what happened by writing 1 to 3 in front of the remaining statements. Put an X in front of the statement that doesn't belong.

_____ They threw him in a cistern (a big pit for water).

_____ They beat him up.

_____ They took his robe.

_____ They sold him to the Ishmaelites to be a slave.

A Jealousy Continuum

Your teacher will read situations where you might feel jealous. Place an X on the line to show how you would feel about each situation.

⟵⟶

Bothers me a little.	Bothers me a lot.
I wish I had that.	That is so NOT FAIR!
How could that happen?	I'm going to get even!

Jealousy and coveting are two of Satan's best weapons against our faith. He wants to make us feel discontent with God's blessings and draw us away from God and His love.

Results of Contentment

Use the code on page 192 to find two blessings that we receive when we are content with what God has given us. We also have these blessings when we remember the assurance of eternal life that we have because of Jesus' suffering, death, and resurrection for the forgiveness of our sins.

___ ___ ___ ___ ___ and ___ ___ ___
16 5 1 3 5   10 15 25

Bible Words to Remember

I have learned in whatever situation I am to be content.
Philippians 4:11

The Command Expanded

The Ninth and Tenth Commandments go hand in hand. Both address the sin of covetousness.

The Tenth Commandment expands the sin to all areas of our lives.

What does God warn us about coveting in the Ninth Commandment? _____

What four things does God warn us about coveting in the Tenth Commandment?

_____

Hearts Changed

Contentment in the hearts of Jacob's family members was hard to find in Genesis 37–43. Let's find out how their hearts became more content as your teacher tells how Joseph's brothers protected Benjamin.

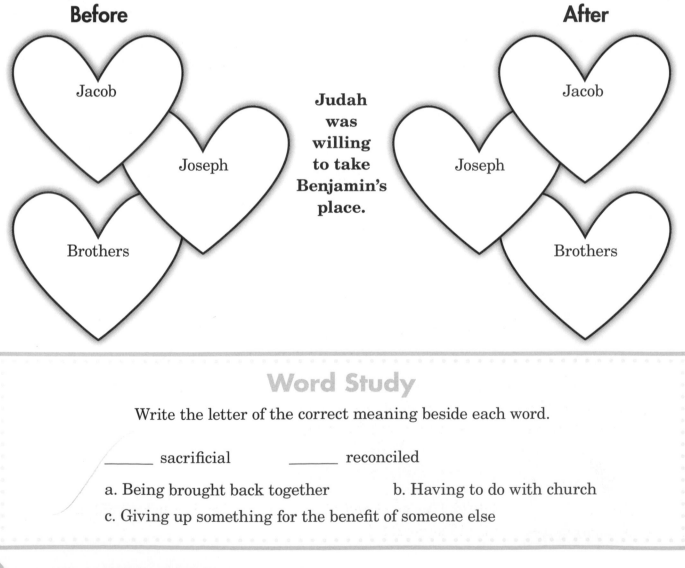

Before

Jacob

Joseph

Brothers

Judah was willing to take Benjamin's place.

After

Jacob

Joseph

Brothers

Word Study

Write the letter of the correct meaning beside each word.

_____ sacrificial _____ reconciled

a. Being brought back together   b. Having to do with church

c. Giving up something for the benefit of someone else

Reconciliation Brings Contentment

Imagine the joy Joseph and his family shared when reunited. Pharaoh gave them the best land in Egypt. Best of all, they were together again and Joseph had forgiven them. The hearts of Joseph's family changed because of love and forgiveness.

Jesus' love and forgiveness changes our hearts too. Our change of heart shows in our relationships.

Before

Jesus' sacrificial offering

God

us   others

us

After

Jesus' sacrificial death on the cross reconciles us to God. Draw a vertical line to connect the "God" and "us" dots. Through Jesus, we are reconciled to others. Draw a horizontal line to make a cross. Reconciliation brings contentment and God's peace.

Be Still, My Soul

With your class, read the lyrics of "Be Still, My Soul" (*LSB* 752). Read it again and circle or underline your favorite lines of the song.

> Be still, my soul;
> The Lord is on your side;
> Bear patiently the cross of grief or pain;
> Leave to your God to order and provide;
> In ev'ry change He faithful will remain.
> Be still, my soul;
> Your best, your heav'nly Friend,
> Through thorny ways leads to a joyful end.

While we live in this sinful world, we will have struggles and difficulties. Things will happen that we do not understand. Still, we can rest in God's peace, knowing that our God will guide us and work all things out for our good.

Bible Words to Remember

Behold, how good and pleasant it is when brothers dwell in unity! Psalm 133:1

95

Joseph and His Brothers

Narrator

Joseph's brothers

Joseph

Messenger 1

Messenger 2

 When Joseph's brothers saw that their father was dead, they said,

 (Fearfully) It may be that Joseph will hate us and pay us back for the evil we did to him.

 So they sent a message to Joseph saying,

 Your father gave this command before he died,

 (Reading from scroll) Say to Joseph, please forgive the transgression of your brothers and their sin because they did evil to you.

 And now, please forgive the transgression of the servants of the God of your father.

 Joseph wept when they spoke to him. His brothers also came and fell down before him and said,

 (Kneeling) Behold, we are your servants.

 But Joseph said to them,

 Do not fear, for am I in the place of God? As for you, you meant evil against me, but God meant it for good, so many people should be kept alive, as they are today. So do not fear; I will provide for you and your little ones.

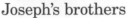 Thus he comforted them and spoke kindly to them.

Word Study

Instructions: Circle the synonyms (the words that means the same).

grudge:	forgive	resentment	animosity
revenge:	retaliation	pardon	punishment
contentment:	covet	peace	satisfaction

Before and After

☐ Before Joseph is sold into slavery . . .

☐ After Joseph was a ruler in Egypt . . .

☐ Before the brothers come to Egypt . . .

☐ After Jacob died . . .

☐ Before we were baptized . . .

☐ After we become God's children . . .

God Gives Contentment

Did Joseph's brothers deserve God's love and forgiveness? Did Joseph? Do you? No. No one does!

But God loves us so much He sent Jesus to be our Savior from sin, death, and the devil. Because of God's big love for us, "We know that . . . all things work together for good" (Romans 8:28).

Write a letter to Joseph to share how God helped you in one of your troubles. Then tell Joseph how knowing God is with you and works all things for your good is teaching you to be content.

Dear Joseph,

Your friend,

_____

Bible Words to Remember

Be content with what you have, for He has said, "I will never leave you nor forsake you." Hebrews 13:5

What Do You Expect?

What might you expect to happen if you . . .

dropped your open water bottle?

forgot to bring your homework?

broke Mom's favorite vase?

finished your book report on time?

wrote a thank-you note to Grandma?

took your sister's hairbrush?

made your bed without whining?

lied about a friend?

Word Study

_____ : not getting the punishment we deserve

_____ : getting what we don't deserve

Reunited!

Bible Words to Remember

The law was given through _____; grace and truth
came through _____. John 1:17

Joy in Jesus

JOY =

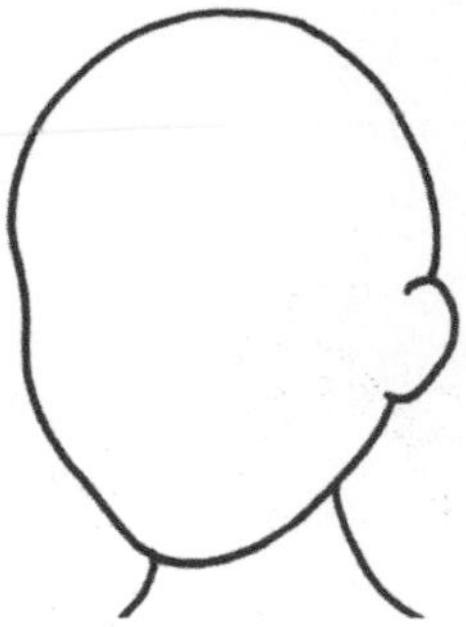

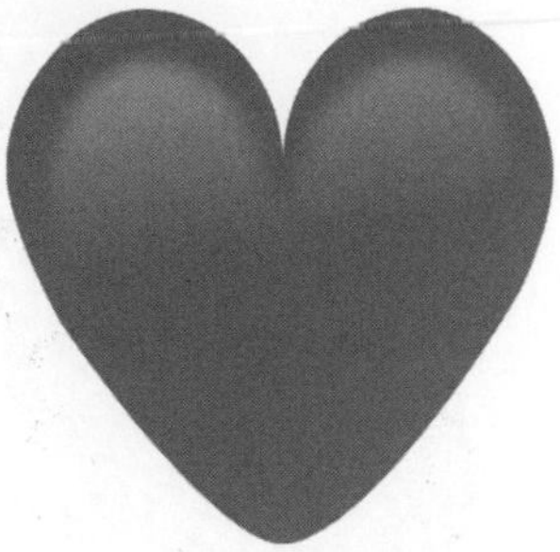

the same _____

the same _____

full _____

one _____

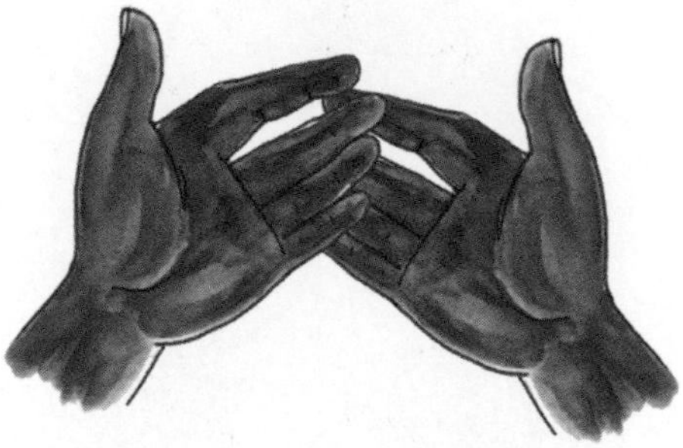

rivalry   conceit   humility

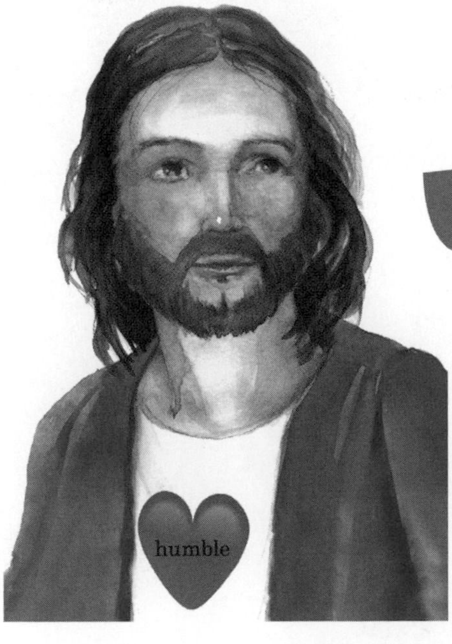

JESUS was humble

Philippians 2:5–8

made Himself _____

taking the form of a _____

born in the likeness of _____

obedient to _____ on a

humble

Word Study

Humble: _____

Jesus said, "I am the Light of the world."

of the world."
John 8:12

Shine as lights in the world.

grumbling   blameless   without blemish

questioning   innocent

Bible Words to Remember

Shine as lights in the world, holding fast to the word of life.
Philippians 2:15–16

John 6:1–15

His Love, Our Response

PSALMS = religious songs prayers we sing

Who God Is

Psalm 111

What God Does

v. 3 _____

_____ _____ v. 2

v. 4 _____

_____ _____ v. 5

v. 4 _____

_____ _____

The fear of the LORD is the beginning of wisdom. Psalm 111:10

v. 7 _____

_____ _____

v. 7 _____

_____ v. 6

v. 7 _____

_____ _____ v. 6

v. 1

v. 9 _____

_____

v. 9 _____

_____ v. 9

_____

v. 1 _____

v. 10 _____

Our Response

Word Study

Prayer is . . .

_____

_____

My Prayers

Jesus thanked God for the five loaves and two fish, then fed over 5,000 people and had leftovers. How? God gave this miracle.

We can talk to God anytime, anywhere, about anything. Show this by writing ends to the following sentences.

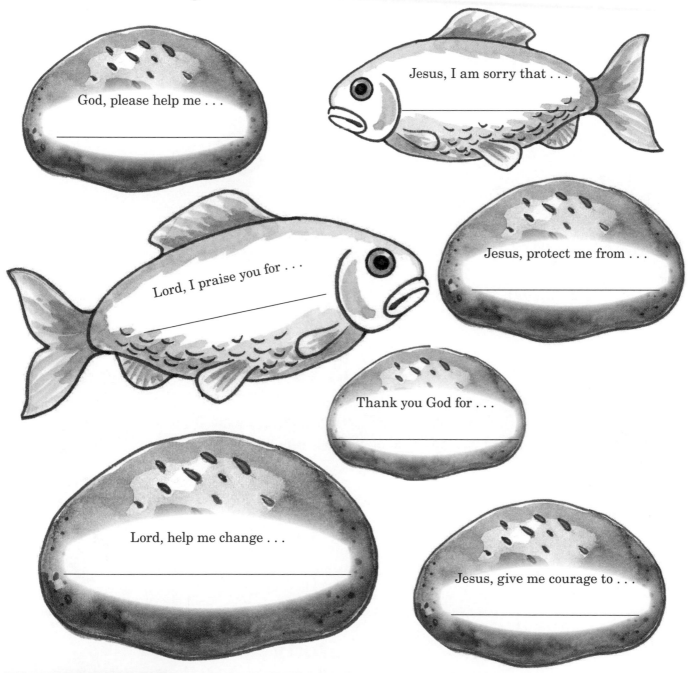

God, please help me . . .

Jesus, I am sorry that . . .

Lord, I praise you for . . .

Jesus, protect me from . . .

Thank you God for . . .

Lord, help me change . . .

Jesus, give me courage to . . .

Bible Words to Remember

Do not be anxious about anything, but in everything by prayer and supplication with thanksgiving let your requests be made known to God. Philippians 4:6–7

God's Word at Work in Us

Directions: Use these words to finish the sentences:
live, sin, serve, Savior, obey, repent, live, forgiveness, thank.

God's Word has *Law* and *Gospel* . We need both. Each shows us

something important about God and us. God is perfect. We are not.

God's our _____ . It us to _____ .

God's our _____ and _____ of sin He provides.

Because of what Jesus did for us, we want to _____ , _____ ,

_____ , and _____ God and _____ for Him.

Walk in Love

In the Bible verse, highlight words that tell what Jesus did for us. Circle words that show our response to Jesus' love.

Ephesians 5:2: Walk in love, as Christ loved us and gave

Himself up for us, a fragrant offering and sacrifice to God.

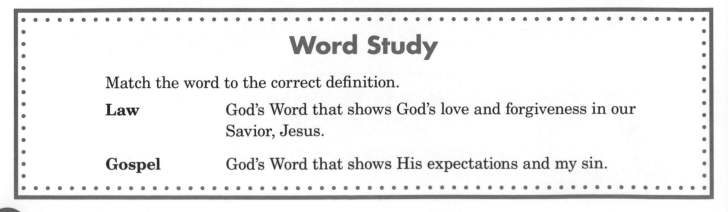

Word Study

Match the word to the correct definition.

Law   God's Word that shows God's love and forgiveness in our Savior, Jesus.

Gospel   God's Word that shows His expectations and my sin.

A Light to My Path

Psalm 119:97–105

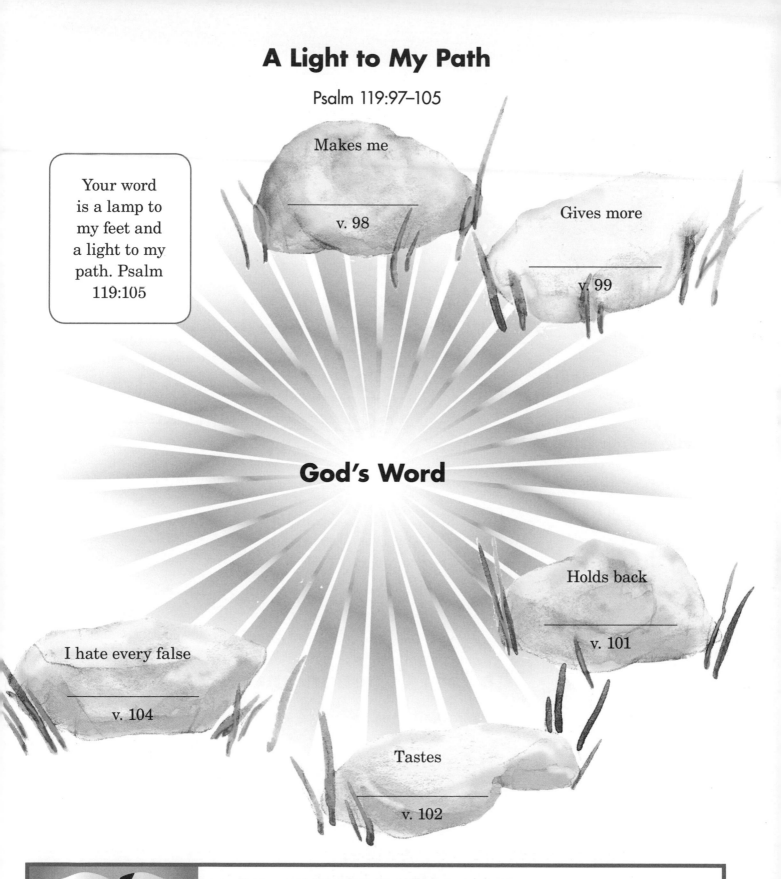

Your word is a lamp to my feet and a light to my path. Psalm 119:105

Makes me

_____

v. 98

Gives more

_____

v. 99

God's Word

Holds back

_____

v. 101

I hate every false

_____

v. 104

Tastes

_____

v. 102

Bible Words to Remember

Your word is a lamp to my feet and a light to my path.
Psalm 119:105

Jesus and Me

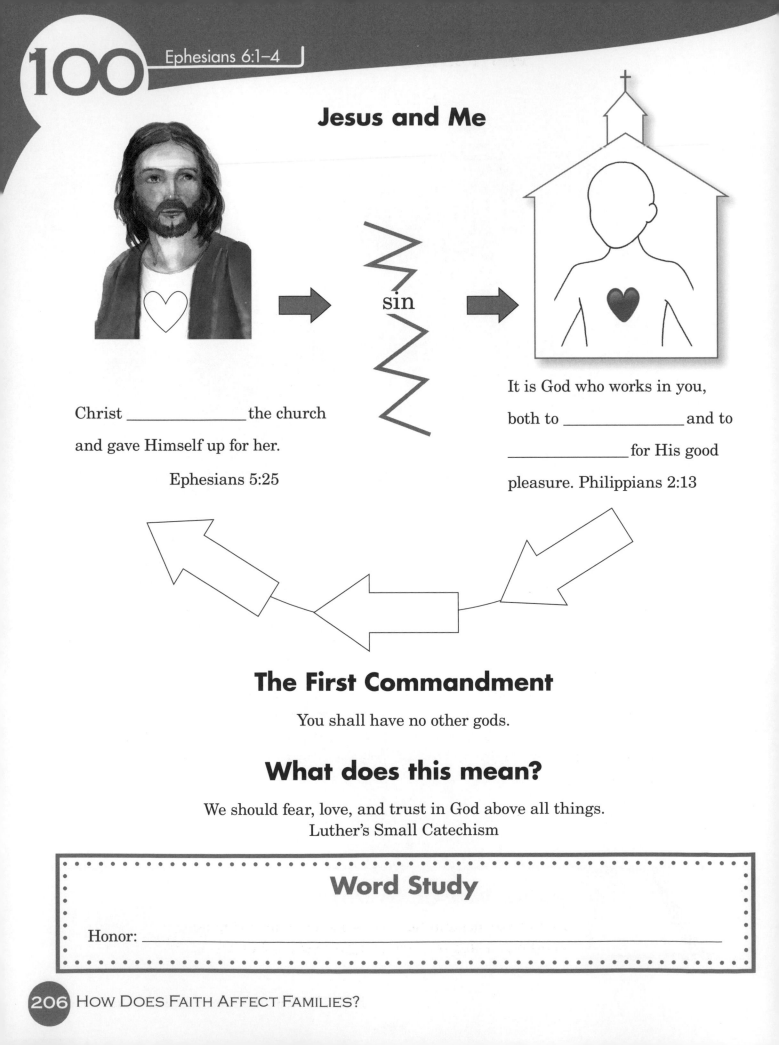

sin

Christ _____ the church and gave Himself up for her.

Ephesians 5:25

It is God who works in you, both to _____ and to _____ for His good pleasure. Philippians 2:13

The First Commandment

You shall have no other gods.

What does this mean?

We should fear, love, and trust in God above all things.
Luther's Small Catechism

Word Study

Honor: _____

My Parents and Me

Do not

Do

Do

Do

Do

Parents, "do not **provoke** your children to anger, but bring them up in the **discipline** and **instruction of the Lord**." Ephesians 6:4

"Children, **obey** your parents in the Lord, for this is right. '**Honor** your father and mother.'" Ephesians 6:1–2

It is a far higher thing to honor someone than to love someone, because honor includes not only love, but also modesty, humility, and submission to a majesty hidden in them. Honor requires not only that parents be addressed kindly and with reverence, but also that, both in the heart and with the body, we demonstrate that we value them very highly and that, next to God, we regard them as the very highest.

—Luther's Large Catechism, the Fourth Commandment

Concordia: The Lutheran Confessions, page 397

Bible Words to Remember

Be kind to one another, tenderhearted, forgiving one another, as God in Christ forgave you. Ephesians 4:32

Weary?

Directions: Circle *weary* in the Bible verse. Highlight the *do* commands. Underline words that mean the same as *church* or *believers in Jesus*.

Let us not grow weary of doing good, for in due season we will reap, if we do not give up. So then, as we have opportunity, let us do good to everyone, and especially to those who are of the household of faith. Galatians 6:9–10

So What?

Sometimes it is hard to do the right thing. It doesn't always feel good. We grow weary of doing good when others do not. When we feel this way, we sin. We have forgotten that God loves us and saved us for a purpose, to serve Him.

Write or draw one thing you get tired of doing.

Write a short prayer to confess this sin to God and ask for His help to do better.

_____

_____

_____

_____

_____

_____

God forgives us in Jesus' name. He sends the Holy Spirit to help us live as His people.

Word Study

Choose the correct definition.

_____ weary   a. full of energy   b. tired, sad, and unfocused   c. happy

Now What?

Set free from sin, we are free to serve God. What does God want us to do? Read the Bible Words to Remember to find out. Then draw a picture that shows you doing each thing.

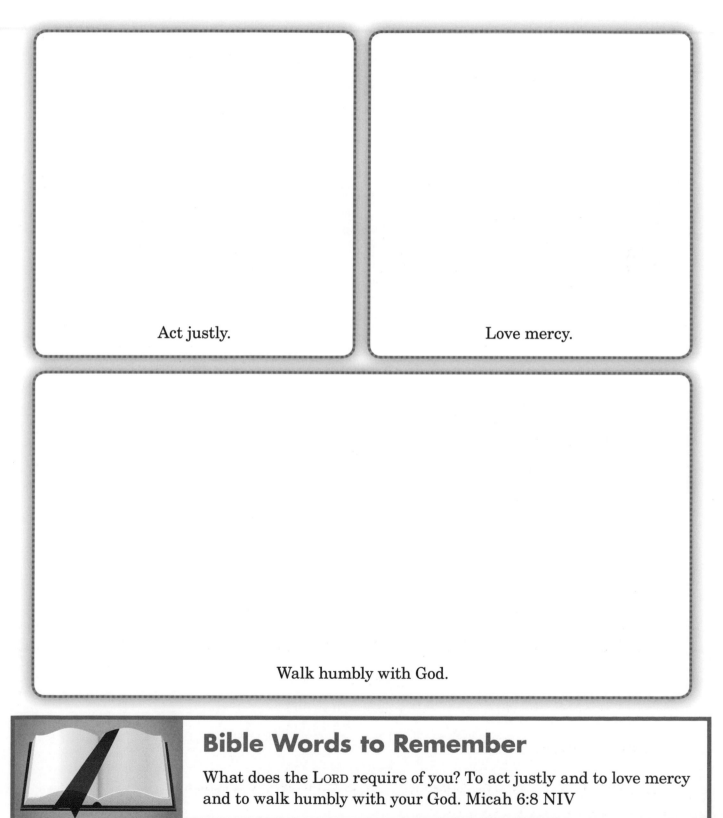

Act justly.

Love mercy.

Walk humbly with God.

Blessings and Problems

Read Acts 6:1–7 and fill in the chart to complete the story.

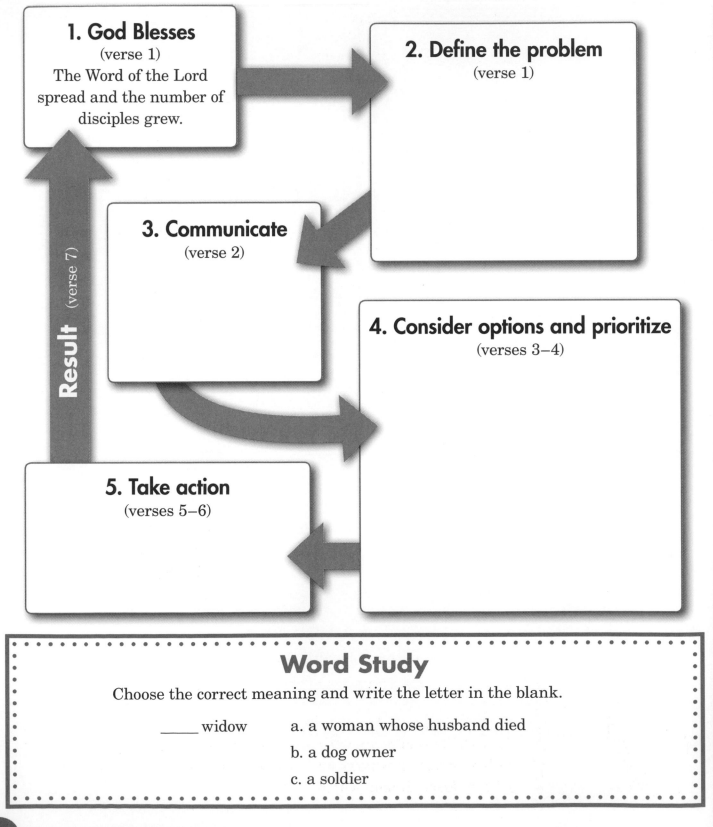

1. God Blesses
(verse 1)
The Word of the Lord spread and the number of disciples grew.

2. Define the problem
(verse 1)

3. Communicate
(verse 2)

Result (verse 7)

4. Consider options and prioritize
(verses 3–4)

5. Take action
(verses 5–6)

Word Study

Choose the correct meaning and write the letter in the blank.

_____ widow

a. a woman whose husband died

b. a dog owner

c. a soldier

Blessings in My Church

Find words in the puzzle that tell things God's Church does. Cross words off the list when you find them.

```
H  F  C  A  R  E  J  X  V  S  O  S
E  W  O  R  S  H  I  P  I  I  C  M
L  G  N  E  C  D  N  R  S  N  O  A
P  C  F  E  H  J  G  A  I  G  M  L
T  A  I  E  O  H  L  Y  T  C  F  L
H  R  R  S  O  Y  G  X  S  N  O  G
E  E  M  O  L  W  C  T  I  P  R  R
P  W  A  S  E  R  V  I  C  E  T  O
O  X  T  K  E  A  T  P  K  B  M  U
O  B  I  B  L  E  S  T  U  D  Y  P
R  F  O  Q  U  I  P  L  A  Y  D  S
S  U  N  D  A  Y  S  C  H  O  O  L
```

Word List

Bible study	help the poor	sing
care	play	small groups
comfort	pray	Sunday School
confirmation	school	visit sick
eat	service	worship

Bible Words to Remember

May the God of endurance and encouragement grant you to live in such harmony with one another, in accord with Christ Jesus. Romans 15:5

One World, One Lord

Now there are varieties of _____ , but the same _____ ; and there are

varieties of _____ , but the same _____ ; and there are varieties of

_____ , but it is the same _____ who empowers them all in everyone.

1 Corinthians 12:4–6

Corinth

Paul came to Corinth
from Athens.

Priscilla and Aquila
came to Corinth from Rome.

Word Bank

baptism   faith   Lord

body   hope   Spirit

God and Father

Timothy and Silas
came to Corinth from Macedonia

one _____ ,

one _____ ,

one _____ ,

one _____ , one _____ ,

one _____ , one _____

Ephesians 4:4–6

Bible Words to Remember

Therefore encourage one another and build one another up.
1 Thessalonians 5:11

Look! Come and See!

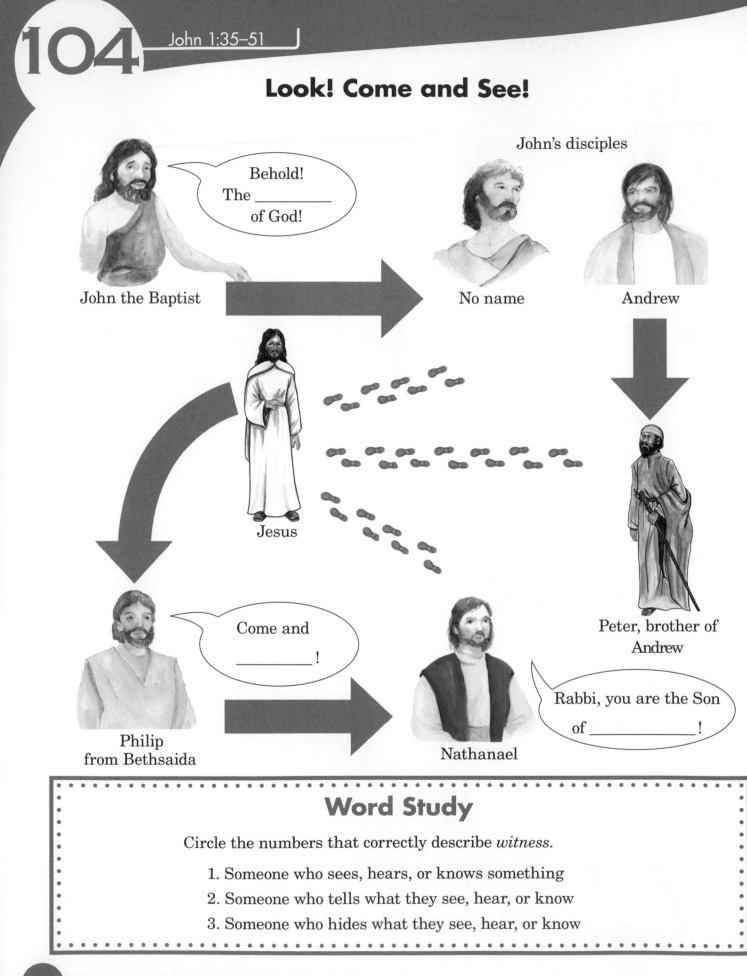

Word Study

Circle the numbers that correctly describe *witness*.

1. Someone who sees, hears, or knows something
2. Someone who tells what they see, hear, or know
3. Someone who hides what they see, hear, or know

Whom Can I Tell about Jesus?

Make the figure look like you. Draw three people you can tell about Jesus in the ovals. Write what you can tell about Jesus in the speech bubble.

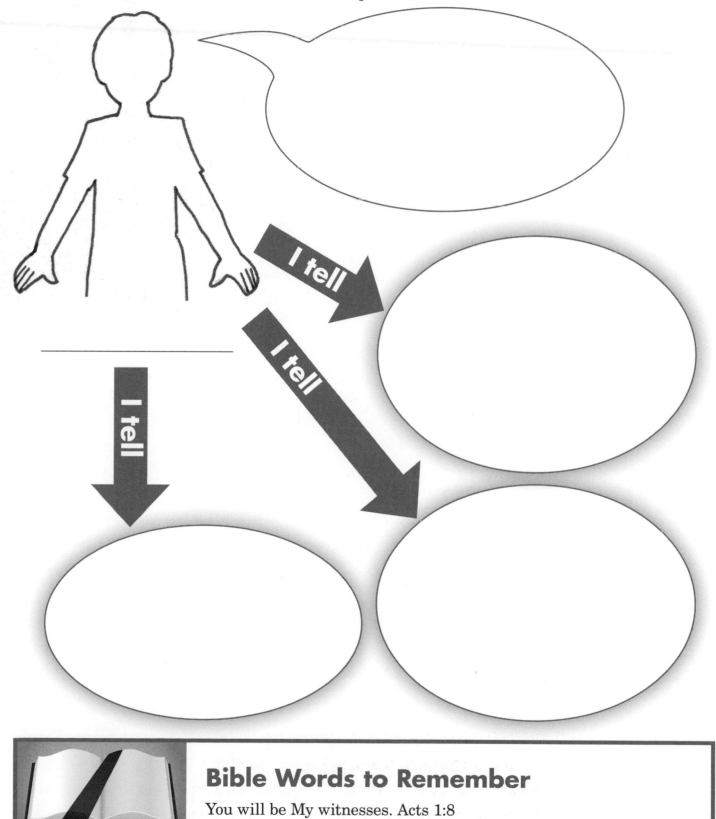

Bible Words to Remember

You will be My witnesses. Acts 1:8

A Day of Ups and Downs

Telling about Jesus has ups and downs. Consider one day for Paul and Silas in the city of Philippi. Circle *up*, *down*, *both*, or *neither* to show how you think their day went.

up =    down =   both = **B**   neither = **N**

1. A slave girl with an evil spirit followed Paul and Silas. She said, "These men are servants of the Most High God who proclaim to you the way of salvation."

      **B**   **N**

2. After many days, Paul was annoyed. He commanded the evil spirit to come out of the girl in Jesus' name.

      **B**   **N**

3. The girl's owners were angry. She would no longer make them lots of money. They took Paul and Silas to the judges.

        B   **N**

4. The crowd attacked Paul and Silas. The judges beat them and sent them to jail.

      **B**   **N**

5. The jailer, a Roman soldier, put their feet in stocks as torture and to keep them from running.

      **B**   **N**

6. At midnight, Paul and Silas prayed and sang hymns to God. The other prisoners listened.

      **B**   **N**

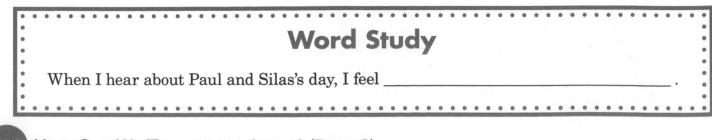

Word Study

When I hear about Paul and Silas's day, I feel _____ .

7. An earthquake shook the prison, opened doors, and broke chains. The jailer saw the open doors, thought everyone escaped, and drew his sword to kill himself.

B   N

8. Paul told the jailer to stop. Everyone was there.

B   N

9. The jailer fell at their feet in fear. He asked, "Sirs, what must I do to be saved?"

B   N

10. They answered, "Believe in the Lord Jesus, and you will be saved."

B   N

11. They shared God's Word with the jailer and his family. He and his family were baptized.

B   N

12. The jailer washed their wounds and fed them.

B   N

What Would You Say?

1. Alex wants his dad to come to church to hear him sing with his school class.

2. Natalie wants to invite Addison to go to Vacation Bible School with her.

3. Paul's friend Mitch has been upset lately. He tells Paul his parents have been fighting a lot.

4. Jack's mom lost her job.

5. Grace has just moved to town and is a new student in class.

Bible Words to Remember

My word . . . shall not return to Me empty, but it shall accomplish that which I purpose, and shall succeed in the thing for which I sent it. Isaiah 55:11

One True Faith

Other religions   **Christianity**

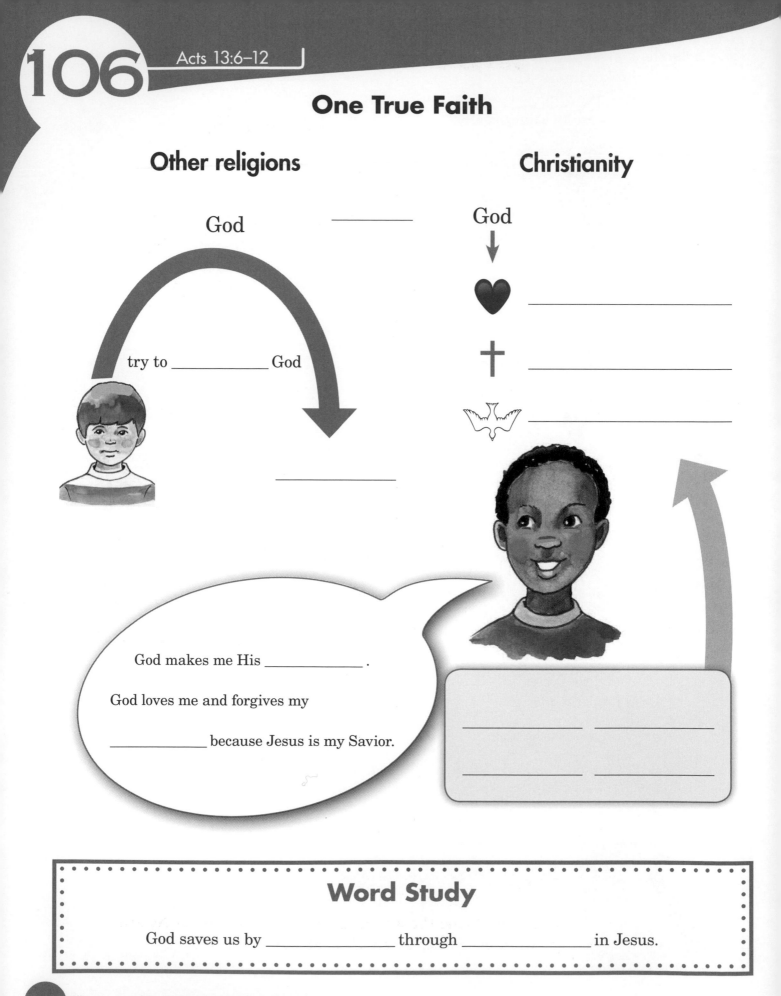

God   _____   God

try to _____ God

God makes me His _____ .

God loves me and forgives my

_____ because Jesus is my Savior.

Jesus or Bar-Jesus?

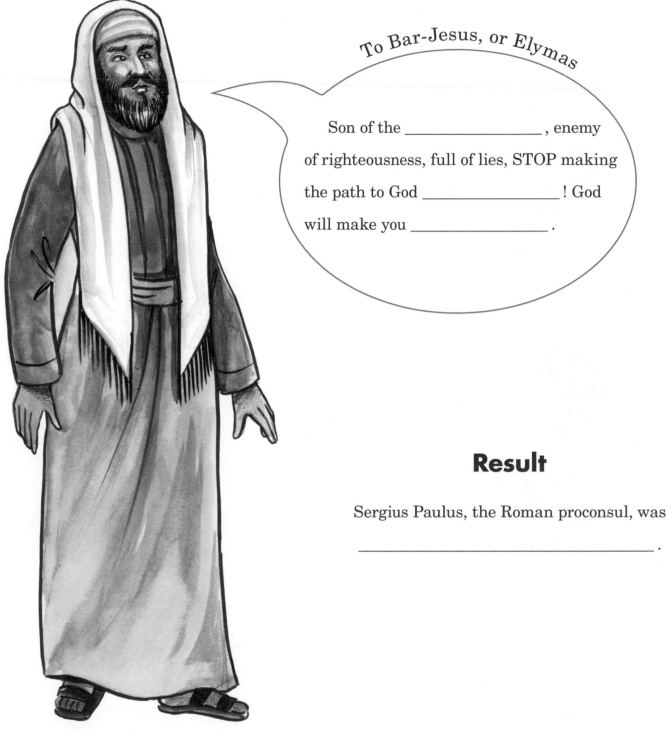

To Bar-Jesus, or Elymas

Son of the _____ , enemy of righteousness, full of lies, STOP making the path to God _____ ! God will make you _____ .

Paul

Result

Sergius Paulus, the Roman proconsul, was

_____ .

Bible Words to Remember

Jesus said, "I am the way, and the truth, and the life. No one comes to the Father except through Me." John 14:6

Courage and Mercy

You read about Peter, John, and the beggar in the temple.
What do you think happened next to each person?

Peter and John

Beggar

People who saw the
healed man

The religious leaders

Word Study

Vocation: _____

Write the name of one of your vocations: _____

My Vocation

God gives us vocations. Through our vocations we serve God and other people.

I am a Christian. I can serve my neighbor as a Christian by

I am a _____ . I can serve my family by

I am a student. I can serve my teacher and classmates by

Bible Words to Remember

If anyone is in Christ, he is a new creation. 2 Corinthians 5:17

The Fruit of the Spirit

Christians have new life in Jesus. The Holy Spirit works in us to grow our faith, helps us live as Christians, and produces fruit in us.

Fruit? That means good things that develop in us because we are connected to Jesus and His Word; because we trust Him as our Savior.

Highlight the words that Galatians 5 says are fruit of the Spirit. Cross out words that do not come from the Spirit.

Fruit of the _____

fighting

fits of anger

envy   joy   jealousy

hatred   goodness

gentleness   revenge

self-control

kindness

patience

conceit   idolatry

love

peace

Works of the flesh

provoking one another

Word Study

Galatians 5:25 says, "Walk by the _____."

The Lord's Treasure

1: God led the people of Israel out of Egypt and into the desert.

2: They set up camp by a mountain called Sinai.

3: Their leader, Moses, went up the mountain to talk to the Lord.

4: The LORD called to him and said,

God: Tell My people: You saw what I did to the Egyptians. I carried you on eagles' wings to Myself. Now, if you obey My voice and keep My covenant, you shall be My treasured possession among all people. The whole earth is Mine, and you shall be a holy nation.

5: So Moses told the people what the LORD said. The people answered together and said,

All: We will do what the LORD said.

6: God made a promise and the people accepted.

7: God loved and treasured His people.

8: Many years later, God showed this love when He sent His own Son, Jesus, to the world as our Savior from sin.

1 and 3: Jesus lived without sin,

2 and 4: and then died on the cross to take the punishment for the sin of all people.

5 and 7: He was buried.

6 and 8: God raised Him from the dead and He lives, our Savior and Lord.

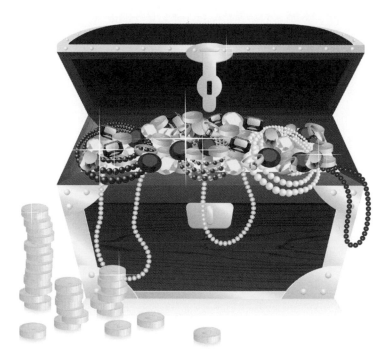

All: In Him, we have life. We are His holy, treasured people.

Teacher: These are written so that you may believe that Jesus is the Christ, the Son of God, and that by believing you may have life in His name.

All: May it be so, now and forever. Amen.

Based on Exodus 19 and John 20:31.

Bible Words to Remember

You shall be My treasured possession among all peoples.
Exodus 19:5

APPENDIX

Table of Contents

Abba An Aramaic word meaning "Daddy" or "Father," often used by little children.

absolution Confirmation of the truth that our sins are forgiven for Jesus' sake.

Adam The first man God created.

adoption When someone chooses you to be their child.

advocate One who speaks for another.

altar Table used for religious sacrifices or prayers.

altar of burnt offering Large table where sacrifices were burned in Israel's tabernacle and temples that followed. In Herod's temple, this altar was made of uncut stone, over fifteen feet high. It had a ramp to walk up and a ledge near the top where priests stood to reach the altar.

altar of incense Gold table in the Holy Place of Israel's tabernacle and later temples where priests burned incense daily. The rising smoke from incense reminded the people of their prayers rising to God. Near this altar, an angel appeared to Zechariah, John the Baptist's father (Luke 1:5–25).

ambition Strong desire to get or achieve one's goal; to want to succeed.

amen Means "so be it" or "we agree."

angel Messenger of God; a created being, not like humans; often depicted with wings. Scripture sometimes describes angels as looking similar to men (Mark 16:5; Luke 24:4).

annunciation The event when the angel Gabriel told Mary she was going to give birth to the Savior of the world, Jesus.

anoint To pour oil on a person's head to set him apart for the Lord's service.

anxiety Worried or nervous feeling about someone or something.

apostles Witnesses who saw Jesus resurrected from the dead; missionaries sent out by Jesus. Jesus' eleven original disciples were called apostles.

ark Large boat. God told Noah to build an ark before He flooded the earth. Noah's ark was 450 feet long and 45 feet high.

ark of the covenant The golden chest God told the people to build for the tabernacle. It held the tablets with the Ten Commandments, Aaron's staff, and a gold jar of manna. The ark had gold rings along the two long sides into which priests ran long sticks to carry it. The ark was captured by the Philistines but returned. It disappeared hundreds of years before Jesus was born.

atonement Payment Jesus made by His death and resurrection for the sins of the world; it is what makes our relationship with God whole (at-one-ment) again.

attitude How you look at things; your viewpoint or personal feeling about something.

authority Reliable source or witness, a judge or an expert; a power or a right to give commands, enforce obedience, take action, or make decisions.

Baal Name of many false gods of the nations around Israel. Each region had its own Baal.

Baptism The sacrament that brings people into God's family through the work of the Holy Spirit. Water is applied in the name of the Father, Son, and Holy Spirit. In Baptism, we receive forgiveness for our sins and are given eternal life through Jesus.

baptize The action of sharing God's grace in Christ by applying water in the name of the Father, Son, and Holy Spirit.

behavior How you act, what you do, and how you respond to something.

Bible The holy and perfect Word of God. The Bible is a written collection of God's Word revealed to men through the inspiration of the Holy Spirit.

bronze Metal that contains copper and tin.

celebrate To give honor and praise in a public setting; to have a joyous time in honor of a special day or person.

chalice A long-stemmed cup that holds the wine for Holy Communion.

chorale Religious song, originally intended for singing in the Lutheran Church.

chosen Selected; wanted.

Christ Name for Jesus. The Greek word *Christos* means "Messiah" or "Anointed One."

Christian A follower of and believer in Jesus Christ; a "little Christ."

Christian Church The people who believe in Jesus as their Savior from sin.

Christ's return See Judgment Day.

Church Year The Church's calendar, organized to observe the events in the life of Christ and the Church.

ciborium A lidded chalice that holds extra bread (wafers) for Holy Communion.

command A rule or a law given by someone with authority.

commandment A rule to follow; a law.

commission The act of doing something.

communion of saints All who believe in Jesus as their Savior; the Holy Christian Church.

compassion Showing care for someone; understanding and feeling sad for someone else's bad feelings or situation and desiring to help the person; pity.

conceit Thinking excessively well of yourself or something you have done.

confession Admitting we have done something wrong; a statement of belief.

confirmation A special celebration of faith in which a person states publicly what he or she believes about God and salvation in Christ Jesus.

congregation A group of Christians who gather in one place to worship God.

consequences The results of a behavior or decision; an outcome.

contentment Feeling satisfied with what you have; peacefulness.

context Setting, situation, surrounding words, and background.

contrition Being truly sorry for one's sin.

convert To change someone's heart or mind from one thing to another. Only the Holy Spirit working through the Word of God can convert sinners into believers in Jesus Christ.

cornerstone The stone in a building that sets the direction for two walls and anchors them together.

covenant An agreement; a promise.

create Make or design something; bring something to life.

creation Something that someone makes or brings to life.

Creator The maker of the universe; a name for God, who made the universe out of nothing in six days.

creed A statement of beliefs.

cross Two wooden beams crossed together that were used especially by the ancient Romans to put people to death. Jesus was crucified on a cross.

Day of Atonement The one day of the year when the High Priest entered the Most Holy of Place to spread the blood of a bull and a goat on the cover of the ark of the covenant, picturing Christ's sacrifice for our sin. See Leviticus 16; 23:26–32.

den A cave or small area where animals are kept.

denomination A group of congregations in a church body who believe the same teachings (doctrines).

deposit Money or valuables given as a down payment in order to purchase something.

devil An evil spirit; an angel who rebelled against God and was cast out of heaven.

disguise To change your appearance or the way you act in order to prevent recognition.

Divine Service The name of the worship service that includes the Lord's Supper.

doctrine Teaching; the beliefs of a religion.

Easter The day on which we celebrate Jesus' rising from the dead.

enmity Hate. See *hostile*.

epistle A letter. In the Bible, epistles are letters written by Paul and other apostles that are now Bible books.

eternal Something with no beginning and no end.

eternal life Living forever with God, a gift God gives by grace through faith in Jesus Christ.

evangelist One who tells the Good News; a special name given the four authors of the Gospels—Matthew, Mark, Luke, and John.

evil Bad actions or intentions; wicked; anything that is against God or denies that Jesus is the Christ; the devil and all his actions and words.

faith Trusting in Jesus to give us forgiveness of sin and eternal life. God the Holy Spirit works faith in our hearts to believe in Jesus as our Savior and to trust God's promises.

fall The result of Adam and Eve's sin of disobedience against God.

flagon The pitcher we use at Holy Communion to hold extra wine.

flood Water that overflows its normal borders or banks; the time when water covered the entire surface of the earth.

foreign From another place or another country.

Gospel The good news that God has given us salvation and forgiven our sins through Jesus, who paid the penalty for our sins on the cross; one of four books of the Bible that tell about Jesus' earthly life.

grace God's love, freely given to us in Jesus; kindness or love we don't deserve. In His grace, God gives us forgiveness, life, and salvation as a free gift.

grudge Having resentment and animosity toward someone with no intention of letting it go.

guilt The bad and sad feeling that we have because of our sin.

hallow To respect or give high honor to; to set apart as holy.

heir One who inherits possessions, property, money, or other blessings from someone else.

herald To make an announcement. An angel (messenger).

Herod's temple Worship center built by Herod the Great for the Jews to worship God. Destroyed in AD 70 by the Roman armies. Later used as a temple to worship the Roman god of Jupiter. Now home to the Dome of the Rock, a Muslim shrine built in AD 689–91. All that remains of Herod's temple is one retaining wall, now called the Wailing Wall.

holy Without sin or perfect; set apart; special.

Holy Baptism A sacrament God uses to bring people into His family; a washing of the Holy Spirit with water applied in the name  of the Father, the Son, and the Holy Spirit. Through Baptism, God gives forgiveness for our sins and eternal life in Jesus. A shell is often used to remind us of Baptism.

Holy Communion The sacrament that Jesus instituted on the night before His death. He gives us His body and blood with the bread and the wine. As  Christians eat His body and drink His blood, they receive Jesus' promise that their sins are forgiven. Communion is a Means of Grace or way that God gives us His grace and gifts.

Also known as the Lord's Supper, the Eucharist, the Lord's Table, the Breaking of the Bread, and the Sacrament of the Altar.

Holy Place Special room in the tabernacle and temple where offerings were made by priests.

Holy Scripture Another name for the Bible, God's Word.

Holy Spirit The Third Person of the Trinity. A real personal being, not just the energy of God, He gives faith and keeps it alive.

honor To respect, regard highly, give credit to; to treat with courtesy.

hosanna A word used to praise God; it means "save us."

host box A small box that can be used instead of a ciborium to hold the bread in Holy Communion.

hostile Full of hatred, anger, and bitterness; unfriendly.

humble Not proud or boastful.

humility Not being proud or boastful.

idol A false god, sometimes shown in human form in a statue.

image of God Knowing God perfectly and having perfect holiness and bodies. People lost the image of God when Adam and Eve fell into sin, but it is now being restored in those who believe in Christ.

imitate Attempt to copy or be like someone or something else.

Immanuel Hebrew word that means "God with us." Jesus is called Immanuel.

incarnate God existing as a human being.

indulgence Document sold with the false understanding that the purchaser would have God's grace and forgiveness.

inheritance Money or items that are passed on to another person when someone dies.

iniquity Sin; wickedness.

instrument A device that makes music.

intercede To pray to God on behalf of someone else.

invisible Not able to be seen.

jealousy A bad feeling or upset mood because someone has something you want; feeling resentful because of something someone else has.

jobs Work that people do to earn money. See page 235.

Judgment Day The final day on earth when Jesus will return to take His people to heaven. Also called the second coming, Last Day, and Christ's return.

justification When God forgives us and treats us as if we have no sins at all because of Jesus' sinless life, His death to pay for our sins on the cross, and His resurrection from the dead.

keeper of the prison Person in charge of prisoners in a jail.

kingdom of grace Christ's rule over and care for all believers.

kingdom of glory Christ's heavenly kingdom that lasts forever.

kingdom of power Christ's almighty rule over all of creation.

Lamb of God A name for Jesus, who gave His life as a sacrifice for us (John 1:29).

lampstand Oil lamps made of gold that sat in the Holy Place in the tabernacle and later the temple.

Last Day See Judgment Day.

laver A basin that held water in the tabernacle and temple; used for washing hands.

Law Words that show our sin and how God wants us to live.

leper A person with the disease of leprosy. Because of the disease, a leper had to leave his or her family and community to live with other lepers.

leprosy A skin disease that was contagious and incurable in ancient times, but now is treatable with modern medicine.

liturgical arts Artwork with a religious, spiritual purpose to guide our understanding of God's Word, to focus our attention in worship, and to remind us of the grace and greatness of God.

liturgical colors Colors designated for use during seasons of the Church Year.

liturgy The pattern that we follow in a worship service, including God's Word, the Sacraments, and our responses to God.

Lord's Prayer The prayer Jesus taught His disciples and us.

Lord's Supper Another name for Holy Communion. Also known as the Eucharist, the Lord's Table, the Breaking of the Bread, and the Sacrament of the Altar. See Holy Communion.

love Deep affection, respect, and devotion.

lyre A stringed instrument like a harp.

Means of Grace The things the Holy Spirit uses to bring us to faith and to strengthen our faith. They are God's Word and Sacraments (Baptism and Holy Communion).

mediator Someone who talks and makes peace between two people.

meditate To think carefully about something; to wonder about or ponder.

memorial A special marker that is put up to remember a person or a special event.

mercy Not getting the punishment you deserve; undeserved love.

Messiah Hebrew word that means the same as the Greek word *Christos* or "Christ"; literally means "the Anointed One."

messianic prophecy A message from God about Jesus even before He was born.

miracle An event that is beyond the ability of nature; an act of God. Jesus' miracles were signs that showed He was God's Son.

missionaries People who tell others about Jesus.

mission offering Money given to support missionaries.

monk A man who has promised to spend his life serving God by leaving his family and living with other monks, praying, and working together.

Most Holy Place Special room in the tabernacle and temple where the ark of the covenant was kept. Only the High Priest could go into this room.

narrative Writing that tells a story.

net Tool used to catch fish.

obey Follow commands, restrictions, wishes, or instructions.

occupations See jobs.

Old Testament The part of the Bible that tells about the history of God's people, the Israelites, before Jesus came to earth.

omission Neglecting to do something.

Ordinary Time Parts of the Church Year after Epiphany until Lent and after Pentecost until Advent.

original sin Sin all people are born with as a result of Adam and Eve's sin; the inclination to sin and inability not to sin. Also called the Old Man or Old Adam.

overflowing When something is so full that it can't hold any more.

overseer A person who directs the work of others; a boss.

Palm Sunday The Sunday before Easter when Jesus rode into Jerusalem and all the people praised Him and put palm branches and their coats on the road in front of Him.

parable A story that Jesus used to teach His followers.

paradise A wonderful place; heaven.

Passover Jewish feast that celebrates Israel's freedom from slavery in Egypt. The name reminds that the angel of death *passed over* their homes during the last plague in Egypt.

paten The plate from which the bread is distributed in Holy Communion.

pax The Latin word for *peace*.

perfect Without sin or mistakes; spotless.

persecute When someone does or says bad things to another person.

persecutor Someone who causes another person pain or suffering.

pollution Something that makes nature spoiled or dirty.

praise To notice and express appreciation for a quality or action; to tell good things about someone or something; to glorify.

prayer Talking to God to praise and thank Him, confess sins, and ask for His help. Jesus taught us to pray to God the Father in the Lord's Prayer.

privately Quietly, with no one else around.

proclaim Tell about.

promise To tell someone that you will do something for him or her at a later time.

Promised Land The country that God promised to His people, the Israelites.

prophecy A message from God, usually intended to bring people to repentance and faith.

prophet Messenger who spoke for God. Messages might include information about the future. Prophets wrote many of the Old Testament books.

propitiation Satisfaction for the demands of God's Law.

prosper To succeed or do well.

proverbs Wise sayings; also the name of a book in the Old Testament.

psalm A sacred song or poem; a biblical hymn.

publicly To do something so that everyone knows about it.

pulpit The place where a pastor stands to deliver a sermon.

Purgatory According to a teaching of the Roman Catholic Church, but not the Bible, this is a place where a person's soul goes after death to prepare for heaven.

purify To make someone clean, good, and wholesome.

purity The quality of being pure, free from evil or sin.

ram A male sheep.

ransom The payment needed to rescue someone.

rebirth To be born again, as in Baptism.

reconcile To be brought back together, to resolve differences.

redeem To pay a price to buy something back; to buy someone out of slavery and set the person free; to trade one thing for another.

redeemer Jesus, the One who paid with His life to save us from our sins.

Reformation The sixteenth-century Christian reform movement that began when Luther published the Ninety-five Theses objecting to the practice of selling indulgences, leading to the establishment of Lutheran and other non-Roman Catholic churches.

reluctant Afraid to do something.

repent To feel sorry for sin and not want to sin again; to turn around.

repentance Being sorry for one's sin and trusting God to forgive for Jesus' sake, leading to changed behavior.

representative One who stands for a whole group.

request Ask.

respect To value; to think most highly of; to treat as special.

resurrection When God raises a dead body back to life.

reunited To be together again with someone that you were separated from.

revenge Giving someone punishment for something that person did; retaliating.

revere To love; to respect; to be in awe of.

Sabbath Day The special day set aside for rest and worship.

sackcloth Special rough clothing that people put on to remind them of their sins.

sacrament A sacred act commanded by God through which He gives forgiveness of sins earned by Jesus through His death and resurrection. We have two sacraments, Baptism and the Lord's Supper.

sacrifice To offer something to God for His use. Something given up or offered to God or someone else.

saint Someone who believes in Jesus as Savior and thus has been forgiven and is a new creation.

salvation God's saving us from our sins by His grace, which we have through faith in Jesus.

sanctification What the Holy Spirit does *in us* to make us holy and to change us more and more into people whose lives resemble Christ's.

sanctify To make holy.

Savior One who saves from sin; Jesus.

Scripture The written Word of God; the Holy Bible.

second coming See Judgment Day.

self-righteous Thinking one can save oneself or that one is always right.

servant A person who serves another person or a family.

shepherd A person who protects, guides, and cares for sheep; a pastor, who cares for the spiritual needs of his people.

sin Doing what God forbids or failing to do what He commands.

sinner Someone who thinks, says, and does wrong things; someone whose heart is against God.

sins of commission When we do what God forbids.

sins of omission When we fail to do what God commands.

slander A lie or untruth told about someone, often with an angry attitude.

slave Person who works for someone else without any pay. He or she may be owned by that person.

slavery The owning or keeping of slaves as a practice. Being a slave.

Solomon's temple Worship center built by King Solomon for the Israelites to worship God. King David began gathering materials and made plans for the temple, but his son Solomon built it.

spirit A personal being without a body.

stanza Part of a religious song, made up of a group of lines that often rhyme.

state of exaltation When Jesus, as a man, fully and always uses His divine powers.

state of humiliation When Jesus, as a man, did not always or fully use His divine powers.

steward A person who takes care of items that belong to someone else.

substitute Person who takes the place of someone else.

tabernacle Tent where the people of Israel worshiped God while wandering in the wilderness and until  Solomon built a temple for the Lord.

talent A God-given skill or ability to do something well.

tax collector A person who collected tax money for the Roman government.

temple The building in Jerusalem where the Israelites worshiped, offered sacrifices, prayed, and learned about God. First built by King Solomon, it was destroyed by the Babylonians in 587 BC. The people rebuilt it after they came back from Babylonian exile.  Later, King Herod the Great remodeled it and added features to make it larger and more beautiful. Herod starting construction in 20 BC, but the temple was not finished until AD 64. The Romans destroyed it in AD 70.

tempt Encourage someone to do something that is wrong, against the Law of God.

temptation Something that lures us to do something that is wrong, against the Law of God.

Ten Commandments The ten rules that God gave His people to live by; stone tablets God gave Moses at Mount Sinai.

testament A statement of truth; a witness's account; the name for a group of books in the Bible.

transform Change into something different.

transgressions Another word for *sins*.

treasure Something of great value.

Trinity Three in one, specifically three persons in one God—God the Father, God the Son, and God the Holy Spirit.

triune God The one true God—Father, Son, and Holy Spirit; the Trinity—one God (*une*), in three persons (*tri*); an incomprehensible mystery.

upper room A second story in many New Testament homes; a room used for guest sleeping or religious dinners and celebrations.

visible Able to be seen.

vocation A person's calling through which he or she serves God and neighbor.

vow A promise, often one that is made to God.

weary Tired, sad, unfocused.

widow Woman whose husband has died.

wilderness A place that is far away from a town or city where very few people live.

will Desire; wish; choice; determination; consent; decision; command.

witch Person who uses the power of evil to make things happen.

witness Person who sees or hears something happen.

works Anything human beings do; doing good deeds.

Aaron Brother of Moses; spokesman for Moses before Pharaoh; Israel's first high priest.

Abednego Young Judean brought by King Nebuchadnezzar into captivity in Babylon; one of four young men chosen by the king to be educated according to Babylonian ways so that they could serve in his palace. Abednego's Judean name was Azariah.

Abel Second son of Adam and Eve; murdered by his older brother, Cain.

Abigail Beautiful wife of Nabal who rescued her cruel and foolish husband. After Nabal's death, she became the wife of David.

Abijah (1) Son and successor of King Rehoboam who reigned for three years. (2) Second son of Samuel. (3) Son of Jeroboam I, king of Israel; only member of his family to go to his grave in peace.

Abimelech Name of more than one of the Philistine kings.

Abinadab Son of Jesse; second of seven sons who were passed over before David was anointed the next king of Israel.

Abner Son of Ner; commander of King David's army.

Abraham (Abram) Father of the Hebrew people; promised by God that his children would make a mighty nation; Sarah's husband; Isaac's father.

Absalom Son of David; murdered his half-brother Amnon; plotted to take over David's throne.

Achan Israelite who kept riches from the battle of Jericho; as a result of his theft, he and his family were stoned to death.

Common jobs in Bible times: farmer (Genesis 4:2); herdsman (Genesis 4:20); fisherman (Matthew 4:18); shepherd (1 Samuel 17:15); hunter (Genesis 10:9); merchant (Proverbs 31:18); winemaker (Matthew 21:33); olive oil maker (Exodus 27:20); baker (Genesis 40:2); cook (1 Samuel 9:24); potter (Isaiah 29:16); seamstress (Proverbs 31:22); engraver, embroiderer, weaver (Exodus 35:35); importer/exporter (2 Chronicles 1:17); priest (Exodus 28:1; Levite (2 Chronicles 13:10); musician (Genesis 4:21; Psalm 68:25); wife, husband, parent; landowner (1 Kings 16:24); carpenter (Isaiah 44:13); woodcutter (Joshua 9:21); builder (1 Kings 5:18); craftsman (Exodus 35:10); silversmith (Acts 19:24); goldsmith (Isaiah 46:6); metalworker (Genesis 4:22); brickmaker (Exodus 5:14); mason, stonecutter (2 Kings 12:12); jeweler (Exodus 28:11); government official (John 4:46; Acts 24:1); tax collector (Luke 5:27); mourner (Luke 8:52); judge (Luke 18:1); soldier (Acts 10:7); slave (Philemon 15–16); banker (Matthew 25:27); expert in the Law (Matthew 22:35)); physician (Colossians 4:14); preacher (1 Timothy 2:7); teacher (Ephesians 4:11); writer (1 Corinthians 16:21).

Adam First man God created; sinned by disobeying God, thereby bringing all people under the curse of sin.

Agrippa I See Herod Agrippa I.

Ahab Wicked king of Israel; together with his wife, Jezebel, caused Israel to worship Baal rather than God.

Ahijah Prophet of Shiloh who told Jeroboam that he would be the ruler over ten tribes of Israel.

Amos Prophet sent to announce God's judgment to the Northern Kingdom (Israelites); worked with flocks and sycamore-fig groves; author of the Book of Amos.

Ananias (1) Husband of Sapphira who was struck dead for lying to God. (2) Disciple who baptized Saul. (3) High priest before whom Paul was tried.

Andrew One of Jesus' twelve disciples; an apostle; witness to Jesus' resurrection; from Bethsaida (John 1:44); first a disciple of John the Baptist, he brought to Jesus his brother Peter, who also became one of the Twelve (John 1:35–42); fished on Sea of Galilee with brother Peter (Mark 1:16–20). Church history says Andrew died for the faith in Greece, crucified on an X-shaped cross.

Anna Prophetess from the tribe of Asher; widow who never left the temple, where she worshiped day and night.

Antipas See Herod Antipas.

Antipater II Firstborn son of Herod the Great, made first heir in Herod's

will. Lived 46–4 BC. Found guilty by a Roman court of trying to kill his father; executed by order of Caesar Augustus.

Apollos Jewish leader in the Early Christian Church; taught by Priscilla and Aquila.

Apostles Original twelve disciples who followed Jesus during His ministry and saw and heard Him (Matthew 10:2–4; Mark 3:16–19; Luke 6:13–16; Acts 1:13). All but Judas were witnesses of Jesus' resurrection from the dead. Jesus sent them out as missionaries to tell the world about Him. Matthias, who replaced Judas, and St. Paul are also called apostles because they too were witnesses to Jesus' resurrection. The New Testament tells what the apostles saw, heard, and wrote down under the guidance (inspiration) of the Holy Spirit.

Aquila Jew who met Paul in Corinth. He and wife Priscilla were leaders and teachers in the Early Christian Church.

Archelaus See **Herod Archelaus.**

Aristobulus IV Son of Herod the Great and Mariamne, the last of the Jewish line of Hasmoneans. Herod the Great ordered him killed in 7 BC.

Artaxerxes King of Persia who permitted the Israelites to return to Jerusalem after their captivity in Babylon.

Asa Son of Abijah and third of Judah's kings; worked to rid the land of heathenism.

Asher Eighth son of Jacob; born to Zilpah, Leah's handmaid.

Athaliah Wicked daughter of Ahab and Jezebel; married Jehoram, king of Judah, and introduced Baal worship into Judah. Athaliah later killed her own grandchildren and usurped the kingdom.

Augustus Caesar See Caesar Augustus.

Baal Name of many false gods in Canaan; each section of Canaan had its own Baal.

Balaam Seer who tried to curse Israel during their journey to the Promised Land, but God would not allow it.

Balak Son of Zippor, king of Moab; wanted Balaam to curse the Israelites so that they could not cross through Moab.

Barabbas A robber who had committed murder during an insurrection; he was released instead of Jesus by Pilate at the will of the people.

Barak Military commander who was led by Deborah, a prophetess of Ephraim, under God's hand, to deliver Israel from its enemies at Jezreel.

Barnabas Apostle and evangelist; co-worker with Paul on his first missionary journey.

Bartholomew One of Jesus' twelve disciples; an apostle; witness to Jesus' resurrection; also known as Nathanael; brought to Jesus by Philip (John 1:45–51); known for  his simple, forthright character; he died for his faith.

Bartimaeus A blind beggar of Jericho who appealed to Jesus and was healed by Him.

Bathsheba Wife of Uriah; committed adultery with David and later became his wife and the mother of Solomon.

Belteshazzar Babylonian name that the king gave to Daniel when the Judeans were taken captive by the Babylonians.

Benjamin Twelfth son of Jacob; Rachel was his mother; younger brother of Joseph.

Bernice Oldest daughter of Herod Agrippa I, who first married her uncle Herod and after his death lived with her brother Agrippa II.

Bethuel Son of Nahor, nephew of Abraham, and father of Rebekah and Laban.

Boaz Husband of Ruth; father of Obed; ancestor of King David and Jesus.

Caesar Title used by the emperors of Rome from 300 BC to about AD 300; a title used by other countries for their king or emperor.

Caesar Augustus First ruler of the Roman Empire; lived 63 BC–AD 14; ruled when Jesus was born; also called Octavian. After Caesar's assassination in 44 BC, Augustus joined forces with Mark Antony and Marcus Aemilius Lepidus in a military dictatorship known as the Second Triumvirate. When this partnership failed, Augustus restored the Roman Republic with power vested in the Roman senate. In practice, he retained power as a dictator. By law, he held a collection of powers granted to him for life by the senate. Augustus expanded the Roman Empire, secured its boundaries, and ruled in relative peace. After his death, the senate declared him a god to be worshiped by the Romans. The month of August is named in his honor.

Caiaphas High priest of the Jews during the time of Jesus' public ministry, death, and resurrection.

Cain Adam and Eve's firstborn son; murdered his brother Abel.

Caleb One of twelve men sent to spy in Canaan; only he and Joshua encouraged Israelites to take possession of Canaan.

Candace Name applied to a dynasty of Ethiopian queens.

Chilion Son of Naomi and Elimelech; husband of Orpah.

Christ Name for Jesus, God's Son. This is a Greek word that means "Messiah" or "Anointed One."

Cleopas One of the two disciples who traveled from Jerusalem to Emmaus on the day of the resurrection.

Cornelius Roman centurion to whom God sent Peter to preach the Gospel; was one of the first Gentiles to become Christian.

Cyrus King of Persia; helped the Judeans return to the Promised Land, giving them gold and silver that King Nebuchadnezzar had taken from them in captivity.

Daniel Young Judean brought by King Nebuchadnezzar into captivity in Babylon; one of four young men chosen by the king to be educated according to Babylonian ways so that they could serve in his palace. Daniel's Babylonian name was Belteshazzar.

Darius King of Persia who wrote a decree that allowed the Judeans to rebuild the temple in Jerusalem.

David Son of Jesse; anointed as young boy to become king of Israel; after Saul's death, became king; author of a portion of Psalms.

Deborah Prophetess and judge who led Israel to victory over the Canaanites.

Delilah Lover of Samson who, after constant pleading, got him to tell her the secret of his great strength.

Demetrius Silversmith from Ephesus; made silver idols; accused Paul of destroying business because Paul preached of the one true God.

devil An evil spirit, an angel who rebelled against God and was cast out of heaven. There are many devils or demons. "The devil" sometimes refers to a specific evil spirit, also called Satan, Lucifer, the evil one.

Dinah Daughter of Jacob and Leah.

Eli High priest of Israel; Samuel spent the early years of his life living in the temple with Eli.

Eliezer Abraham's chief servant who journeyed to the home of Bethuel to secure a wife for Isaac.

Elijah Prophet of the Lord during the reign of Ahab; taken to heaven in a whirlwind and later appeared with Moses at the transfiguration of Jesus.

Elimelech Husband of Naomi; moved from Bethlehem to Moab because of a famine. After Elimelech and his sons died, Naomi and daughter-in-law Ruth returned to Bethlehem.

Elisha Prophet who succeeded Elijah when he was taken up to heaven.

Elizabeth Wife of Zechariah who miraculously became the mother of John the Baptist at an advanced age.

Elkanah Zuphite from Ephraim; Hannah's husband and father of Samuel.

Enoch Man who "walked with God"; later in life was taken to heaven by God without dying.

Ephraim Second son of Joseph by Leah.

Esau Firstborn son of Isaac and Rebekah and twin of Jacob; sold his birthright to Jacob for a pot of stew; was tricked out of his blessing by Jacob; later in life, he and Jacob met and were reconciled.

Esther Beautiful Jewish woman from Persia; King Xerxes chose her out of many women to be his queen.

Eunice God-fearing mother of Timothy.

Eutychus A youth at Troas who, having fallen asleep during Paul's sermon and out of a window to his death, was brought back to life by Paul.

Eve First woman God created. Her name means "mother of all the living."

Ezra Priest and teacher of the Law; led a group of exiles back to Judah and helped them rebuild the temple in Jerusalem.

Felix Roman governor who heard the complaints of the Jews against Paul and then heard Paul's explanation.

Gabriel Archangel who appeared to Mary to tell her she would become the mother of the Savior of the world.

Gamaliel Most famous Jewish teacher of his time; was president of the Sanhedrin (the Jewish Council); Saul of Tarsus was one of his students.

Gideon Youngest son of Joash of an undistinguished family; nicknamed Jerubbaal, which means "let Baal contend against him"; fifth and greatest judge of Israel; tested God with a woolen fleece.

Goliath Famous Philistine giant who may have been nine or ten feet tall; slain by David in the power of God.

Hagar Egyptian handmaid of Sarah; mother of Ishmael (Abraham's son).

Haggai Prophet who encouraged the Israelites to rebuild the temple after they returned from exile in Babylon; author of the Book of Haggai.

Ham One of Noah's three sons.

Haman Enemy of the Jews who was a leader in the court of the king of Persia; was hanged on the gallows he had built for Mordecai the Jew.

Hannah Wife of Elkanah; prayed for a son, after which God gave her Samuel.

Hasmoneans The ruling family of the Kingdom of Israel (Northern Kingdom) from 140–37 BC; established under leadership of Simon Maccabaeus two decades after his brother Judas defeated the Seleucid army (Greek-speaking people from Alexander the Great's kingdom). Intertestamental Apocryphal books 1 and 2 Maccabees provide some of their history. Roman leaders Mark Antony and Octavian stopped a brief Hasmonean uprising that resulted in Herod the Great becoming king in 37 BC and ended Hasmonean rule.

Herod Family name of five kings who ruled Palestine under the Roman emperor: Herod the Great (Matthew 2:1–8, 16); Herod Antipas (Mark 6:14–29); Herod Philip (Matthew 14:3); Herod Agrippa I (Acts 12:1–4, 19–23); Herod Agrippa II (Acts 23:35; 25:13–26:32).

Herod the Great Also called King Herod; ruled Judea for Rome from 37–4 BC; called "the Great" because he built many large and impressive structures, including the third temple in Jerusalem, sometimes called Herod's Temple. He was known as a ruthless man who killed his favorite wife, his own sons, many rabbis, and others who got in his way. His land was divided between his three sons after his death.

Herod Agrippa I Grandson of Herod the Great, eaten by worms for defying God (Acts 12:20–23).

Herod Agrippa II Great-grandson of Herod the Great; called Herod in the report in the Book of Acts of St. Paul's trial before Agrippa before being sent to Rome. Agrippa ruled without a Roman procurator, the only king of the time to do so except for Herod the Great.

Herod Antipas Son of Herod the Great; ruled as a tetrarch over Galilee and Perea (the east side of the Jordan River) after his father's death; ordered the death of John the Baptist. Jesus called him "that fox" to indicate his sneakiness (Luke 13:32). After Jesus' arrest, Pontius Pilate sent Him to be tried by Herod Antipas, but he sent Jesus back to Pilate.

Herod Archelaus Son of Herod the Great; ruled Judea, Idumaea, and Samaria as an ethnarch (not king) after his father's death.

Herod Philip Son of Herod the Great who ruled the region beyond the Sea of Galilee and to Bashan after his father's death.

Hezekiah King of Judah who restored the temple, reinstituted proper worship, and sought the Lord's help against the Assyrians.

high priest The main priest who served God in the Israelite tabernacle and temples.

Hilkiah High priest during the reign of Josiah.

Hophni One of Eli's wicked sons; died in battle in fulfillment of the Lord's prophecy.

Hosea First of the minor prophets; wrote the Book of Hosea.

Huldah Prophetess during the time of King Josiah.

Ichabod Son of Phinehas and grandson of Eli; born shortly after the death of both.

Isaac Promised son of Abraham and Sarah; offered as a sacrifice by Abraham; married Rebekah; father of Jacob and Esau.

Isaiah Prophet called by God to prophesy to Judah; many of his prophecies were about the coming Messiah.

Ishbosheth Youngest of Saul's sons and his likely successor.

Ishmael Son of Abraham by Hagar the Egyptian, born when Abraham was 86 years old.

Jacob (Israel) Second son of Isaac and Rebekah; twin brother of Esau; bought Esau's birthright with a pot of stew; later tricked Isaac into giving him the blessing that belonged to Esau; wrestled with God, and his name was changed to Israel; had twelve sons, all of whom eventually went to Egypt during a famine; settled in Egypt; buried by his son Joseph in Canaan, the Promised Land.

Jael Woman who killed Israel's enemy Sisera by driving a tent stake into his head.

Jairus Official who asked Jesus to come and make his sick daughter well. Jesus raised her from the dead.

James One of Jesus' half brothers, a son of Mary and Joseph, along with Joseph, Judas, and Simon (Matthew 12:46; 13:55; Mark 6:3); did not believe in Jesus as the Messiah until after witnessing Jesus' resurrection (1 Corinthians 15:7); leader in the Jerusalem Church (Acts 12:17; 15:1–21; 21:17–18; Galatians 1:18–19; 2:9–12); author of the Book of James; died by stoning for his faith in Christ.

James the Greater
One of Jesus' twelve disciples; an apostle; witness to Jesus' resurrection; son of Zebedee and Mary, also called Salome (Matthew 27:56);  fished with his brother John (also one of the Twelve) and father on the Sea of Galilee (Mark 1:19–20); Jesus called the brothers "Sons of Thunder" (Mark 3:17); one of Jesus' trusted inner circle along with Peter and John (Matthew 17:1; Mark 5:37; 13:3; 14:33). James was the first of the remaining eleven disciples to die for believing in Jesus, killed by sword at the command of King Herod Agrippa I in Jerusalem (Acts 12:1–2). Shells in his shield refer to his travels.

James the Lesser
One of Jesus' twelve disciples; an apostle; witness to Jesus' resurrection; son of Alphaeus; died for his faith in Christ.

Japheth Youngest of Noah's three sons.

Jason A friend of the apostle Paul.

Jehoahaz King of Judah after his father Josiah's death; became king when he was twenty-three years old and reigned for only three months; did evil in the eyes of the Lord.

Jehoiachin King of Judah; became king when he was eighteen years old and reigned for only three months and ten days; did evil in the eyes of the Lord.

Jehoiakim King of Judah after Jehoahaz's death; became king when he was twenty-five years old and reigned for eleven years; did evil in the eyes of the Lord.

Jehoshaphat King of Judah; son of Asa who began to reign when he was thirty-five years old and reigned for twenty-five years.

Jehu King of Israel; known for driving like a madman (2 Kings 9:20).

Jephthah Judge of Israel whose foolish pledge resulted in the loss of his daughter.

Jeremiah Prophet called by God to prophesy to Judah; often referred to as the "prophet of gloom" because he prophesied the destruction of Judah; also told about the coming of the Savior, Jesus Christ.

Jeroboam Official in Solomon's court; rebelled and became king of the northern Kingdom of Israel.

Jesse Father of David; all of his sons were looked at by Samuel, but only the last and youngest, David, was chosen to be the king of Israel.

Jesus God's only begotten Son, Second Person of the Trinity, true God and true man; our Savior from sin who lived without sinning and died on the cross to pay for our sins, who rose from the grave, ascended into heaven, and promises to return to earth on the last day. *Jesus* means "the Lord saves." Other forms of the name are *Joshua* and *Jeshua*. Jesus' life in the flesh is told about in the Gospels, the first four books of the New Testament— Matthew, Mark, Luke, and John.

Jethro (Reuel) Priest of Midian; father-in-law of Moses who offered Moses good advice on leadership.

Jezebel Sidonian wife of King Ahab who promoted the worship of Baal in Israel.

Joab Nephew of David; general in David's army.

Joash (1) Son and successor of Israel's king Jehoahaz. (2) Father of Gideon.

Job God-fearing wealthy man of Uz who lost and regained much, yet remained faithful to the one true God throughout his life's experiences.

Jochebed Wife of Amram and mother of Moses and Aaron.

John One of Jesus' twelve disciples; an apostle; witness to Jesus' resurrection; son of Zebedee and Mary, also called Salome (Matthew 27:56); fished with his  brother James (also one of the Twelve) and father on the Sea of Galilee (Mark 1:19–20); Jesus called the brothers "Sons of Thunder" (Mark 3:17); one of Jesus' trusted inner circle along with Peter and James (Matthew 17:1; Mark 5:37; 13:3; 14:33). Church history says that enemies tried to kill John by poisoning his drink, but the Lord spared him. John was the only one of the Twelve to die a natural death, around the age of ninety-four in AD 100. He is the author of the Gospel of John; 1, 2, and 3 John; and Revelation.

John the Baptist Son of Zechariah and Elizabeth; preached in the desert, preparing the people for Jesus; baptized Jesus in the Jordan River; was arrested and executed by Herod.

Jonah Reluctant prophet sent to Nineveh; God caused him to be swallowed by a big fish.

Jonathan Son of King Saul; David's best friend; always tried to keep David out of trouble.

Joseph (1) Son of Jacob and Rachel; sold by brothers into slavery but in turn of events became ruler of Egypt; instrumental in saving God's people by bringing them to Egypt during a time of severe famine. (2) Mary's husband; Jesus' earthly father. (3)

(of Arimathea) Follower of Jesus; provided his tomb as the burial place for the body of Jesus. (4) One of Jesus' half brothers, a son of Mary and Joseph, along with James, Judas, and Simon (Matthew 12:46; 13:55; Mark 6:3).

Joshua Moses' aide and successor; led the people into Canaan and in the battle of Jericho.

Josiah King of Judah; became king when he was eight years old and reigned for thirty-one years; did what was right in the eyes of the Lord.

Judah Fourth son of Jacob by Leah; ancestor of King David and ultimately of Christ.

Judas One of Jesus' half brothers, a son of Mary and Joseph, along with James, Joseph, and Simon (Matthew 12:46; 13:55; Mark 6:3).

Judas Iscariot One of Jesus' twelve disciples; held the money bag for Jesus and the disciples, and was a thief (John 12:6; 13:29); conspired with  the chief priests to betray Jesus with a kiss in the Garden of Gethsemane (Matthew 26:14–16, 47–50); received thirty pieces of silver for betraying Jesus; killed Himself soon after Jesus was crucified (Matthew 27:3–10).

Jude One of Jesus' twelve disciples; an apostle; witness to Jesus' resurrection; also called Judas and Thaddaeus (Matthew 10:2–4;  Mark 3:16–19). Church history says he traveled many places to share the Gospel, accompanied by the apostle Simon; a ship on his shield reminds us of his travels.

Julius Roman centurion charged with taking Paul from Caesarea to Rome.

Keturah Married Abraham after Sarah's death; she bore him six children.

Kish Father of King Saul.

Korah Son of Izhar; Levite who rebelled against Moses and Aaron; he and his followers and family went to their graves alive when the earth swallowed them.

Laban Brother of Rebekah and father of Rachel and Leah; tricked Jacob into marrying both Leah and Rachel.

Lamech Father of Noah.

Lazarus Brother of Martha and Mary whom Jesus brought back from the dead.

Leah First wife of Jacob; had six sons and one daughter.

Levi Third son of Jacob by Leah; his descendants formed the priestly line among God's people.

Levite A man from the tribe of Levi; Levites served God's tabernacle and temple as priests, musicians, singers, cleaners, guards, and builders, as well as in other functions.

Lois Godly grandmother of Timothy.

Lot Nephew of Abraham; chose the richer lands near the wicked cities of Sodom and Gomorrah when he and Abraham separated.

Luke Author of the Gospel of Luke and the Acts of the Apostles; physician; co-worker and traveling companion of St. Paul; work as an evangelist is shown by a winged calf, which reminds us of the sacrificial death of our Lord Jesus.

Lydia First European convert of St. Paul, whom she hosted in her home in Philippi.

Maccabees A Jewish family group who led a revolt against the Seleucid king and obtained a 25-year freedom from Roman rule from 167–142 BC; ruled Israel in the first century BC. See **Hasmonean.**

Magi Name used for the people who brought gifts to the baby Jesus; the Wise Men.

Mahlon First husband of Ruth; son of Naomi and Elimelech.

Malachi Last prophet of the Old Testament; name means "my messenger"; author of the Book of Malachi.

Mark Author of the Gospel of Mark; his work as an evangelist is often shown by a winged eagle, which reminds us of the grace of the Holy Spirit, which was always with Jesus, or of Jesus' ascension. (Sometimes Mark is represented by a lion and John is represented by an eagle.)

Martha Sister of Mary and Lazarus; hostess who showed concern for Jesus' comfort while He taught at her home.

Mary (1) Mother of Jesus. (2) (Magdalene) Woman whom Jesus freed from demons; became faithful follower of Jesus and His ministry. Among the first to whom Jesus appeared after His resurrection. (3) Sister of Martha and Lazarus, faithful followers of Jesus. (4) (Salome) Mother of James and John, traveled with Jesus and the disciples, witnessed the resurrection.

Matthew One of Jesus' twelve disciples; an apostle; witness to Jesus' resurrection; a tax collector and son of Alphaeus (Matthew 9:9–13; Mark 2:13–17); also called Levi (Mark 2:14); author of the Gospel of Matthew; his work as an evangelist is shown as a winged man, which reminds us of the human nature of the Lord Jesus or his incarnation, or by moneybags to show his first profession. Church history says Matthew died for his faith by crucifixion in Ethiopia.

Matthias Apostle elected to replace Judas after Jesus' ascension.

Mephibosheth Son of Jonathan; born lame in both feet; King David showed him kindness for Jonathan's sake.

Meshach Young Judean brought by King Nebuchadnezzar into captivity in Babylon; one of four young men chosen by the king to be educated according to Babylonian ways so that they could serve in his palace. Meshach's Judean name was Mishael.

Methuselah Son of Enoch; sixth in descent from Seth, the son of Adam; father of Lamech; lived 969 years, the oldest man in recorded history.

Micaiah Faithful prophet of God in Samaria.

Michael Archangel; described in Daniel as the "prince" of Israel.

Michal Daughter of King Saul and wife of David; helped David escape when Saul sought to kill him; ridiculed David for dancing before the Lord.

Miriam Sister of Moses who watched him when, as a baby, he floated in the Nile; later led Israel in praising God for delivering them from Egypt at the time of the exodus.

Mordecai Uncle of Esther who raised her; contributed to saving the life of the king.

Moses Hebrew slave adopted by an Egyptian princess; later killed an Egyptian who was abusing a Hebrew slave; fled to Midian, where he herded sheep; chosen by God to be leader of Israelites in their journey out of Egypt and across the desert to the Promised Land.

Naaman Commander of the army of the king of Aram; healed of leprosy by the prophet Elisha.

Nabal Foolish and cruel husband of Abigail who showed disrespect to David and therefore to the Lord.

Naboth Jezreelite who owned a vineyard in Jezreel; would not sell his vineyard to King Ahab because it was the inheritance of his fathers, so Ahab had him killed.

Naomi Wife of Elimelech; moved from Bethlehem because of a famine. After her husband and both sons died, she returned with daughter-in-law Ruth to Bethlehem, where Ruth married Boaz, a relative of Elimelech's.

Nathan Prophet during the reign of kings David and Solomon; pointed out David's sin when he committed adultery.

Nathanael See **Bartholomew.**

Nebuchadnezzar King of Babylon; brought the people of Judah into captivity in Babylon.

Nehemiah Cupbearer to King Artaxerxes of Persia; author of Book of Nehemiah.

Nicodemus Pharisee who visited Jesus at night and learned about being born again; prepared Jesus' body for burial with Joseph of Arimathea.

Noah "A righteous man" in early Bible times; built an ark as God commanded him; God made a covenant with him never again to cover the entire earth with a flood.

Obadiah (1) Believer in the Lord; in charge of King Ahab's palace; sheltered a hundred of the Lord's prophets from Jezebel when she wished to have them killed. (2) Prophet who wrote the Book of Obadiah.

Obed Son of Ruth and Boaz; ancestor of King David.

Og King of Bashan; one of the last of the giant race of Rephaim.

Omri King of Israel; became king after Tibni son of Ginath died; did evil in the eyes of the Lord.

Onesimus Runaway slave of Philemon who was a believer in Christ; was sent back to his master by Paul.

Orpah Moabite woman who married Chilion, son of Naomi and Elimelech; sister-in-law to Ruth.

Paul Missionary and apostle of the Early Church; met the risen Christ on the road to Damascus, where he intended to arrest Christians on authority  of the Jewish leaders in Jerusalem; took three missionary trips recorded in the Book of Acts, and possibly others; arrested by Romans in Jerusalem and eventually taken to Rome to plead his case to Caesar. The Book of Acts ends with Paul under house arrest in Rome. Church tradition says he was released from prison in Rome and traveled to Spain before being once again imprisoned in Rome, where he died for his faith in AD 68 during Nero's persecution of Christians. Paul suffered much for Christ, enduring flogging, jail, stoning, hunger, and other trials.

Peleg Ancestor of Christ; born 101 years after the flood. His name is associated with a dividing.

Peter One of Jesus' twelve disciples; an apostle; witness to Jesus' resurrection; from Bethsaida (John 1:44); also called Simon (Matthew 4:18; 10:2), Simon Peter (Luke  5:8; John 1:40; 13:6) and Cephas (John 1:42; 1 Corinthians 1:12; 3:22; 9:5; 15:5; Galatians 1:18; 2:9, 11, 14); fished with brother Andrew (also one of the Twelve) on the Sea of Galilee (Mark 1:16–20); one of a trusted inner circle along with James and John (Matthew 17:1; Mark 5:37; 13:3; 14:33); considered the leader of the Early Church; imprisoned by Herod Agrippa I in Jerusalem, but set free by an angel (Acts 12:1–19). Church history says Peter died for his faith in Rome in AD 68 during Nero's persecution of Christians, crucified upside down because he said he wasn't good enough to die as Jesus did.

Pharisee A religious leader during the time of Jesus; demanded rigid adherence to God's Law.

Philemon Slave-owning believer who received a letter from Paul asking him to welcome back his runaway slave Onesimus.

Philip One of Jesus' twelve disciples; an apostle; witness to Jesus' resurrection; from Bethsaida (John 1:44); brought  Nathanael to Jesus (John 1:45–51); ministered in Samaria after Pentecost (Acts 8:5–13); baptized the Ethiopian eunuch (Acts 8:26–39); bread in his shield refers to his part of the feeding of the 5,000 (John 6:1–14). Church tradition says Philip died for his faith in Christ by stoning and crucifixion.

Philip (Herod) See Herod Philip.

Phinehas Wicked son of Eli who, together with his brother Hophni, died in battle in fulfillment of God's words to Samuel.

Phoebe Important early Christian referred to in Romans 16.

Pompey Roman general who conquered Judea in 63 BC.

Pontius Pilate Roman governor of Judea; questioned Jesus and sent Him to Herod; finally consented to Jesus' crucifixion when crowds chose Barabbas rather than Jesus.

Potiphar Egyptian captain of Pharaoh's guard; owner of Joseph.

priest A man from the tribe of Levi; served in the temple, offering sacrifices to God.

Rachel Daughter of Laban; Jacob's second but favorite wife; mother of Joseph and Benjamin.

Rahab Prostitute who hid Israelite spies before the battle of Jericho.

Rebekah Sister of Laban; wife of Isaac; mother of Esau and Jacob. With her encouragement, Jacob tricked his father into giving him the blessing that normally would be given to the oldest son, Esau.

Rehoboam Son of Solomon; reigned during and after the division of the kingdom; reigned seventeen years as king of Judah.

Reuben Firstborn son of Jacob and Leah.

Rhoda Servant girl who failed to open the door for Peter in her excitement at knowing he was freed from prison.

Ruth Moabite woman who married Mahlon, a son of Naomi and Elimelech; traveled with Naomi to Bethlehem after Mahlon's death; met Boaz and later married him; ancestor of King David and Jesus.

Sadducee Jewish religious group of priests who opposed the Pharisees from the second century BC. Ceased to exist sometime after the destruction of the temple in Jerusalem in AD 70.

Salome Daughter of Herodias; was granted her request for the head of John the Baptist after dancing for Herod Antipas on his birthday.

Samaritan A person from the area of Samaria. Samaritans and Jews were related. When the Assyrians took Israel into captivity, they repopulated the area with people from other lands. Those people intermarried with the small remnant of Israelites left behind. Though they retained some aspects of their faith in the one true God, they did not worship God in Jerusalem. Because of this, the Jews considered them outcasts and traitors to the faith.

Samson Judge of Israel; his mother was told of his birth by an angel; granted great strength from the Lord.

Samuel Last of Israel's judges; after his birth, his mother, Hannah, dedicated him to the Lord; at age 3 he went to live in the temple and was raised by Eli the priest.

Sanhedrin Jewish Council of seventy religious leaders plus the high priest; responsible for the temple and the worship and religious life of the Jews; sometimes called the Supreme Court of Israel. During early New Testament times, the Sanhedrin met in the Hall of Hewn Stones in the temple in Jerusalem.

Sapphira Wife of Ananias; was struck down for lying to God.

Sarah (Sarai) Wife of Abraham; laughed at the word from God that she would bear a son in her advanced age; mother of Isaac.

Satan Another name for the devil.

Saul (1) First king of Israel; disobeyed God; David's father-in-law. (2) Jewish name of the apostle Paul; persecuted those who believed in God; was called by Jesus to be His disciple; apostle and missionary to the Early Church. See **Paul**.

Scribe Person who learned the Jewish Law and copied it onto scrolls by hand. During New Testament times, scribes were often very wealthy and agreed with the Pharisees about many things.

Sennacherib Enemy of Israel; the angel of the Lord killed 185,000 of his soldiers when they marched against the people of God.

Seth Son of Adam and Eve; born after Cain killed Abel; ancestor of Jesus.

Shadrach Young Judean brought by King Nebuchadnezzar into captivity in Babylon; one of four young men chosen by the king to be educated according to Babylonian ways so that they could serve in his palace. Shadrach's Judean name was Hananiah.

Shaphan Court secretary to King Josiah; read the Book of the Law when it was found in the presence of the king.

Shem One of Noah's three sons; ancestor of Jesus.

Sihon King of the Amorites when Israel arrived at the Promised Land.

Silas Prophet who was a co-worker with Paul on his second missionary journey.

Simeon Servant of the Lord; in the temple when Jesus was presented.

Simon (1) Peter's given name; see **Peter**. (2) (of Cyrene) Man whom the guards forced to carry the cross of Jesus at His crucifixion. (3) One of Jesus' half brothers, a son of Mary and Joseph, along with James, Joseph, and Judas (Matthew 12:46; 13:55; Mark 6:3).

Simon the Zealot One of Jesus' twelve disciples; an apostle; witness to Jesus' resurrection; died for his faith in Christ; church history says he traveled many places to share his faith in Christ, along with the apostle Jude.

Sisera Commander of King Jabin of Canaan who reigned in Hazor; his army was defeated and he fled to the tent of Jael, who killed him there with a tent stake and a hammer.

Solomon Son of David and Bathsheba who became king when David died; known for his great wisdom and for building the temple in Jerusalem.

Stephen Leader in the Early Church who was arrested and put on trial; after a rousing speech before the Council (Sanhedrin), he was stoned to death.

Tabitha (Dorcas) Godly and generous woman; raised from the dead by Peter.

Terah Father of Abraham who worshiped idols.

Tertullus Orator who accused Paul before Felix.

Thaddaeus See Jude.

Thomas One of Jesus' twelve disciples; an apostle; witness to Jesus' resurrection, yet doubted it until he put his hands in Jesus' wounds (John 20:24–29; 21:1–14); a twin (John 11:16).

Timothy Fellow traveler and official representative of the apostle Paul; his mother and grandmother believed in God; joined Paul on his second missionary journey, and at one point in this journey Paul sent him to minister to the Church in Corinth; was leader in the Church at Ephesus and co-writer with Paul.

Uriah Bathsheba's husband; King David arranged for him to be killed in battle after David committed adultery with Bathsheba.

Uzziah (Azariah) King of Judah who, for most of his reign, proved a wise, godly ruler.

Vashti First queen of King Xerxes until banished from the kingdom because of disobedience, after which Esther became queen.

Xerxes King of Persia who ruled over 127 provinces stretching from India to Cush; banished his first queen, Vashti, because of her disobedience; chose Esther to be his second queen.

Zacchaeus Short tax collector who climbed a tree in order to see Jesus; upon coming to faith, promised to restore ill-gotten wealth.

Zadok Priest during the reign of David; remained faithful to David all through his reign.

zealot (1) Member of a religious group in Jesus' time who were extremely loyal to Jewish traditions and against the Roman government. (2) A person who is very excited about a certain subject.

Zebedee Fisherman and father of James and John, disciples of Jesus.

Zebulun Tenth son of Jacob and sixth of Leah. Jacob's blessing to Zebulun was that he would "dwell at the shore of the sea; he shall become a haven for ships" (Genesis 49:13).

Zechariah Elderly priest to whom John the Baptist was born.

Zedekiah (Mattaniah) Son of Josiah; last king of Judah; puppet ruler for Nebuchadnezzar, king of Babylon.

Zerubbabel Head of the tribe of Judah at the time of Israel's return from Babylonian captivity.

Ziba Servant of King Saul's household; presented Mephibosheth to David when he was looking for someone in the house of Saul to whom he could show God's kindness.

Zimri King of Israel who reigned for seven days; died when he set the palace on fire around himself after being besieged by Omri and the Israelites.

Zipporah Daughter of Jethro (Reuel) and wife of Moses.

Books of the Bible
(66 Books)

Old Testament
(39 Books)

Genesis: This is a book of beginnings: the beginning of the world, the beginning of sin, the beginning of God's promise (to Adam and Eve) to send a Savior to rescue His people from sin and death, and the beginnings of the family (of Abraham, Isaac, and Jacob) that passed on this promise from God.

Exodus: The story of God's chosen people (known as the Hebrews or Israelites) continues in the Book of Exodus, which means "to go out." The people "go out" of slavery in Egypt, led by the Lord and His appointed leader, Moses, toward the Promised Land.

Leviticus: The third of five books known as the Books of Moses, or the Books of the Law, it focuses on the worship, sacrifices, feasts, and offerings that point to the Messiah, Jesus, the perfect sacrifice to come.

Numbers: The name of this book refers to the counting of the people and their property; but it is mostly about the Israelites' wandering in the desert wilderness, as God faithfully provided for His people.

Deuteronomy: This is the retelling of God's Law—a review of what God has done and of God's will for His people, preparing them for their life in the Promised Land. God calls His people to rededicate their lives to Him.

Joshua: The section of the Bible from Joshua to Esther is called "the history section" of the Old Testament. Joshua, whose name means "the Lord is salvation," becomes the new leader, taking the people into the Promised Land (Canaan) after the death of Moses.

Judges: This tells of the continuing cycle of the people turning away from God and then being conquered by evil enemies, followed by God's call to repentance and His deliverance through His chosen leaders (such as Gideon, Deborah, and Samson).

Ruth: The story of Ruth is about a woman who was not an Israelite, but came to faith in God and became one of the ancestors of Jesus, reminding us that God's kingdom is for all people who have faith in Him.

1 and 2 Samuel: These books tell the story of Samuel, a prophet, priest, and judge. Until the time of Samuel, leaders were chosen by God to carry out His will because God Himself was the true ruler of the people. However, the people wanted a king like nations around them. The first two kings, Saul and David, were anointed by God's prophet Samuel.

1 and 2 Kings: These books continue the history from the time when David and Solomon ruled over a united kingdom, through the times of the divided kingdom, with Israel to the north and Judah in the south. The northern Kingdom of Israel never had a king who was faithful to God; the southern Kingdom of Judah was mostly unfaithful too, though occasionally it was ruled by God-fearing kings who tried to lead the people back to the Lord.

Eventually, both kingdoms were taken into captivity.

1 and 2 Chronicles: These books focus on the reigns of King David and his son Solomon (who built the temple), and continue the history of this royal family in the southern Kingdom of Judah. The family line of David carried the promise of the Messiah, who came centuries later in Christ Jesus.

Ezra: The Books of Ezra, Nehemiah, and Esther continue the story of God's people who had been in captivity in Babylon for seventy years and finally began to see their need for hope in the true God. Ezra was part of a group that returned to Jerusalem to complete the rebuilding of the temple.

Nehemiah: Without the protection of city walls, the people who had returned to Jerusalem from captivity were in constant danger. This is the story of Nehemiah, chosen by God to guide the people to rebuild the walls (in just fifty-two days).

Esther: This book tells of Jewish people who stayed in Persia instead of returning to Judah. Again we see how God can work through ordinary people, such as Esther, to accomplish His will. This ends the historical section of the Old Testament.

Job: This begins a section of five books of poetry. These were originally written in Hebrew and do not rhyme as do poems in English. This is the story of a man who loses everything and suffers much. Job's life is a witness to others that even troubles can provide opportunities to praise God.

Psalms: This is a book of prayer and praise that gives examples of how God's people deal with both joys and sorrows.

David (as shepherd, warrior, and king) wrote about half of the psalms. There is frequent mention of the coming Messiah.

Proverbs: This is a collection of wise sayings that tell how to live a godly life. There is practical advice on many subjects such as making friends, handling money, and caring for the poor; but real wisdom is based on honoring and faithfully following God.

Ecclesiastes: The author of this book speaks of the real purpose of life and encourages us to stay away from things that are meaningless. Some things in life are empty, but life with God brings true joy and direction.

Song of Solomon: Also known as *Song of Songs*, this book tells of the relationship between a husband and wife. We can compare this to the love God has for us, which is perfect and faithful.

Isaiah: He prophesied concerning Judah and Jerusalem during the reigns of Uzziah, Jotham, Ahaz, and Hezekiah, kings of Judah. Isaiah foretold the Messiah's virgin birth and His innocent suffering and death. Isaiah was the son of Amoz.

Jeremiah: Jeremiah loved his nation enough to speak out the truth about their sin and the coming punishment. His harsh warnings often made him unpopular with his countrymen, who ridiculed him; but he remained faithful to God.

Lamentations: This is a poetic book of weeping. The author, thought to be Jeremiah, is crying over the destruction of Jerusalem—the consequence of sin, as prophesied. However, even in the middle of terrible sadness, with God there is hope.

Ezekiel: The prophet Ezekiel lived in difficult times, calling the unfaithful people to repentance. He used picture language and even acted out some of the prophecies to explain the visions he had received from the Lord.

Daniel: This book has two parts, one telling the stories of Daniel and his friends, and the other telling of prophecies and visions from God about the future. God is in charge of all history, and He directs all things for the purpose of saving His people through Christ Jesus.

Hosea: This is the first book of the twelve Minor Prophets. It tells of the prophet Hosea's relationship to his unfaithful wife, Gomer, which is a symbol of God's constant, continual love for His unfaithful people.

Joel: The prophet speaks of a swarm of locusts that destroyed the crops in Judah. Joel warns that if the people do not repent, there will be even greater destruction, caused by the swarm of an enemy's army. He says that the "day of the Lord" will come to punish sin, but those who trust in God will be saved.

Amos: Amos was a shepherd who became God's prophet to warn the people at a time when they were rich and thought things were going well. He warned the people not to trust in money or idols, but to trust in the true God.

Obadiah: Obadiah is the shortest book in the Old Testament. The prophet speaks against the people of Edom, who were glad to see Judah suffering when taken captive by Babylon. The prophet repeats God's promise to one day restore His people to their land.

Jonah: Jonah was an unwilling prophet who tried to run from God's command. He did not want God's message of repentance and forgiveness to be shared with the people of Nineveh, Israel's Assyrian enemy. God clearly wants all people to hear His Word and to come to faith—a message for us today to share with all people.

Micah: The Book of Micah explains that God hates sin but loves the sinner. Though the people would be punished for their refusal to repent of sin, the prophet also speaks a message of hope in the coming Messiah. Micah points to Bethlehem as the birthplace of the Savior who would care for His sheep and lead them like a shepherd.

Nahum: Nahum pronounced God's judgment on the nation that had taken Israel captive. Nahum said that God is slow to anger, but He brings justice on those who are guilty and is a refuge in times of trouble for those who trust in Him.

Habakkuk: This is a conversation as the prophet asks God many questions and God answers, revealing His plan. God assures us that we can hope in Him even when surrounded by troubles, because He is still in control.

Zephaniah: The book begins with sorrow over the sin of the people, but that sadness turns to joy as the prophet speaks of God's deliverance and salvation. The prophet says that when the people return to the Lord, He will bless them, and through them the whole earth will be blessed. That blessing for all the earth is the Promised Savior.

Haggai: The prophet Haggai encouraging the people returning from captivity to rebuild Jerusalem. While the rebuilt temple would not be as beautiful as Solomon's, it would have greater glory because the Savior would one day come to this new temple.

Zechariah: As Zechariah encourages the rebuilding of the temple, he gives even greater encouragement through prophecies about the Promised Savior, such as foretelling Jesus' triumphant entry into Jerusalem on Palm Sunday.

Malachi: The last Old Testament prophet, Malachi, prophesied about the messenger (John the Baptist) who would get people ready for the coming of the Messiah (Jesus). Four hundred years would pass before the Savior was born.

New Testament
(27 books)

Matthew: The four Gospels tell the stories of Jesus' life, death, and resurrected life, each from a special point of view. Matthew, writing mostly to Jewish people, emphasized that Jesus indeed is the promised Messiah, showing over and over how Jesus fulfilled the prophecies of old.

Mark: The style of the Gospel of Mark is full of action, telling what Jesus did. The primary audience was Roman Christians, who would appreciate this active style of writing, which is brief and to the point.

Luke: The author of this book, Luke, was a doctor who had a second career as a missionary and writer. Luke emphasizes Jesus' compassion for people as he tells of Jesus' parables and healing miracles.

John: John's viewpoint tends to be more philosophical than the other Gospels, focusing more on the teachings of Jesus. This would relate especially well to John's Greek audience. His constant theme is the love of Jesus for all people.

Acts: Luke wrote this book of history called the Acts of the Apostles. It tells of the early growth of the Christian Church and how the Holy Spirit worked in the lives of believers such as Stephen, Peter, Paul, Philip, Lydia, and Dorcas.

Romans: This begins the section of *epistles* (letters). Romans was written by the apostle Paul to the Christian Church in Rome around the time of the emperor Nero. It gives basic details about our Christian faith, emphasizing the grace and mercy that is a gift from God through Christ Jesus.

1 and 2 Corinthians: These epistles were written to people in the Greek seaport city of Corinth, a city known for its many idols to false gods. Paul heard that the Church in Corinth had many problems. He wrote these letters to guide them and also encourage them about salvation through Jesus.

Galatians: Some of the people in Galatia (part of modern-day Turkey) were demanding that new Christians follow old Jewish law. Paul emphasizes that faith in Jesus alone is all that is necessary for salvation, not rules or works.

Ephesians: Ephesus was a very large commercial city. As Paul writes to the Church in Ephesus, he is telling us today too, that the Church is not a building; the Church is people—believers in Christ Jesus who want to serve Him.

Philippians: Philippi was a wealthy Roman colony in Macedonia. Paul's letter is full of joy, encouraging the people to be faithful even when troubles come, knowing that in Christ they can do all things.

Colossians: Paul writes to the Church in the city of Colossae that they should be careful of false teachings. He wants them to know that human knowledge is nothing compared to the greatness of God and the saving truth He offers us.

1 and 2 Thessalonians: Thessalonica was a busy seaport. These epistles were written to Christians there who were being persecuted. Paul encourages them to continue in their faith and look forward to the hope that is theirs in Christ Jesus.

1 and 2 Timothy: Having been raised in a godly home, Timothy was led to Christ by Paul and was trained by him as he accompanied Paul on several mission trips. Paul wrote these two letters to Timothy to explain how workers in the Church should teach and live.

Titus: This letter is to Titus, a Greek church worker on the island of Crete who had traveled with Paul on some of his missionary journeys. Paul emphasizes that godly living is always motivated by God's love for us in Christ Jesus.

Philemon: This is a personal letter to Philemon, who is a slave owner. Paul asks for mercy for Philemon's runaway slave, Onesimus, offering to pay off his debts and asking that Philemon welcome him back. This is a picture of us as sinners who are slaves to sin. Jesus has paid the debt for our guilt and now welcomes us back to His family.

Hebrews: This was written to Jewish communities, who were familiar with the priesthood, to teach about the work of Jesus. It shows that not only is Jesus the great High Priest but He is also the perfect and complete sacrifice for the forgiveness of our sins.

James: James wants people to understand that works are an important sign of faith and that "faith without works" is dead. Good works do not create saving faith, but when saving faith in Jesus exists, it is always followed by Christian living.

1 and 2 Peter: Peter sends these letters to people who were being persecuted for their faith. He reminds them that Jesus understands because He suffered for us. The people are encouraged to be faithful until Christ comes again.

1, 2, and 3 John: John was an old man when he wrote these letters, and he often refers to the readers as his "dear children." He summarizes the love and mercy we have in Christ Jesus, which leads us to show love and mercy to others.

Jude: Jude reminds Christians that they are kept in their faith by Jesus. Jude challenges believers of all times and all ages to stand up for what they believe in—Christ—and to clearly protect the true faith.

Revelation: This book of prophecy uses picture language to tell about Jesus' coming on the Last Day to take us to heaven. As Genesis starts with the beginning of time, Revelation speaks of the end of time, when we will see Jesus Christ's complete victory over sin, death, and the power of the devil.

THE TEN COMMANDMENTS

The First Commandment

You shall have no other gods

What does this mean? We should fear, love, and trust in God above all things.

The Second Commandment

You shall not misuse the name of the Lord your God.

What does this mean? We should fear and love God so that we do not curse, swear, use satanic arts, lie, or deceive by His name, but call upon it in every trouble, pray, praise, and give thanks.

The Third Commandment

Remember the Sabbath day by keeping it holy.

What does this mean? We should fear and love God so that we do not despise preaching and His Word, but hold it sacred and gladly hear and learn it.

The Fourth Commandment

Honor your father and your mother.

What does this mean? We should fear and love God so that we do not despise or anger our parents and other authorities, but honor them, serve and obey them, love and cherish them.

The Fifth Commandment

You shall not murder.

What does this mean? We should fear and love God so that we do not hurt or harm our neighbor in his body, but help and support him in every physical need.

The Sixth Commandment

You shall not commit adultery.

What does this mean? We should fear and love God so that we lead a sexually pure and decent life in what we say and do, and husband and wife love and honor each other.

The Seventh Commandment

You shall not steal.

What does this mean? We should fear and love God so that we do not take our neighbor's money or possessions, or get them in any dishonest way, but help him to improve and protect his possessions and income.

The Eighth Commandment

You shall not give false testimony against your neighbor.

What does this mean? We should fear and love God so that we do not tell lies about our neighbor, betray him, slander him, or hurt his reputation, but defend him, speak well of him, and explain everything in the kindest way.

The Ninth Commandment

You shall not covet your neighbor's house.

What does this mean? We should fear and love God so that we do not scheme to get our neighbor's inheritance or house, or get it in a way which only appears right, but help and be of service to him in keeping it.

The Tenth Commandment

You shall not covet your neighbor's wife,
or his manservant or maidservant, his ox or donkey,
or anything that belongs to your neighbor.

What does this mean? We should fear and love God so that we do not entice or force away our neighbor's wife, workers, or animals, or turn them against him, but urge them to stay and do their duty.

The Close of the Commandments

What does God say about all these commandments? He says, "I, the Lord your God, am a jealous God, punishing the children for the sin of the fathers to the third and fourth generation of those who hate Me, but showing love to a thousand generations of those who love Me and keep My commandments." (Exodus 20:5–6)

What does this mean? God threatens to punish all who break these commandments. Therefore, we should fear His wrath and not do anything against them. But He promises grace and every blessing to all who keep these commandments. Therefore, we should also love and trust in Him and gladly do what He commands.

THE CREED

The First Article *(Creation)*

I believe in God, the Father Almighty, Maker of heaven and earth.

What does this mean? I believe that God has made me and all creatures; that He has given me my body and soul, eyes, ears, and all my members, my reason and all my senses, and still takes care of them.

He also gives me clothing and shoes, food and drink, house and home, wife and children, land, animals, and all I have. He richly and daily provides me with all that I need to support this body and life.

He defends me against all danger and guards and protects me from all evil.

All this He does only out of fatherly, divine goodness and mercy, without any merit or worthiness in me. For all this it is my duty to thank and praise, serve and obey Him.

This is most certainly true.

The Second Article *(Redemption)*

And in Jesus Christ, His only Son, our Lord, who was conceived by the Holy Spirit, born of the Virgin Mary, suffered under Pontius Pilate, was crucified, died and was buried. He descended into hell. The third day He rose again from the dead. He ascended into heaven and sits at the right hand of God, the Father Almighty. From thence He will come to judge the living and the dead.

What does this mean? I believe that Jesus Christ, true God, begotten of the Father from eternity, and also true man, born of the Virgin Mary, is my Lord,

who has redeemed me, a lost and condemned person, purchased and won me from all sins, from death, and from the power of the devil; not with gold or silver, but with His holy, precious blood and with His innocent suffering and death, that I may be His own and live under Him in His kingdom and serve Him in everlasting righteousness, innocence, and blessedness,

just as He is risen from the dead, lives and reigns to all eternity.

This is most certainly true.

The Third Article *(Sanctification)*

I believe in the Holy Spirit, the holy Christian church, the communion of saints, the forgiveness of sins, the resurrection of the body, and the life everlasting. Amen.

What does this mean? I believe that I cannot by my own reason or strength believe in Jesus Christ, my Lord, or come to Him; but the Holy Spirit has called me by the Gospel, enlightened me with His gifts, sanctified and kept me in the true faith.

In the same way He calls, gathers, enlightens, and sanctifies the whole Christian church on earth, and keeps it with Jesus Christ in the one true faith.

In this Christian church He daily and richly forgives all my sins and the sins of all believers.

On the Last Day He will raise me and all the dead, and give eternal life to me and all believers in Christ.

This is most certainly true.

THE LORD'S PRAYER

The Introduction
Our Father who art in heaven.

What does this mean? With these words God tenderly invites us to believe that He is our true Father and that we are His true children, so that with all boldness and confidence we may ask Him as dear children ask their dear father.

The First Petition
Hallowed be Thy name.

What does this mean? God's name is certainly holy in itself, but we pray in this petition that it may be kept holy among us also.
How is God's name kept holy? God's name is kept holy when the Word of God is taught in its truth and purity, and we, as the children of God, also lead holy lives according to it. Help us to do this, dear Father in heaven! But anyone who teaches or lives contrary to God's Word profanes the name of God among us. Protect us from this, heavenly Father!

The Second Petition
Thy kingdom come.

What does this mean? The kingdom of God certainly comes by itself without our prayer, but we pray in this petition that it may come to us also.
How does God's kingdom come? God's kingdom comes when our heavenly Father gives us His Holy Spirit, so that by His grace we believe His holy Word and lead godly lives here in time and there in eternity.

The Third Petition
Thy will be done on earth as it is in heaven.

What does this mean? The good and gracious will of God is done even without our prayer, but we pray in this petition that it may be done among us also.
How is God's will done? God's will is done when He breaks and hinders every evil plan and purpose of the devil, the world, and our sinful nature,

which do not want us to hallow God's name or let His kingdom come;

and when He strengthens and keeps us firm in His Word and faith until we die.

This is His good and gracious will.

The Fourth Petition

Give us this day our daily bread.

What does this mean? God certainly gives daily bread to everyone without our prayers, even to all evil people, but we pray in this petition that God would lead us to realize this and to receive our daily bread with thanksgiving.

What is meant by daily bread? Daily bread includes everything that has to do with the support and needs of the body, such as food, drink, clothing, shoes, house, home, land, animals, money, goods, a devout husband or wife, devout children, devout workers, devout and faithful rulers, good government, good weather, peace, health, self-control, good reputation, good friends, faithful neighbors, and the like.

The Fifth Petition

And forgive us our trespasses as we forgive those who trespass against us.

What does this mean? We pray in this petition that our Father in heaven would not look at our sins, or deny our prayer because of them. We are neither worthy of the things for which we pray, nor have we deserved them, but we ask that He would give them all to us by grace, for we daily sin much and surely deserve nothing but punishment. So we too will sincerely forgive and gladly do good to those who sin against us.

The Sixth Petition

And lead us not into temptation.

What does this mean? God tempts no one. We pray in this petition that God would guard and keep us so that the devil, the world, and our sinful nature may not deceive us or mislead us into false belief, despair, and other great shame and vice. Although we are attacked by these things, we pray that we may finally overcome them and win the victory.

The Seventh Petition

But deliver us from evil.

What does this mean? We pray in this petition, in summary, that our Father in heaven would rescue us from every evil of body and soul, possessions and reputation, and finally, when our last hour comes, give us a blessed end, and graciously take us from this valley of sorrow to Himself in heaven.

The Conclusion

For Thine is the kingdom and the power and the glory forever and ever. Amen.

What does this mean? This means that I should be certain that these petitions are pleasing to our Father in heaven, and are heard by Him; for He Himself has commanded us to pray in this way and has promised to hear us. Amen, amen means "yes, yes, it shall be so."

THE SACRAMENT OF HOLY BAPTISM

FIRST

What is Baptism? Baptism is not just plain water, but it is the water included in God's command and combined with God's word.

Which is that word of God? Christ our Lord says in the last chapter of Matthew: "Therefore go and make disciples of all nations, baptizing them in the name of the Father and of the Son and of the Holy Spirit." (Matthew 28:19)

SECOND

What benefits does Baptism give? It works forgiveness of sins, rescues from death and the devil, and gives eternal salvation to all who believe this, as the words and promises of God declare.

Which are these words and promises of God? Christ our Lord says in the last chapter of Mark: "Whoever believes and is baptized will be saved, but whoever does not believe will be condemned." (Mark 16:16)

THIRD

How can water do such great things? Certainly not just water, but the word of God in and with the water does these things, along with the faith which trusts this word of God in the water. For without God's word the water is plain water and no Baptism. But with the word of God it is a Baptism, that is, a life-giving water, rich in grace, and a washing of the new birth in the Holy Spirit, as St. Paul says in Titus, chapter three:

"He saved us through the washing of rebirth and renewal by the Holy Spirit, whom He poured out on us generously through Jesus Christ our Savior, so that, having been justified by His grace, we might become heirs having the hope of eternal life. This is a trustworthy saying." (Titus 3:5–8)

FOURTH

What does such baptizing with water indicate? It indicates that the Old Adam in us should by daily contrition and repentance be drowned and die with all sins and evil desires, and that a new man should daily emerge and arise to live before God in righteousness and purity forever.

Where is this written? St. Paul writes in Romans chapter six: "We were therefore buried with Him through baptism into death in order that, just as Christ was raised from the dead through the glory of the Father, we too may live a new life." (Romans 6:4)

CONFESSION

What is Confession? Confession has two parts.

First, that we confess our sins, and

second, that we receive absolution, that is, forgiveness, from the pastor as from God Himself, not doubting, but firmly believing that by it our sins are forgiven before God in heaven.

What sins should we confess? Before God we should plead guilty of all sins, even those we are not aware of, as we do in the Lord's Prayer; but before the pastor we should confess only those sins which we know and feel in our hearts.

Which are these? Consider your place in life according to the Ten Commandments: Are you a father, mother, son, daughter, husband, wife, or worker? Have you been disobedient, unfaithful, or lazy? Have you been hot-tempered, rude, or quarrelsome? Have you hurt someone by your words or deeds? Have you stolen, been negligent, wasted anything, or done any harm?

What is the Office of the Keys? The Office of the Keys is that special authority which Christ has given to His church on earth to forgive the sins of repentant sinners, but to withhold forgiveness from the unrepentant as long as they do not repent.

Where is this written? This is what St. John the Evangelist writes in chapter twenty: The Lord Jesus breathed on His disciples and said, "Receive the Holy Spirit. If you forgive anyone his sins, they are forgiven; if you do not forgive them, they are not forgiven." (John 20:22–23)

What do you believe according to these words? I believe that when the called ministers of Christ deal with us by His divine command, in particular when they exclude openly unrepentant sinners from the Christian congregation and absolve those who repent of their sins and want to do better, this is just as valid and certain, even in heaven, as if Christ our dear Lord dealt with us Himself.

THE SACRAMENT OF THE ALTAR

What is the Sacrament of the Altar? It is the true body and blood of our Lord Jesus Christ under the bread and wine, instituted by Christ Himself for us Christians to eat and to drink.

Where is this written? The holy Evangelists Matthew, Mark, Luke, and St. Paul write:

> Our Lord Jesus Christ, on the night when He was betrayed, took bread, and when He had given thanks, He broke it and gave it to the disciples and said: "Take, eat; this is My body, which is given for you. This do in remembrance of Me."

> In the same way also He took the cup after supper, and when He had given thanks, He gave it to them, saying, "Drink of it, all of you; this cup is the new testament in My blood, which is shed for you for the forgiveness of sins. This do, as often as you drink it, in remembrance of Me."

What is the benefit of this eating and drinking? These words, "Given and shed for you for the forgiveness of sins," show us that in the Sacrament forgiveness of sins, life, and salvation are given us through these words. For where there is forgiveness of sins, there is also life and salvation.

How can bodily eating and drinking do such great things? Certainly not just eating and drinking do these things, but the words written here: "Given and shed for you for the forgiveness of sins." These words, along with the bodily eating and drinking, are the main thing in the Sacrament. Whoever believes these words has exactly what they say: "forgiveness of sins."

Who receives this sacrament worthily? Fasting and bodily preparation are certainly fine outward training. But that person is truly worthy and well prepared who has faith in these words: "Given and shed for you for the forgiveness of sins." But anyone who does not believe these words or doubts them is unworthy and unprepared, for the words "for you" require all hearts to believe.

DAILY PRAYERS

MORNING PRAYER

In the morning when you get up, make the sign of the holy cross and say:
In the name of the Father and of the Son and of the Holy Spirit. Amen.

I thank You, my heavenly Father, through Jesus Christ, Your dear Son, that You have kept me this night from all harm and danger; and I pray that You would keep me this day also from sin and every evil, that all my doings and life may please You. For into Your hands I commend myself, my body and soul, and all things. Let Your holy angel be with me, that the evil foe may have no power over me. Amen.

EVENING PRAYER

In the evening when you go to bed, make the sign of the holy cross and say:
In the name of the Father and of the Son and of the Holy Spirit. Amen.

I thank You, my heavenly Father, through Jesus Christ, Your dear Son, that You have graciously kept me this day; and I pray that You would forgive me all my sins where I have done wrong, and graciously keep me this night. For into Your hands I commend myself, my body and soul, and all things. Let Your holy angel be with me, that the evil foe may have no power over me. Amen.

ASKING A BLESSING

The eyes of all look to You, [O Lord,] and You give them their food at the proper time. You open Your hand and satisfy the desires of every living thing. (Psalm 145:15–16)

RETURNING THANKS

Give thanks to the Lord, for He is good. His love endures forever. [He] gives food to every creature. He provides food for the cattle and for the young ravens when they call. His pleasure is not in the strength of the horse, nor His delight in the legs of a man; the Lord delights in those who fear Him, who put their hope in His unfailing love. (Psalm 136:1, 25; 147:9–11)

We thank You, Lord God, heavenly Father, for all Your benefits, through Jesus Christ, our Lord, who lives and reigns with You and the Holy Spirit forever and ever. Amen.

TABLE OF DUTIES

Certain passages of Scripture for various holy orders and positions, admonishing them about their duties and responsibilities

To Bishops, Pastors, and Preachers

The overseer must be above reproach, the husband of but one wife, temperate, self-controlled, respectable, hospitable, able to teach, not given to drunkenness, not violent but gentle, not quarrelsome, not a lover of money. He must manage his own family well and see that his children obey him with proper respect. (1 Timothy 3:2–4)

He must not be a recent convert, or he may become conceited and fall under the same judgment as the devil. (1 Timothy 3:6)

He must hold firmly to the trustworthy message as it has been taught, so that he can encourage others by sound doctrine and refute those who oppose it. (Titus 1:9)

What the Hearers Owe Their Pastors

The Lord has commanded that those who preach the gospel should receive their living from the gospel. (1 Corinthians 9:14)

Anyone who receives instruction in the word must share all good things with his instructor. Do not be deceived: God cannot be mocked. A man reaps what he sows. (Galatians 6:6–7)

The elders who direct the affairs of the church well are worthy of double honor, especially those whose work is preaching and teaching. For the Scripture says, "Do not muzzle the ox while it is treading out the grain," and "The worker deserves his wages." (1 Timothy 5:17–18)

We ask you, brothers, to respect those who work hard among you, who are over you in the Lord and who admonish you. Hold them in the highest regard in love because of their work. Live in peace with each other. (1 Thessalonians 5:12–13)

Obey your leaders and submit to their authority. They keep watch over you as men who must give an account. Obey them so that their work will be a joy, not a burden, for that would be of no advantage to you. (Hebrews 13:17)

Of Civil Government

Everyone must submit himself to the governing authorities, for there is no authority except that which God has established. The authorities that exist have been established by God. Consequently, he who rebels against the authority is rebelling against what God has instituted, and those who do so will bring judgment on themselves. For rulers hold no terror for those who do right, but for those who do wrong. Do you want to be free from fear of the one in authority? Then do what is right and he will commend you. For he is God's servant to do you good. But if you do wrong, be afraid, for he does not bear the sword for nothing. He is God's servant, an agent of wrath to bring punishment on the wrongdoer. (Romans 13:1–4)

Of Citizens

Give to Caesar what is Caesar's, and to God what is God's. (Matthew 22:21)

It is necessary to submit to the authorities, not only because of possible punishment but also because of conscience. This is also why you pay taxes, for the authorities are God's servants, who give their full time to governing. Give everyone what you owe him: If you owe taxes, pay taxes; if revenue, then revenue; if respect, then respect; if honor, then honor. (Romans 13:5–7)

I urge, then, first of all, that requests, prayers, intercession and thanksgiving be made for everyone—for kings and all those in authority, that we may live peaceful and quiet lives in all godliness and holiness. This is good, and pleases God our Savior. (1 Timothy 2:1–3)

Remind the people to be subject to rulers and authorities, to be obedient, to be ready to do whatever is good. (Titus 3:1)

Submit yourselves for the Lord's sake to every authority instituted among men: whether to the king, as the supreme authority, or to governors, who are sent by him to punish those who do wrong and to commend those who do right. (1 Peter 2:13–14)

To Husbands

Husbands, in the same way be considerate as you live with your wives, and treat them with respect as the weaker partner and as heirs with you of the gracious gift of life, so that nothing will hinder your prayers. (1 Peter 3:7)

Husbands, love your wives and do not be harsh with them. (Colossians 3:19)

To Wives

Wives, submit to your husbands as to the Lord. (Ephesians 5:22)

They were submissive to their own husbands, like Sarah, who obeyed Abraham and called him her master. You are her daughters if you do what is right and do not give way to fear. (1 Peter 3:5–6)

To Parents

Fathers, do not exasperate your children; instead, bring them up in the training and instruction of the Lord. (Ephesians 6:4)

To Children

Children, obey your parents in the Lord, for this is right. "Honor your father and your mother"—which is the first commandment with a promise—"that it may go well with you and that you may enjoy long life on the earth." (Ephesians 6:1–3)

To Workers of All Kinds

Slaves, obey your earthly masters with respect and fear, and with sincerity of heart, just as you would obey Christ. Obey them not only to win their favor when their eye is on you, but like slaves of Christ, doing the will of God from your heart. Serve wholeheartedly, as if you were serving the Lord, not men, because you know that the Lord will reward everyone for whatever good he does, whether he is slave or free. (Ephesians 6:5–8)

To Employers and Supervisors

Masters, treat your slaves in the same way. Do not threaten them, since you know that He who is both their Master and yours is in heaven, and there is no favoritism with Him. (Ephesians 6:9)

To Youth

Young men, in the same way be submissive to those who are older. All of you, clothe yourselves with humility toward one another, because, "God opposes the proud but gives grace to the humble." Humble yourselves, therefore, under God's mighty hand, that He may lift you up in due time. (1 Peter 5:5–6)

To Widows

The widow who is really in need and left all alone puts her hope in God and continues night and day to pray and to ask God for help. But the widow who lives for pleasure is dead even while she lives. (1 Timothy 5:5–6)

To Everyone

The commandments . . . are summed up in this one rule: "Love your neighbor as yourself." (Romans 13:9)

I urge . . . that requests, prayers, intercession and thanksgiving be made for everyone. (1 Timothy 2:1)

SECTION 4

CHRISTIAN QUESTIONS WITH THEIR ANSWERS

Prepared by Dr. Martin Luther for those who intend to go to the Sacrament.

After confession and instruction in the Ten Commandments, the Creed, the Lord's Prayer, and the Sacraments of Baptism and the Lord's Supper, the pastor may ask, or Christians may ask themselves these questions:

1. Do you believe that you are a sinner?

   Yes, I believe it. I am a sinner.

2. How do you know this?

   From the Ten Commandments, which I have not kept.

3. Are you sorry for your sins?

   Yes, I am sorry that I have sinned against God.

4. What have you deserved from God because of your sins?

   His wrath and displeasure, temporal death, and eternal damnation. See Romans 6:21, 23.

5. Do you hope to be saved?

   Yes, that is my hope.

6. In whom then do you trust?

   In my dear Lord Jesus Christ.

7. Who is Christ?

   The Son of God, true God and man.

8. How many Gods are there?

   Only one, but there are three persons: Father, Son, and Holy Spirit.

9. What has Christ done for you that you trust in Him?

   He died for me and shed His blood for me on the cross for the forgiveness of sins.

10. Did the Father also die for you?

    He did not. The Father is God only, as is the Holy Spirit; but the Son is both true God and true man. He died for me and shed His blood for me.

11. How do you know this?

    From the Holy Gospel, from the words instituting the Sacrament, and by His body and blood given me as a pledge in the Sacrament.

12. What are the Words of Institution?

    Our Lord Jesus Christ, on the night when He was betrayed, took bread, and when He had given thanks, He broke it and gave it to the disciples and said: "Take eat; this is My body, which is given for you. This do in remembrance of Me."

    In the same way also He took the cup after supper, and when He had given thanks, He gave it to them, saying: "Drink of it, all of you; this cup is the new testament in My blood, which is shed for you for the forgiveness of sins. This do, as often as you drink it, in remembrance of Me."

13. Do you believe, then, that the true body and blood of Christ are in the Sacrament?

> Yes, I believe it.

14. What convinces you to believe this?

> The word of Christ: Take, eat, this is My body; drink of it, all of you, this is My blood.

15. What should we do when we eat His body and drink His blood, and in this way receive His pledge?

> We should remember and proclaim His death and the shedding of His blood, as He taught us: This do, as often as you drink it, in remembrance of Me.

16. Why should we remember and proclaim His death?

> First, so that we may learn to believe that no creature could make satisfaction for our sins. Only Christ, true God and man, could do that. Second, so we may learn to be horrified by our sins, and to regard them as very serious. Third, so we may find joy and comfort in Christ alone, and through faith in Him be saved.

17. What motivated Christ to die and make full payment for your sins?

> His great love for His Father and for me and other sinners, as it is written in John 14; Romans 5; Galatians 2; and Ephesians 5.

18. Finally, why do you wish to go to the Sacrament?

> That I may learn to believe that Christ, out of great love, died for my sin, and also learn from Him to love God and my neighbor.

19. What should admonish and encourage a Christian to receive the Sacrament frequently?

> First, both the command and the promise of Christ the Lord. Second, his own pressing need, because of which the command, encouragement, and promise are given.

20. But what should you do if you are not aware of this need and have no hunger and thirst for the Sacrament?

> To such a person no better advice can be given than this: first, he should touch his body to see if he still has flesh and blood. Then he should believe what the Scriptures say of it in Galatians 5 and Romans 7.
>
> Second, he should look around to see whether he is still in the world, and remember that there will be no lack of sin and trouble, as the Scriptures say in John 15–16 and in 1 John 2 and 5.
>
> Third, he will certainly have the devil also around him, who with his lying and murdering day and night will let him have no peace, within or without, as the Scriptures picture him in John 8 and 16; 1 Peter 5; Ephesians 6; and 2 Timothy 2.

APOSTLES' CREED AND LORD'S PRAYER

The Apostles' Creed

I believe in God, the Father Almighty, Maker of heaven and earth.

And in Jesus Christ, His only Son, our Lord, who was conceived by the Holy Spirit, born of the Virgin Mary, suffered under Pontius Pilate, was crucified, died and was buried. He descended into hell. The third day He rose again from the dead. He ascended into heaven and sits at the right hand of God the Father Almighty. From thence He will come to judge the living and the dead.

I believe in the Holy Spirit, the holy Christian church, the communion of saints, the forgiveness of sins, the resurrection of the body, and the life everlasting. Amen.

The Lord's Prayer

Our Father who art in heaven, hallowed be Thy name, Thy kingdom come, Thy will be done on earth as it is in heaven. Give us this day our daily bread; and forgive us our trespasses as we forgive those who trespass against us; and lead us not into temptation, but deliver us from evil. For Thine is the kingdom and the power and the glory forever and ever. Amen.

Old Testament Israel

CITIES

CITIES OF REFUGE

0   50 KM.
0   30 MI.

Sidon

LEBANON MTS.

VALLEY OF LEBANON

LITANI R.

MOUNT HERMON

Tyre

Dan

Kedesh

LAKE HULEH

Hazor

Acco

SEA OF CHINNERETH

Golan

KISHON R.

YARMUK R.

MOUNT TABOR

MOUNT CARMEL

Dor

Megiddo

Jezreel

Ramoth-gilead

MOUNT GILBOA

Beth-shan

GREAT SEA

Jabesh-gilead

JORDAN R.

Dothan

Samaria

MOUNT EBAL

Penuel

Shechem

Succoth

JABBOK R.

MOUNT GERIZIM

KANAH B.

Mahanaim

Joppa

Shiloh

Rabbah

Bethel

Gilgal

Gezer

Aijalon

Jericho

Heshbon

Gibeon

Ashdod

Ekron

Jerusalem

KIDRON R.

Bezer

Gath

MOUNT NEBO

Ashkelon

Bethlehem

Lachish

Hebron
[Kiriath-arba]

SALT SEA

Dibon

Gaza

ARNON R.

Gerar

Debir

Arad

Beersheba

BROOK OF BESOR

BROOK OF EGYPT

BROOK OF ZERED

The Twelve Tribes

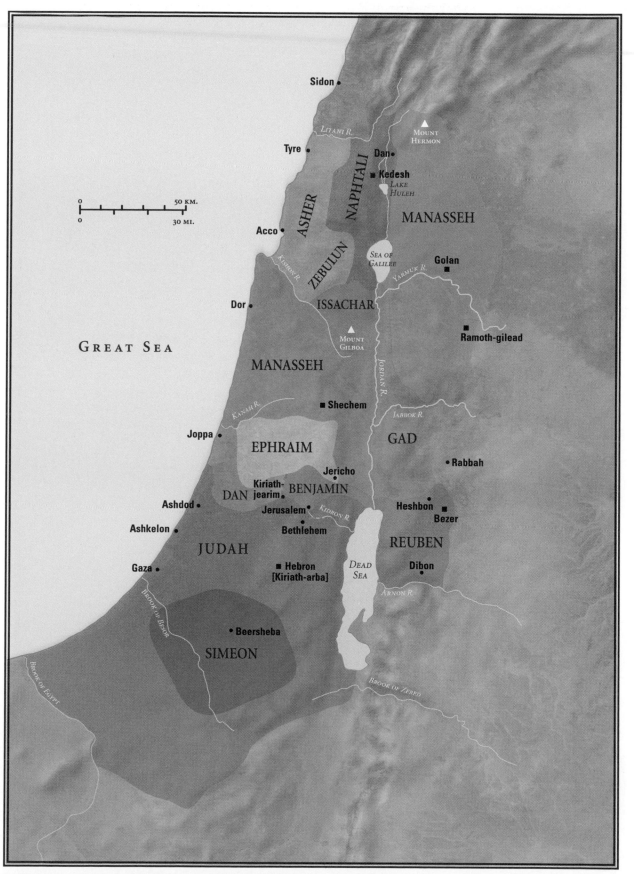

Old Testament Regions

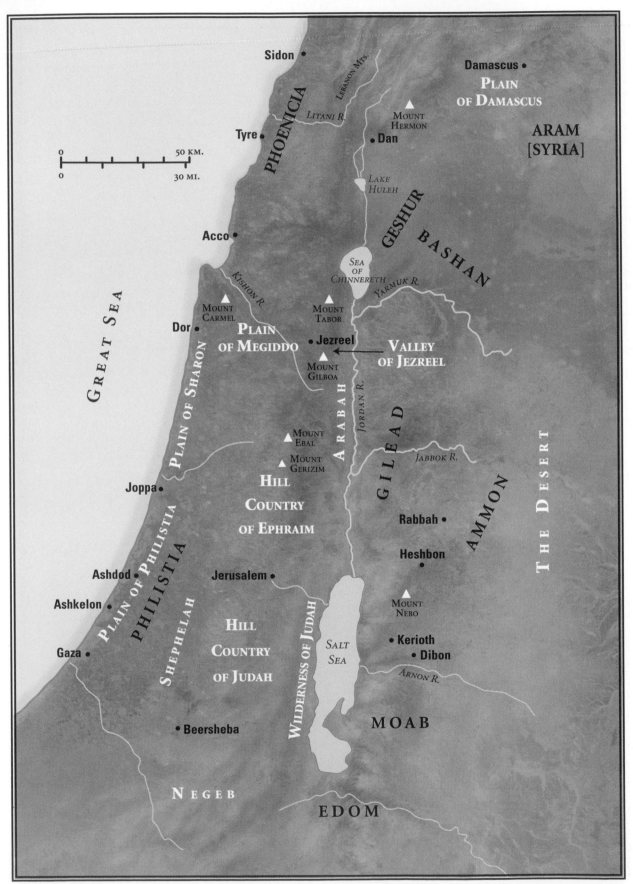

© 2009 Concordia Publishing House. Excerpted from *The Lutheran Study Bible*.

United Kingdom Period

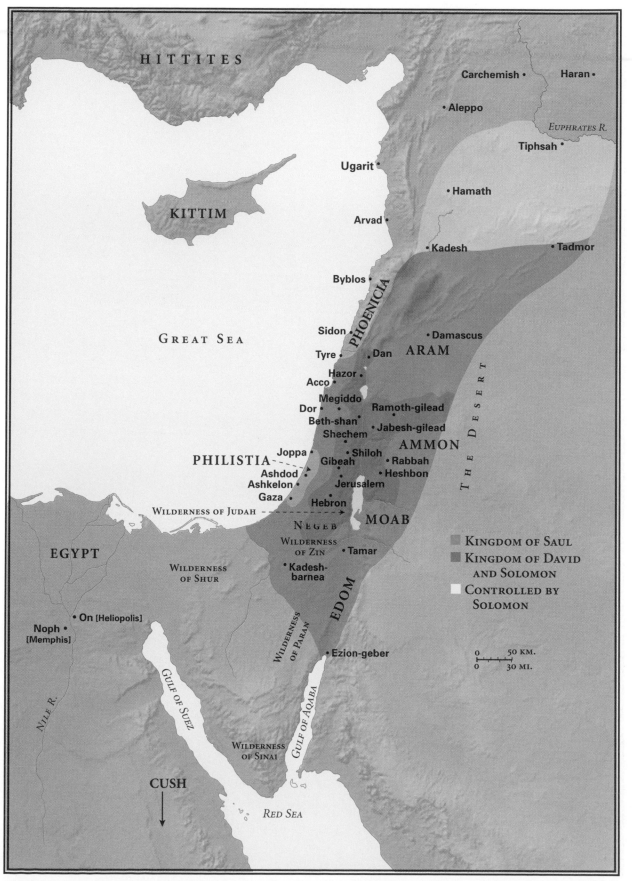

HITTITES

Carchemish •   Haran •

• Aleppo

Euphrates R.

Ugarit •   • Tiphsah

• Hamath

KITTIM

Arvad •   • Tadmor

• Kadesh

Byblos   PHOENICIA

GREAT SEA

Sidon •   • Damascus

Tyre •   • Dan   ARAM

Hazor •   *THE DESERT*

Acco •

Megiddo •

Dor •   Ramoth-gilead •

Beth-shan •   • Jabesh-gilead

Shechem •

Joppa •   • Shiloh   AMMON

PHILISTIA   Gibeah •   • Rabbah

Ashdod •   • Heshbon

Ashkelon •   Jerusalem •

Gaza •   Hebron •

WILDERNESS OF JUDAH   MOAB

NEGEB

WILDERNESS OF ZIN   • Tamar

EGYPT

WILDERNESS OF SHUR   • Kadesh-barnea

EDOM

On [Heliopolis] •

Noph •
[Memphis]

WILDERNESS OF PARAN

• Ezion-geber

NILE R.

GULF OF SUEZ

GULF OF AQABA

WILDERNESS OF SINAI

CUSH

RED SEA

■ KINGDOM OF SAUL
■ KINGDOM OF DAVID AND SOLOMON
□ CONTROLLED BY SOLOMON

0   50 KM.
0   30 MI.

New Testament Cities

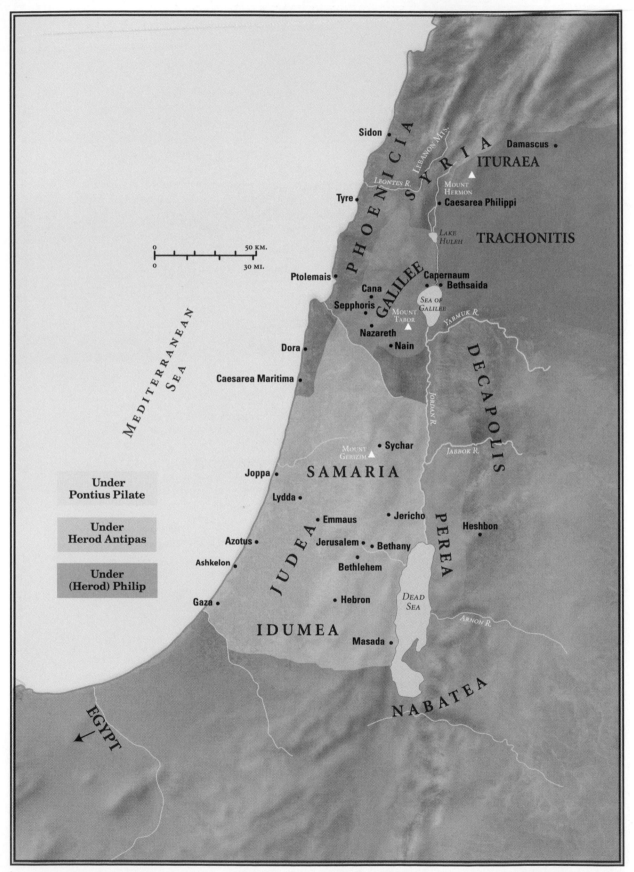

Under
Pontius Pilate

Under
Herod Antipas

Under
(Herod) Philip

MEDITERRANEAN SEA

Sidon

Damascus

SYRIA

ITURAEA

PHOENICIA

LEONTES R.

LEBANON MTS.

MOUNT HERMON

Tyre

Caesarea Philippi

LAKE HULEH

TRACHONITIS

Ptolemais

Capernaum
Bethsaida

Cana

GALILEE

SEA OF GALILEE

Sepphoris

MOUNT TABOR

YARMUK R.

Nazareth

DECAPOLIS

Dora

Nain

JORDAN R.

Caesarea Maritima

JABBOK R.

MOUNT GERIZIM

Sychar

SAMARIA

Joppa

Lydda

Jericho

PEREA

Emmaus

Heshbon

Azotus

Jerusalem

Bethany

Ashkelon

Bethlehem

JUDEA

DEAD SEA

Gaza

Hebron

ARNON R.

IDUMEA

Masada

NABATEA

EGYPT

0   50 KM.
0   30 MI.

Jesus' Ministry in the Gospels

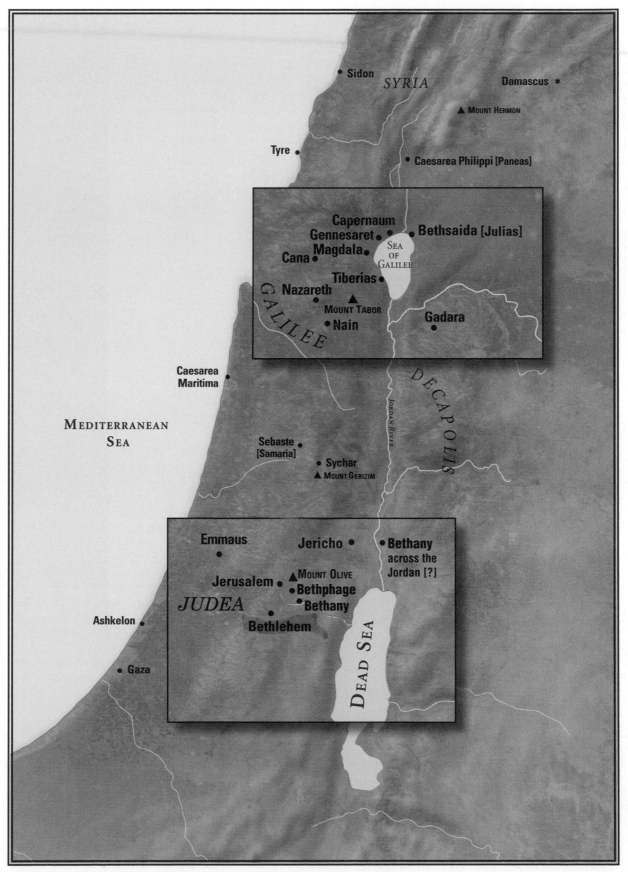

- Sidon
- SYRIA
- Damascus •
- ▲ Mount Hermon
- Tyre •
- • Caesarea Philippi [Paneas]
- Capernaum
- Gennesaret •
- • Bethsaida [Julias]
- Magdala
- Cana •
- Sea of Galilee
- Nazareth
- Tiberias •
- ▲ Mount Tabor
- • Nain
- GALILEE
- Gadara
- Caesarea Maritima
- DECAPOLIS
- MEDITERRANEAN SEA
- JORDAN RIVER
- Sebaste [Samaria] •
- • Sychar
- ▲ Mount Gerizim
- Emmaus •
- Jericho •
- • Bethany across the Jordan [?]
- ▲ Mount Olive
- Jerusalem •
- • Bethphage
- JUDEA
- • Bethany
- Ashkelon •
- Bethlehem
- DEAD SEA
- • Gaza

Paul's Missionary Journeys

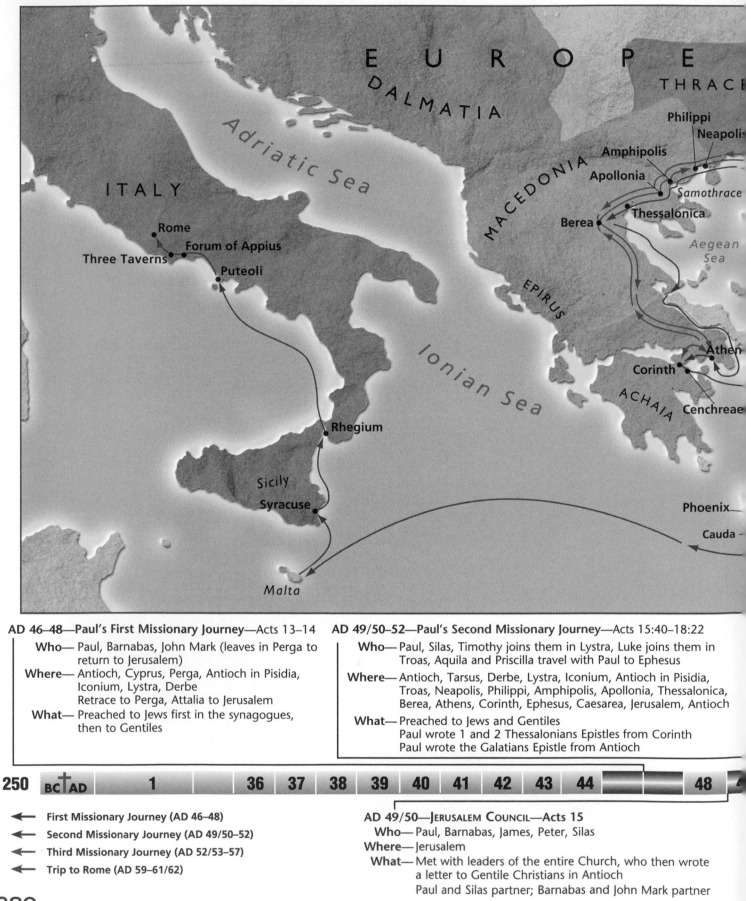

AD 46–48—Paul's First Missionary Journey—Acts 13–14

> **Who—** Paul, Barnabas, John Mark (leaves in Perga to return to Jerusalem)
>
> **Where—** Antioch, Cyprus, Perga, Antioch in Pisidia, Iconium, Lystra, Derbe
> Retrace to Perga, Attalia to Jerusalem
>
> **What—** Preached to Jews first in the synagogues, then to Gentiles

AD 49/50–52—Paul's Second Missionary Journey—Acts 15:40–18:22

> **Who—** Paul, Silas, Timothy joins them in Lystra, Luke joins them in Troas, Aquila and Priscilla travel with Paul to Ephesus
>
> **Where—** Antioch, Tarsus, Derbe, Lystra, Iconium, Antioch in Pisidia, Troas, Neapolis, Philippi, Amphipolis, Apollonia, Thessalonica, Berea, Athens, Corinth, Ephesus, Caesarea, Jerusalem, Antioch
>
> **What—** Preached to Jews and Gentiles
> Paul wrote 1 and 2 Thessalonians Epistles from Corinth
> Paul wrote the Galatians Epistle from Antioch

| 250 | BC†AD | 1 | 36 | 37 | 38 | 39 | 40 | 41 | 42 | 43 | 44 | | 48 | |

← First Missionary Journey (AD 46–48)

← Second Missionary Journey (AD 49/50–52)

← Third Missionary Journey (AD 52/53–57)

← Trip to Rome (AD 59–61/62)

AD 49/50—Jerusalem Council—Acts 15

> **Who—** Paul, Barnabas, James, Peter, Silas
>
> **Where—** Jerusalem
>
> **What—** Met with leaders of the entire Church, who then wrote a letter to Gentile Christians in Antioch
> Paul and Silas partner; Barnabas and John Mark partner

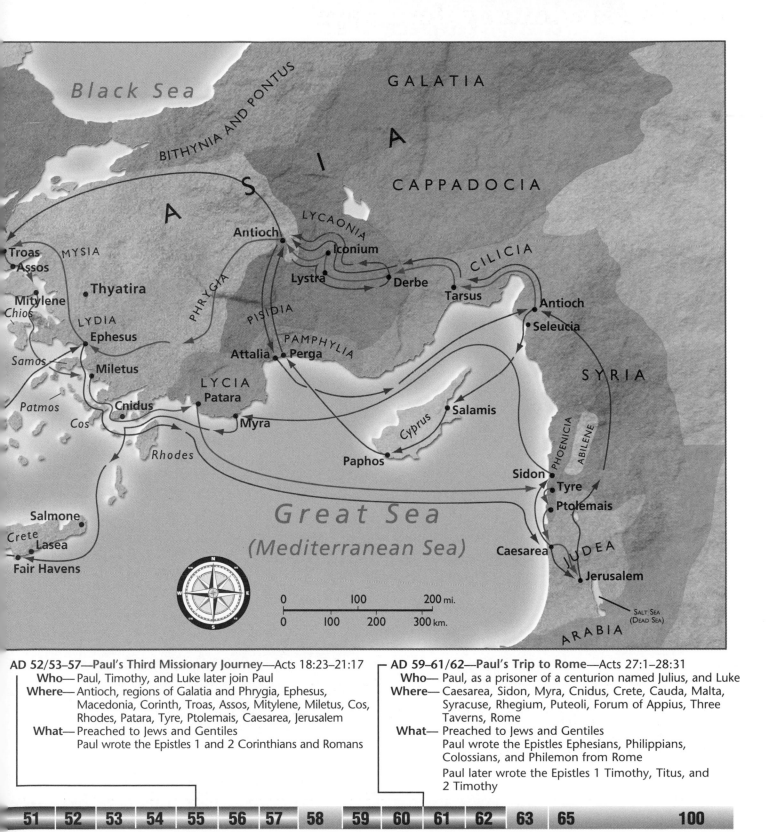

Black Sea

GALATIA

BITHYNIA AND PONTUS

CAPPADOCIA

A S I A

LYCAONIA

Troas
Assos
MYSIA

Thyatira

Mitylene
Chios

LYDIA

Ephesus

Samos

Miletus

Patmos

Cos

Cnidus

Rhodes

Salmone
Crete
Lasea
Fair Havens

Antioch
Iconium

Lystra
Derbe
Tarsus

PHRYGIA

PISIDIA

PAMPHYLIA

Attalia
Perga

LYCIA
Patara

Myra

CILICIA

Antioch
Seleucia

SYRIA

Salamis

Cyprus

Paphos

PHOENICIA
ABILENE

Sidon
Tyre
Ptolemais

Caesarea

JUDEA

Jerusalem

Great Sea
(Mediterranean Sea)

SALT SEA
(DEAD SEA)

ARABIA

N
W   E
S

0   100   200 mi.
0   100   200   300 km.

AD 52/53–57—Paul's Third Missionary Journey—Acts 18:23–21:17
Who— Paul, Timothy, and Luke later join Paul
Where— Antioch, regions of Galatia and Phrygia, Ephesus, Macedonia, Corinth, Troas, Assos, Mitylene, Miletus, Cos, Rhodes, Patara, Tyre, Ptolemais, Caesarea, Jerusalem
What— Preached to Jews and Gentiles
Paul wrote the Epistles 1 and 2 Corinthians and Romans

AD 59–61/62—Paul's Trip to Rome—Acts 27:1–28:31
Who— Paul, as a prisoner of a centurion named Julius, and Luke
Where— Caesarea, Sidon, Myra, Cnidus, Crete, Cauda, Malta, Syracuse, Rhegium, Puteoli, Forum of Appius, Three Taverns, Rome
What— Preached to Jews and Gentiles
Paul wrote the Epistles Ephesians, Philippians, Colossians, and Philemon from Rome
Paul later wrote the Epistles 1 Timothy, Titus, and 2 Timothy

51	52	53	54	55	56	57	58	59	60	61	62	63	65	100

The Roman Empire and Paul's Journey to Rome

ATLANTIC OCEAN

Londinium

RHINE R.

Colonia Agrippina [Cologne]

Augusta Treverorum [Trier]

Lutetia

Augusta Vi [Augsburg]

Burdigala

Lugdunum [Lyon]

Cremona

Venetia A

Genua

Tolosa

Pisae

Salmantica

Rome

Toletum

Puteoli Neapo.

Corduba   Valentia

Hispalis

Malaca

Gades

Caralis

Mes

Utica   Carthage

Icosium [Algiers]

Hippo Regius

MI [M

Oea [Tripoli

Paul's Journey to Rome in AD 57–58

0   500 MI.

0   500 KM.

DANUBE R.

DANUBE R.

BLACK SEA

Trapezus

ㅡIC SEA

Byzantium

Philippi

Brundisium

Thessalonica

Pergamum

Tarsus

EUPHRATES R.

AEGEAN SEA

Ephesus

Antioch

Rhegium

ACHAIA

Athens

Myra

yracuse

Sparta

Cnidus

CYPRUS

CRETE

Sidon

Damascus

Fair Havens

Caesarea Maritima

MEDITERRANEAN SEA

Jerusalem

Major

Alexandria

Cyrene

Petra

Aelana

Memphis

NILE R.

RED SEA

The Apostles' Ministry

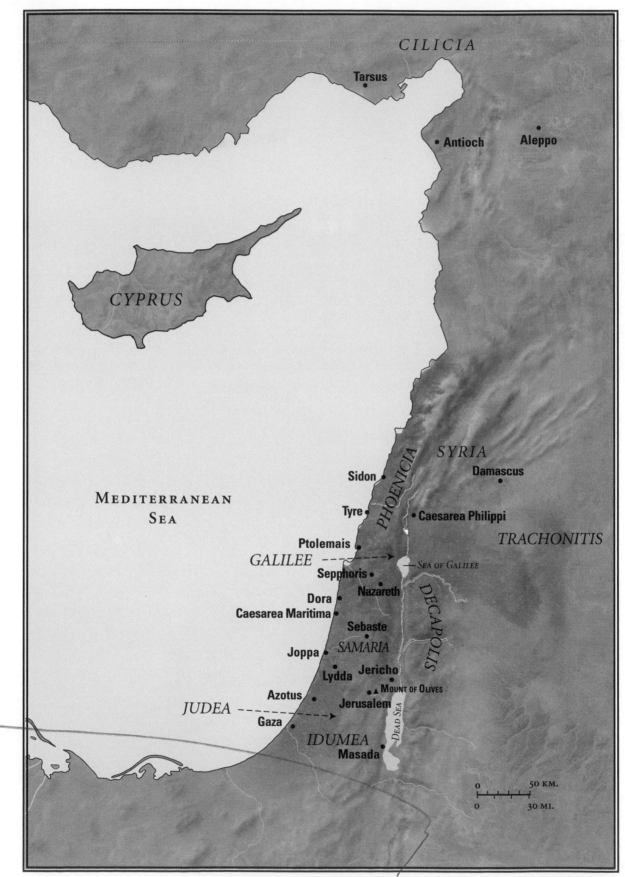

CILICIA

Tarsus

Antioch   Aleppo

SYRIA

Damascus

PHOENICIA

Sidon

Tyre   Caesarea Philippi

TRACHONITIS

MEDITERRANEAN
SEA

Ptolemais

GALILEE - - - →   SEA OF GALILEE

Sepphoris

Nazareth

Dora

Caesarea Maritima

DECAPOLIS

Sebaste

Joppa   SAMARIA

Lydda   Jericho

Mount of Olives

Azotus

JUDEA - - - →   Jerusalem

DEAD SEA

Gaza

IDUMEA

Masada

CYPRUS

0   50 KM.

0   30 MI.

Table of Contents

(repeated here for convenience)